Telling Narratives

Secrets in African American Literature

Leslie W. Lewis

University of Illinois Press

Urbana and Chicago

Library of Congress Cataloging-in-Publication Data
Lewis, Leslie W., 1960–
Telling narratives : secrets in African American
literature / Leslie W. Lewis.
p.   cm.
Includes bibliographical references and index.
ISBN 978-0-252-03211-0 (alk. paper)
ISBN 0-252-03211-x (alk. paper)
 1. American literature—African American authors—
History and criticism. 2. African Americans in
literature.
I. Title.
PS153.N5L467   2007
810.9'896073—dc22   2007015800

CONTENTS

◆◦§ ʒ◦◆

ACKNOWLEDGMENTS

This project has a history that mirrors my own intellectual biography and includes early serious study of classical Western philosophy and other "great books," including Hegel; eye-opening engagement with feminist and gender theory and feminist and queer activism; and the lifesaving discovery of African American literature, African American studies, and critical race theory. I am indebted, therefore, to people who represent these three distinct scholarly communities: Lawrence and Gisela Berns, Eva Brann, Patricia Cook, Peter Drucker, Peter Kalkavage, and Barbara Leonard, just a few of the many people at St. John's College, Annapolis, whose conversations are with me still; Ann Ardis, Sharon Davie, Caroline Gebhard, Holly Laird, Charles Rowell, Margaret Stetz, and other members of the *Iris* editorial collective and the feminist theory group of the mid-1980s at the University of Virginia; and Elizabeth Hadley, Herman Hudson, Phyllis Klotman, Adrian Livingston, Portia Maultsby, John McCluskey, Rita Organ, Bill Pincheon, Gayle Tate, Bill Wiggins, and a host of other scholars, teachers, and friends connected with the Afro-American Studies department at Indiana University. Without these three distinct communities and my involvement in them, this project would not be; I thank you all for the ways I have been tutored, taught, and schooled.

I wish to thank those who read or talked with me about this manuscript in its earliest stages: Eva Cherniavski, Gail Cohee, Kathy Greenlee, Joyce Grover, Jim Justus, John McCluskey, and Carolyn Mitchell. I also thank the American Association of University Women for fellowship support at a crucial time in the development of this project.

I am indebted to the College of Saint Rose for research support during the preparation of this manuscript. Also, Pete Koonz, Kate Moss, and other Saint Rose library staff members provided key help in a timely manner. My thanks to students at both Emporia State University and the College of Saint Rose who have played an important role in the development of the ideas this book represents, and to two anonymous readers at the University of Illinois Press for their close attention to this manuscript. Special thanks to Joan Catapano for years of encouragement that stretch back to shared time at Indiana University.

Finally, my thanks and love go to Marjorie Pryse, to whom I am deeply indebted intellectually and emotionally, and without whom I cannot imagine this project.

Telling Narratives

Introduction:
Positioning Secrets

This project began as a study of racial and sexual secrets within an African American literary context. It remains rooted in feminist and African American cultural theory and focuses specifically on the problems of voice that both feminists and African Americanists have identified as a consequence of white (and/or) male dominance. I trace part of this project's origins to feminists who do rape crisis and domestic violence work, and particularly to the insistence that women must "break the silence" about all forms of violence against women. While this activist imperative was my starting point, conceptually speaking I am suggesting that a different model, that of keeping and telling secrets, is more useful to an exploration of the articulation and absence of articulation that occurs when people survive the kind of violence that threatens life or identity, or both. Looking at secrets, I suggest, is a way to explore the muted articulations that a strict dichotomy between speech and silence would indicate does not exist. Secrets focus us *not* on what is not, or cannot be, or is finally said, but on what has always been said quietly, carefully, despite the odds or consequences.

Along the way, this study has also come to incorporate specific societal questions that African American women, in particular, raise about their own place and power in late twentieth-century American life. When Patricia Hill Collins declares, "Afro-American women have long been privy to some of the most intimate secrets of white society," she articulates a connection between Black women and secrets whose interrogation has driven this project in surprising directions ("Learning" 35). Ultimately, I have been led to posit an origin story for American consciousness that relies upon the dialectical acknowledgment between master and female slave, where the Hegelian moment of self-consciousness is both raced and gendered. By revising Hegelian thought in this way, I mean to be specifically addressing a question raised by Nell Irvin Painter in *Sojourner Truth: A Life, a Symbol*, where she wonders in her "Coda" how "the assertive words of a black woman can halt the world they pierce" (287). The symbolic power of Sojourner Truth and, in Painter's anecdote, Painter's own power as she comments upon a paper at the 1995 Organization of American Historians, gives evidence that Black women sometimes represent a very significant counterforce to patriarchal power. When a Black woman's words can "halt the world they pierce," I suspect this is not just because they are unexpected, as Painter speculates, but because white listeners understand that these words come from a privileged position of knowledge, from the position of the "outsider within," as Patricia Hill Collins names it, a position from which much truth has been told. To make this case even more strongly, I turn to my revised Hegelian model of an American coming-to-conscious-ness, which suggests that such words as they are spoken are inflected with the force of the "other" consciousness that has existed from the beginning, the consciousness that confronts and recognizes the "master," defines him, if you will, and so both witnesses and makes possible American origin stories.

While the focus of this study is the narrative history of telling secrets in earlier African American texts, and the consequences of gender with regard to those secrets, my analysis is shaped by the projects of contemporary African American novelists. I remain convinced that the role of secrets in African American literature profoundly affects the very definition of modern and contemporary African American literary production. It is no accident that James Weldon Johnson's *Autobiography of an Ex-Coloured Man*, by all accounts a significant modern text, opens with the line, "I know that in writing the following pages I am divulging the great secret of my life." Nor is it surprising that Toni Morrison's first novel, *The Bluest Eye*, begins with the words, "Quiet as it's kept,"[1] while her *Beloved*, focused on the interior of slavery's legacy, insists, "This is not a story to pass on." As Morrison implies, and Johnson's *Ex-Coloured Man* makes explicit, twentieth-century African American narrative production is all about telling secrets.

There are so many instances in contemporary African American litera-ture of significant, "telling" moments when secrets are shared that, in fact, the keeping and telling of secrets has developed into a significant narrative mode of production. This is a point explored by Ashraf Rushdy as he analyzes what he calls palimpsest narratives of the 1970s, which show that "slavery is the family secret of America" (2). While not a narrative about slavery, and not explored by Rushdy, Maya Angelou's *I Know Why the Caged Bird Sings* contains a popular example of a "telling" moment, and one that also helps to illustrate the theoretical territory opened up by shifting, conceptually, from silences to secrets. After being raped by her mother's lover, the young Marguerite, according to the narrator, stops talking. About this phase of her life she says: "I discovered that to achieve perfect personal silence all I had to do was to attach myself leechlike to sound. I began to listen to everything. . . . I walked into rooms where people were laughing, their voices hitting the walls like stones, and I simply stood still—in the midst of the riot of sound. After a minute or two, silence would rush into the room from its hiding place because I had eaten up all the sounds" (73). Literary critics take Angelou's cue and also speak of her trauma-induced silence, but in fact the young Angelou is only silent sometimes. The narrator makes it quite clear that Marguerite continues to talk, but only to her older brother, Bailey, and that the rest of her family understands and accepts this: "They understood that I could talk to Bailey, but to no one else" (73). I suspect that critical analysis of *Caged Bird* shifts dramatically when we revise Marguerite's silence into careful talk and see the young Angelou's traumatic experience as something that compels her to speak secretly, but not publicly. Most significantly, this shift from silence to secrets suggests that Bailey is the audience who hears what we, as readers, do not.

Bailey's role in *Caged Bird* as his sister's confidant also points to an important conceptual distinction between silence and secrets: the number of people involved. Silence implies a duality, that is, one person *not* saying something to another person or party. Secrets, however, involve a triad: one person who keeps something from someone, but at the same time tells that something to someone else. Because in-groups and out-groups of knowers are suggested by secrets, this model works well as a representation of color-line literature, particularly African American writing concerned with slavery or memories of it, as Ashraf Rushdy suggests. This is directly related to slavery's existence as an institution founded upon practices about which one dared not speak. Secrets are not just a subject *within* African American texts, however. Just as denial shapes the structure of white American texts, as Toni Morrison points out in "Unspeakable Things Unspoken" and *Playing in the Dark*, so, too, do secrets shape the structure of African American narratives—of what gets said to whom and how. Secret telling, which might be best characterized as that kind of telling that depends upon a third party who hears, and implies a second party who does not, becomes a recognizable structure within African American narrative literature.

David Bradley's novel, *The Chaneysville Incident*, one of the narratives that Rushdy explores, presents in its most profound moment of dramatic action an example of secret telling, perhaps most remarkable for the way that telling and listening are completely intertwined, so that listening clearly affects the shape and meaning of the story being told. John, a gifted historian, tells the story that gives significance to his father's and great-grandfather's deaths; Judith, John's white lover, hears him. Structurally, the novel works by forcing readers to determine whether they hear what Judith hears, or not, and this in turn influences the readers' interpretation of Bradley's purposely ambiguous ending to the novel. At *Chaneysville*'s most poignant moment, after John has ended his story, he tells Judith that he believes the white miller, Iames, was responsible for burying the fugitive slaves in family groupings that respect their relations to one another. When Judith questions this, asking, "Why would a white man . . . why would you think a white man . . .?" could care: with breaks in the text to indicate words that Judith does not speak, we understand that John, because of Judith, believes that someone white might care enough about a fugitive slave family, even while Judith, in the same moment, has been swept away by the story and does not think Iames possible of such humanity because he is a white man. Thus, Bradley engages the formal structure of secret telling and listening as a model for cross-racial understanding, and he suggests also the empathic possibility of shifting positionalities, so that listener-response, and reader-response, might become unmoored from fixed race and gender identities. This, I want to suggest, is a specific strategy developed so as to deal with unreliable readers, as Robert Stepto names them in *From Behind the Veil*—a way to offer to a reading audience the possibility of really "hearing" a story. Using Stepto's terminology, and generalizing from Bradley's novel, we might say that the textual keeping and telling of secrets is a way for African American authors to mark the existence of (and respond to) societal, racially inflected structures that guarantee unreliable readers who will have difficulty hearing what they are being told.

There is yet another way to consider secrets as they influence the ways that writers understand audience. Both Houston A. Baker and Henry Louis Gates Jr., in their respective works within vernacular theory, discuss the classic African American interpretive figure that Ralph Ellison presents as the "little man hidden behind the stove" in his essay "The Little Man at Chehaw Station" (Baker, *Blues* 12–13; Gates, *Signifying Monkey* 64–65). According to Ellison, it was his music teacher at Tuskegee, the world-renowned Black American classical composer and pianist Hazel Harrison, who taught him what it really means to be an American musician and artist. After Ellison performed poorly during his trumpet recital, "substituting a certain skill of lips and fingers for the intelligent and artistic structuring of emotion that was demanded in performing the music," he sought solace from Harrison. Rather than give comfort, Harrison presented a puzzle: "But, baby," she said, "in this country you must always prepare yourself to play your very best wherever you are, and on all occasions. . . . You must *always* play your best, even if it's only in the waiting room at Chehaw Station, because in this country there'll always be a little man hidden behind the stove" (4). While Baker refers to the "little man" as Ellison's tribute to the blues vernacular (the little man being situated in a railroad way-station), and Gates refers to the "little man" as a trickster figure who surfaces when you least expect him—two interpretations of this image that each establish a significant trope within African American literature—my interest is in the "little man" as secret, as someone *hidden*, presumably Black, who is, according to Ellison later in his essay, the "representative of the American audience writ small" (7).

As audience, Ellison's little man is not the untrustworthy reader who Robert Stepto says will need to be "told" or "told off" in order to hear (*From Behind the Veil* 202). He is, instead, the hearer already in existence who encourages the artist to reach for a profound level of truthfulness, to "say it" each and every time he or she performs, to always play from the heart, or soul. Yet, Ellison's tale is cautionary. His point is that no artist, or writer, can fake it. No matter where you are or what you are saying, you must always play for that hidden person who will inevitably hear, who somehow already knows the point you express and so will judge if you have "gotten it right." Ironically enough, this, according to Ellison, is what it means to perform according to an *American* aesthetic.

I conclude with a telling anecdotal moment from my current life. During a visit to Brooklyn in late spring, in the middle of revisionary reflection upon this project, I found myself engaged in family talk while sitting on a bench in Prospect Park. Musing, mostly listening, but sometimes a third-party participant in a conversation best categorized as between mother and daughter, I became somewhat concerned that our family scene was mightily disturbing the serious reader two benches to our right. Because of my concern, I surreptitiously eyed this reader carefully and so can report him to be a tall, dark-skinned, dreadlocked, African American man perhaps in his late twenties. What might have been a simple day in the park became much more significant, however, when I caught a glimpse of the text that this reader held in his hands, a text very prominently titled *Hegel*. Given my revisionary juxtaposition of nineteenth-century texts about slavery against twentieth-century interpretations of Hegel's dialectic between master and slave, given my project here, which dramatically shifted as I began to see African American slavery in the context of Western philosophy's history of consciousness, even I am tempted to think that I characterize a specter of my imagination. But this coincidental meeting of another reader of Hegel at a rather unlikely place and time, when my thoughts were focused on connections between Hegelian and African American literary ideas, indeed happened, and happened for a reason: Prospect Park Hegelian, I dedicate this book to you.

I

The Master/Female Slave Moment
as Slavery's Legacy

My father had a little joke that made light of our legacy as a family that had
once owned slaves.
"There are five things we don't talk about in the Ball family," he would say.
"Religion, sex, death, money, and the Negroes."
"What does that leave to talk about?" my mother asked once.
"That's another of the family secrets," Dad said, smiling.

—Edward Ball, *Slaves in the Family*

Secrets are at the heart of African American narrative literature and are a
legacy of slavery. The institution of slavery itself engendered secrets because it
created a group of people (masters) who could forbid another group of people
(slaves) to share certain kinds of information, thus assuring that the information would be shared outside the masters' presence. While I specifically embed
this study in African American cultural and literary history, I also mean to
suggest, through the above parenthetical insertion of the language of master
and slave, the trope of the Hegelian subject, which represents, in Western
philosophy, perhaps the most significant construct of the origins and stages of
human consciousness and human knowledge. In making this reference, I am
quite aware that Hegel's subject, and his master/slave moment in the history
of consciousness, is generally read by later philosophers as exclusively masculine (Simone de Beauvoir being the exception). Nevertheless, my intent here
is to explore, in Hegelian terms, the contours of male master/female-slave
relationships.[1] In doing so, I am decidedly not following Beauvoir's efforts
toward developing an analogy between slave status and the status of women as
wives and mothers, since in that analogy the lived experiences of the women
upon whom I focus here are erased, just as they are also erased in exclusively
masculine versions of the life of slaves. Instead, I take seriously the both/and

claim that African American women make about race and gender status, and so begin with the idea that since the peculiar American institution enslaved women as well as men, these women are as representative of slave status as men, in Hegelian terms.

Typically, women are thought to be excluded from the master/slave dialectic because it is one of many public moments in the history of consciousness, and women are excluded from the public stage. Arguments against Beauvoir's inclusion of women within the master/slave dialectic focus on the ways that Beauvoir's privileged women cannot hold the slave position because they do not experience the two crucial elements that characterize slave status for Hegel: they do not face death, and they do not labor as slaves.[2] Yet even the most cursory glance at the historical record of American slavery demonstrates that African American women's experiences in slavery include these elements. Simply thinking through the stories of the two most famous American ex-slave women, Harriet Tubman and Sojourner Truth, gives us specific examples of each: Harriet Tubman, as Moses, risks death repeatedly as she leads other fugitives to freedom; and Sojourner Truth not only works, she famously claims that she "has as much muscle as any man," "can do as much work as any man," and has "plowed and reaped and husked and chopped and mowed, and can any man do more than that?" (Painter, *Sojourner Truth* 125).[3] As these two representatives demonstrate, women partake of slave experience, even as characterized within the masculinist Hegelian dialectic, fully and completely. Yet, of course, there are also dimensions of enslaved women's experience that are gendered female, and in this study I will also consider the all-American drama of the gendered, and sexualized, struggle between master and slave. In the context of American slavery what we have, however, is not so much the meeting of two travelers on the road to a new stage of self-consciousness as, more significantly, the mutual recognition of two beings—both, as we shall see, socially defined—whose struggle resonates within the collective American consciousness, and whose issue, literally, is a new generation of mixed-race children.

While later chapters of this volume examine secret *telling*, that is, the telling of secrets as speech acts that become inscribed in African American narrative literature so significantly as to become a structuring element of the literature, this chapter focuses on secrets as slavery's legacy and examines the content of the secrets springing from slavery, as well as the relational implications of keeping and telling such secrets. The institution of slavery, as I will demonstrate, brings with it two fundamental secrets. The first is the "slaves' secret," kept by and about people of slave status, which concerns the existence of a collective consciousness springing from the kind of self-discovery that is inscribed in moments of religious conversion. The second of slavery's secrets is the "masters' secret," kept primarily by enslaved but sometimes by free women, and concerning the sexual behavior of the slave master. Historical evidence makes clear the existence of such secrets, kept explicitly *as* secret, which also implies a triadic speech act, defined as both speaking/not speaking simultaneously, determined by the relation between master and slave. This model involving three, rather than two, parties configured variously in subject/object positions not only complicates the dichotomy between language and silence, but also suggests a radical alternative to the many current readings of the dialectical process.

Hegel's origin of self-consciousness, which is characterized through the master/slave moment, has, of course, influenced tremendous numbers of Marxist and existential thinkers, among others (Singer 75). Further, the early twentieth-century French reception of Hegel, shaped as it was by Jean Hyppolite and Alexandre Kojève, who in turn taught or influenced Michel Foucault, Jacques Derrida, Simone de Beauvoir, Jean-Paul Sartre, and Jacques Lacan, means that "most of the work of Anglo-American literary and cultural criticism can be explained by relegating it to this Hegelianism," which centers upon the lord and bondsman (master/slave) chapter of Hegel's *Phenomenology of Spirit* (Barnett 20).[4] Hyppolite offered the first French translation of Hegel's *Phenomenology*, carefully explicated the difficult text, and then, according to Stuart Barnett, positioned "the issue of self-consciousness as a moment in the unfolding of the Absolute" (Barnett 15). Kojève, who had "the greater immediate impact," offered the master/slave dialectic as "the centerpiece" of his reading of Hegel (Barnett 15). Judith Butler goes further, saying that "Kojève halts the *Phenomenology* at the end of 'Lordship and Bondage,' and retells Hegel's narrative from the point of view of that struggling individual on the brink of collective identity" (*Subjects of Desire* 58), "the bondsman emerging into collective identity" (75).

Firmly mapping how we might understand this collective identity to which Butler refers would take us into the deepest recesses of phenomenological, existential, structuralist, and psychoanalytic thinking. Most significantly, however, African American experience as recorded in narrative literature suggests that the collective identity into which the bondsman transforms himself is implicit in slave self-consciousness. In other words, to know oneself as a slave is to have a collective understanding of self, in slavery, which suggests that collective identity already (or always already) exists in the master/slave moment. Further, while the dialectical process as it is most commonly understood (thesis-antithesis-synthesis) seems to involve two terms that merge into a unity, Hegel's word for the synthetic transformation, *Aufhebung*, which negates, transcends, and preserves all at once, really suggests three terms implicit in the dialectical relationship itself, a point Charles Taylor also makes when he says that "we might better understand [dialectical movement] as a relation involving not just two terms but three" (133).[5] This third term as I am naming it here, the collective identity of those enslaved, exists even as master and slave confront one another, yet might best be understood to exist in secret.

As should now be evident, examining slavery's secrets has consequences beyond our specific understanding of African American experience, consequences that I will continue to suggest throughout this chapter. In order to do so, I turn now to Hegel's master/slave allegory as it has been read within African American and African diasporic cultural and literary history, particularly by Orlando Patterson, Eric Sundquist, and Paul Gilroy; as well, I examine additional and poignant master/slave moments that these critics do not consider. For Patterson, slavery is an experience that generates honor for masters and dishonor for slaves, and his comparative study of slavery, *Slavery and Social Death*, defines the condition as the "permanent, violent domination of natally alienated and generally dishonored persons" (13). Accordingly, Patterson turns to Frederick Douglass's account of his conflict with the slave-driver Edward Covey as an example of what is "universal in the master-slave relationship" (11).[6] Eric Sundquist, who works with Patterson's model, elaborates: "In this celebrated scene . . . Douglass accentuates his own conversion to mastery—mastery of Covey, in a reversal of the relationship of power, and mastery of himself, in a release from the condition of chattelism" (*Wake* 123). As Paul Gilroy notes in *The Black Atlantic*, however, what is produced here is specifically gendered and not universal, is "a liberatory definition of masculinity" rather than personhood (63). According to Gilroy, there are indeed other stories that "raise complex questions about the mediating role of gender categories in racial politics and in particular about the psychological structures of identification facilitated by the idea of maternity" (68). Unfortunately, even Gilroy finds it "impossible to explore these important matters" (68), yet by pointing toward maternity as key he suggests just the loophole that must be explored as we rethink Patterson's and Sundquist's patriarchal structuring of both the production of freedom, and, ultimately, modernity.

The gendering that Gilroy names but does not explore further, and that Sundquist and Patterson do not acknowledge at all, is clearly significant in Sundquist's and Patterson's description of the Douglass/Covey master/slave moment. Sundquist continues: "A 'boy of sixteen,' Douglass has vanquished his master, assumed his place psychologically, and fathered himself in the dramatic act of resistance. In doing so, he has nearly made literal the Hegelian dialectic of master and slave" (*Wake* 123). While chapter 2 of this study examines in detail the significance of this ex-slave generation of identity as an exclusively male construct, often fixated on father-son relations, here I want to suggest, in theoretical terms, why the celebration of this moment between Douglass and Covey is not adequate to a full understanding of the relation between slavery and freedom, nor to the way in which these concepts engender modernity. If Kojève's reading of Hegel is taken seriously, then the master/slave moment brings the "master" self-consciousness to an impasse from which no development is possible, whereas the "slave" self-consciousness develops, "transform[s] the given (social) conditions of his existence . . . realize[s] a historical progress" (Kojève 50). In other words, it is "slave" self-consciousness that offers real possibility for the future of human consciousness, but, crucially, this is so only if we remember that there is always a third term in the process and recognize that the third term of this dialectical movement is, here, an "other" social order, "the world the slaves made."[7] Further, as I will demonstrate in detail, telling secrets is key: women, as slaves, have the power to tell secrets and with such tellings can shift the private to the public, thereby changing, and often recreating, social orders.

Orlando Patterson's understanding of the dynamics of slavery depends on the idea that slavery means social death, that the slave is "a socially dead person" who has "ceased to belong in his own right to any legitimate social order" (5). Yet at the same time, he recognizes the participation of slaves in what he might call "illegitimate" social orders, speaking of the way in which slaves "mask" true feelings "in their relations with those who had parasitized them" while "in their statements to one another . . . they revealed what they knew and what they were" (338). Further, while natal alienation is part of the definition of enslavement, for Patterson "the fierce love of the slave mother for her child is attested in every slaveholding society" (337). While, then, Patterson's own investigations suggest that mothers are the bedrock of slave community, and that community is an inherent aspect of the experience of slavery, Patterson's analysis—in the interest of the "political psychology of the everyday life of masters and slaves" (11), with its primary focus on the relations between men—overlooks what many narratives suggest to be crucial to the experience of slavery, that is, the personal relations among slaves, including women. Claiming that "we can say little or nothing about the private lives of the members of either [master or slave] group"; that "we know next to nothing about the way they [slaves] felt about one another"; and that because "the data are just not there" it would be "the height of arrogance, not to mention intellectual irresponsibility" (11) to generalize about the inner psychology of the group, the group's significance, itself, is lost in Patterson's account of the dynamics of slavery.

However, the data are there if we include early African American narrative literature as part of the data set. Utterances marked as secret define the personal and private. Telling narratives, narratives that tell secrets, voice what can and cannot be said as they mark a consciousness of saying, and not saying, in their acts of telling or keeping secrets, and doing so gives us the information about the private lives of masters and slaves that Patterson believes does not exist. Further, by devising narrative strategies that depend on telling secrets, writers acknowledge the doubleness of African American life in America, even acknowledge the great schism between public and private talk, yet through the narrative vehicle of telling secrets they maintain a narrative—and psychic—integrity. Since the publication of Toni Morrison's "Unspeakable Things Unspoken: The Afro-American Presence in American Literature," followed by *Playing in the Dark: Whiteness and the Literary Imagination*, Americanists have been working with Morrison's notion of the palpable moments of denial of an African American presence in American literature, as well as her delineation of an *Africanist* presence in American literature, not representatively African American but reflexive so as to profoundly demonstrate what "blackness" signifies in white America's writerly imagination. In the context of Morrison's work, this project, which focuses within African American literary traditions, examines a related phenomenon: African American secrets inscribed within texts also mark key understandings of the vagaries of the larger society's denial of an African American presence.[8] Studying the secrets in African American literature, then, is another way of studying the particulars of what has been denied by the larger society, as well as a way to understand matters of importance within African American communities.

While secret information and denied information have an aspect of illegitimacy in common, they exist in different realms. Denial implies a conscious refusal to acknowledge subconscious truths, all of this taking place within an individual (or group) consciousness. Secrecy, on the other hand, operates in the realm of communication. It is "a method of handling concealed information," a "metacommunicative" device used to give information about information (Bellman 8). While telling a secret, "doing secrecy," communicates that the information told secretly is restricted to a particular "membership group," it is important to realize that all secrets are told to someone: by definition they must be communicated (Bellman 9–11). Thus, secrets in African American literature are easily identified as such because they are spoken as secrets: they are told by someone within the membership group to someone else who is also within that group. As complement to Morrison's project, which depends upon reading the nuances within white American texts, the project of looking to secrets in African American literature for information about the African American presence denied has the advantage of explicit textual references.

As critics' misreadings of Maya Angelou's *I Know Why the Caged Bird Sings* make clear, secret tellings are often misconstrued as silence, an idea explored by Adrienne Rich in her essay "Women and Honor: Some Notes on Lying." In this essay, written at the height of second-wave feminism, Rich recognizes and accepts lying and keeping secrets as behaviors necessary to women in their dealings with men, even while she defines an ethical code that precludes such behavior among women. Rich presents two paradoxes: "'Women have always lied to each other.' 'Women have always told the truth to each other.' Both these axioms are true. 'Women have always been divided against each other.' 'Women have always been in secret collusion.' Both these axioms are true" (189). These paradoxes suggest that lies and secrets are necessitated by relations between people of unequal social status, and that this dishonorable behavior is sometimes, but not always, carried into relations among people of roughly the same social status. Most important, however, is the sense that these sets of paradoxical statements take the place of two other, very familiar sentiments: that women do not talk to one another and that women have no relationships among themselves. Rich's implication, then, is that between groups of people disparate in social status, the dominant group may hear nothing and assume silence when, in fact, members of the subordinate group are quietly whispering to one another.

Records from slavery suggest just this scenario of quiet or coded talk among slaves being mistaken for no talk at all. Numerous accounts by slaveholders emphasize "the faithful slave" and his or her exemplary conduct during the Civil War. As historian Leon Litwack notes, this led to "the paeans of praise that would be heaped upon those black men and women who had stood with their masters and mistresses, the oratorical tributes to their loyalty, the monuments erected to their memory, and the romantic images and legends that would be elaborated upon to comfort and entertain generations of whites" (17). Both Thomas Nelson Page and Joel Chandler Harris, famous as "plantation school" apologists for slavery, write short stories depicting the faithful personal servant who saves his master (or his deceased master's body) from the Yankees.[9] In Page's "Marse Chan: A Tale of Old Virginia," the first tale of the collection *In Ole Virginia*, the slave's loyalty is emphasized by the story he tells of how "old master," when "young master" was a newborn, put the baby in his arms and, as the slave remembers, tells him, "Now, Sam, from dis time you belong to yo' young Marse Channin'; I wan' you to tek keer on 'im ez long ez he lives. You are to be his boy from dis time" (9). The 1906 "Plantation Edition" of *In Ole Virginia* includes a color illustration of this moment.[10]

This familiar picture of the faithful slave makes clear the denial by white slaveholders that slaves were discontent with their slave status. There was even stronger denial that slaves might be so discontent as to rebel against their circumstances. And yet, as Litwack points out, slaveholders were just too "insistent about their sense of security and equanimity" to be completely believable (18). Many slaveholders may have desperately wanted that slaves be loyal to them and to the Confederate cause, but they could not count on that loyalty. They were aware, in spite of themselves, "of the slaves' demonstrated capacity for evasiveness and dissimulation in the presence of whites" (18). As the war continued and it became clearer that the Confederates' position was untenable, "the ambiguities in the slave response . . . tend[ed] to dissolve and the whites who had proclaimed the loudest the faithfulness of their blacks were among those forced to reassess their perceptions in accordance with personal experience" (18). In many cases, it was not until slavery seemed clearly to be drawing to a close that slaves felt secure enough to let slaveholders in on their "secret" discontent.

That those enslaved understood and abhorred their condition was a secret of slavery: a point of information shared with one another but kept from whites, particularly white Southerners. As Melvin Dixon and others have pointed out, slaves constructed an elaborate critique of the plantation system, but it was not recognized as such because it was in the secretive, coded form of the religious songs known as spirituals.[11] Other instances of coded speech by slaves involved the transmission of information about the war: "Few plantation whites were fully aware of the inventiveness with which their slaves transmitted information to other blacks. Extensive black communication networks, feeding on a variety of sources, sped information from plantation to plantation, county to county, often with remarkable secrecy and accuracy. What slaves called the 'grapevine telegraph' frequently employed code words that enabled them to carry on conversations about forbidden subjects in the very presence of their masters and mistresses" (Litwack 23). One example of the "grapevine telegraph" at work is found in Frances E. W. Harper's novel

W. T. Smedley illustration from Thomas Nelson Page, *In Ole Virginia*.
Plantation Edition. New York: Charles Scribner's Sons, 1906.

Iola Leroy, which opens with a conversation between Robert Johnson and Thomas Anderson, both slaves. While seeming to talk about the produce market, they are in fact passing along information about the most recent Civil War battle victory of the North over the South. As Harper's example shows, coded talk allows those enslaved to speak of information "forbidden" to them. In other instances, the forbidden information passed on by slaves pertained to acts of rebellion against, or resistance to, slavery itself.

While a resistant or rebellious attitude is clearly one secret engendered by the slave system, there is a secret at the core of this attitude that marks the community as a community and points to the collective identity of those enslaved that becomes the crucial third term in the master/slave dialectic. Melvin Dixon's article, "Singing Swords: The Literary Legacy of Slavery," describes this core secret by focusing on the religious experiences of the slave community. Dixon begins by defining the "church" built by this community as a combination of traditional African religious practices and American Christianity, but heavily influenced by the day-to-day "social experience in the slave quarters" (300–301). From these influences, according to Dixon, came a religion "centered in a conversion-like initiation" (301). It was this conversion experience that determined whether those held as slaves were "of the group" or not; and the experience itself "prepared them to fight for freedom by becoming morally free of an intrusive and debilitating white out-group and by becoming more responsible to the inner slave community" (302). If we accept this description of the conversion of slaves in the quarters, then the primary secret kept by slaves is that they did, in fact, keep secrets; that is, slaves kept as secret their consciousness of themselves as a distinct group with its own communication practices and an identity distinguishable from that of the larger society.[12]

Dixon sums up his own argument by emphasizing that "slaves were not converting themselves to God, but *were converting themselves to each other*" (302; emphasis in the original). In Black experience, he says, the moment of self-discovery is "the beginning of a collective consciousness and group identity" (306), which, to return to Hegelian terms, suggests that the self-consciousness of the bondsman as such is as much tied to the collective consciousness of the group as to a confrontation with the master. Because the existence of this collective consciousness is denied by, and, so, kept from those people who are outside the group, by definition, too, this collective consciousness is secret. A rebellious or resistant attitude toward slavery, made manifest by standing up to a slaveholder, slavedriver, or master, is one demonstration of this consciousness; escaping from slavery is another. In sum, then, the primary slaves' secret is that through forming a collective consciousness springing from self discovery, those enslaved will not be slaves forever, and they know themselves not to be slaves by nature. In terms of Hegel's dialectic, then, the moment of confrontation between master and slave contains within it the collective identity of those enslaved, who know themselves to be not socially dead, but secretly, "otherly" social, and the existence of this collective consciousness also guarantees that the dialectical engine will continue to move consciousness toward freedom.

Secrets kept within the slave community are not always about that community, however; frequently they are about the slaveholding family, particularly the master. In terms of the paradigm of the master/slave dialectic, one significance of these secrets is the way in which they transform masters from subjects to objects of discourse. Because secrets of this type most often concern sexual relations between white slavemasters and enslaved women, gendered master/slave moments take on great significance. These "masters' secrets" are kept and told primarily by female slaves; sometimes they are also kept by the wives and daughters of slaveholders, as well as other white women, and sometimes the community that shares these secrets includes male slaves. To what degree these groups communicate with one another and form cross-racial or cross-gender membership groups depends on specific circumstances, but narratives and diaries document a number of moments when these actions of masters become the point of conversation about them. Harriet Jacobs, in her narrative *Incidents in the Life of a Slave Girl*, gives us specific evidence of the existence of these secrets about sex between white men and enslaved women, as well as evidence of the difficult membership groups created by these secrets. According to Jacobs, it is quite clear that slavery breeds secrets shared among enslaved women about sex between white men and themselves: "The secrets of slavery are concealed like those of the Inquisition. My master was, to my knowledge, the father of eleven slaves. But did the mothers dare to tell who was the father of their children? Did the other slaves dare to allude to it, except in whispers among themselves? No indeed! They knew too well the terrible consequences" (35). Whispered secrets of paternity result from the master's (and father's) command that slave women keep their knowledge of their children's paternity to themselves. While to the slaveholder this is as good as silence, it is not the same as silence, as we are by now well aware.

Mary Boykin Chesnut and Ella Gertrude Clanton Thomas, two Southern white diarists writing during the era of the Civil War, are also clear about "secret" liaisons between white men and enslaved women. In C. Vann Woodward's *Mary Chesnut's Civil War*, Chesnut recalls a meeting of Confederate officers' and politicians' wives, during which one woman asks the question: "Are our men worse than the others? Does Mrs. Stowe know? You know?" (168).[13] This, as the answers make clear, is a veiled reference to the character of Simon Legree in *Uncle Tom's Cabin*, as well as to Southern white women's own knowledge of their husbands' infidelity. In reply, one woman says that she knew "the dissolute half of Legree," who had children by his female slaves but was kind. The children of this man were not sold, but "provided for handsomely in his will" (169). In testament not just to secret sexual relations, but also to the psychology of denial among white Southern females, Chesnut continues: "His wife and daughters in the might of their purity and innocence are supposed never to dream of what is as plain before their eyes as the sunlight, and they play their parts of unsuspecting angels to the letter" (169). What this analysis of slaveholding women's lives suggests is that these women know secret information about their husbands and fathers, information that has been marked as forbidden. But women playing the part of "unsuspecting angels," however many secrets they may know, do not *tell* any of them. Ella Thomas's diaries also contain what Nell Painter refers to as Thomas's "great secret": that "her father had had children and that her husband had had a child outside their marriages" and with slave women (*Secret Eye* 59). Thomas does not share this information with others, however, nor does she even fully disclose it in her diary. Torn by her need to play her part, she only "hints by indirection at her husband's adultery," thus, according to Painter, "keeping secrets from herself and from her readers" (62). Her denial, in other words, marks the secret information that she knows but dares not tell. Telling secrets, however, is distinctly different from denying them, and means telling something to someone and constructing a membership group that excludes those men who have enjoined silence. For wives and daughters like Thomas, whose primary identification remains with their husbands and fathers, this is obviously not possible.

As a further complication to the keeping and telling of the "masters' secrets," some white women are a part of Harriet Jacobs's secret-keeping community, and helping her escape becomes their own secret. The slaveholding woman who initially hides Jacobs in her attic, for example, tells Jacobs she must be very careful "for my sake as well as your own." Further, she says, "You must never tell my secret [that is, that she has helped Jacobs]; for it would ruin me and my family" (Jacobs 100).[14] This woman is sympathetic to Jacobs's situation even though she, herself, holds a number of slaves in her own name and is the wife of a man who holds many slaves, and buys and sells slaves. Jacobs's grandmother tells this woman Jacobs's story, and it is after "she listened attentively to the details of [her] story, and sat thinking for a while" that she offers her help (99). Presumably, this slaveholding woman wants to help Jacobs because she is sympathetic to her plight as a sexually abused and harassed female, thus suggesting her own (secret) involvement in this membership group.

In another passage from Harriet Jacobs's narrative, Dr. Flint beats a male slave whom he had "accused of . . . stealing corn." This accusation hides the real reason this slave is punished: he had "quarrelled with his wife, in the presence of the overseer, and had accused his master of being the father of her child" (13). When this husband refused to be quiet about the father of his wife's baby, Dr. Flint "handed them both over to a slavetrader," telling his former concubine, "You have let your tongue run too far; damn you!" (13). This incident, as quoted by Jacobs, illustrates not just that slave mothers whose children have been fathered by slavemasters must keep these paternal secrets, but also that slave husbands of the women so treated have a difficult relationship to these secrets. In fact, here, the slave husband is not a member of the community of secret keepers; his relation to secret keeping is so difficult that he most wants to tell the secret publicly, even though he does not have the power to do so with impunity.

Writing about *Incidents in the Life of a Slave Girl*, William Andrews uses Adrienne Rich's essay "Women and Honor," as well as Shirley Ardener's *Perceiving Women*, to analyze the communication that takes place among the women, white and Black, slave and free, determined to save Linda Brent from the sexual aggression of Dr. Flint. According to Andrews, these women constitute a "muted group," where "mutedness" is defined as "'not some condition of linguistic silence,' but as a mode of expression on 'a reduced level of perceptibility' to the dominant group and only marginally connected to 'the dominant communicative system of society'" (*To Tell* 255). Andrews's formulation of Jacobs's secret-keeping community as a "muted group" indicates precisely why the male slave who confronts his wife and/or his master about her light-skinned baby is not part of that group: he refuses to speak on a "reduced level of perceptibility." He desires to tell the secret of white paternity not in a muted fashion but in an amplified voice. He seeks, in other words, to engage the white slaveholder and speak as part of the dominant discourse.

In an essay written much later than Jacobs's, Chesnut's, or Thomas's narratives, Lillian Smith, imagining the 1920s, describes white and Black women talking with one another about white men, clearly forming a membership group of their own: "The thing was a spontaneous reaction. Mother in her old age told daughter strange truths that had gnawed on her lonely heart too long. And daughter told other women. Colored and white women stirring up a lemon-cheese cake for the hungry males in the household looked deep into each other's eyes and understood their common past. A mistress, reading the Bible to her colored maid polishing silver, would lay aside Holy Writ and talk of things less holy but of immense importance to both of them" (126). According to Smith, these conversations were the beginning of the white women's movement against lynching, which led to the formation of the influential Association of Southern Women for the Prevention of Lynching in 1930. Through their political work against lynching, these white women emphatically did form a membership group exclusive of white men. And as Smith notes, these women had more power than they knew: "They had the power of spiritual blackmail over a large part of the white South. . . . No one, of thousands of white men, had any notion how much or how little each woman knew about his private goings-on" (127). The threat to make secrets public, to tell of the "private goings-on" of men, to wrest the public discourse from the hands of "lying" men has, for Smith, immense consequences, and makes possible the prospect of a new South.

There is an important relation between the question of who controls the public discourse and the question of how and by whom honor is defined. Orlando Patterson characterizes slavery as honoring the master and dishonoring the slave; in this scenario, he notes, "The slave . . . could have no honor because he had no power and no independent social existence" (10). Adrienne Rich's essay "Women and Honor: Some Notes on Lying," however, points us in a very different direction regarding a conceptualization of honor. For Rich, honor can exist among women, among "powerless people," but it is defined much differently than "the old, male idea of honor" (186). As earlier suggested, Rich's idea of honor among women is tied to speech acts, and particularly to the telling of secrets. Her definition of honor springs from her idea of "right" behavior in personal relationships; for her, honor involves the refusal to lie, the willingness to make "the effort to speak honestly" (187). As she defines it, then, those women whom Lillian Smith imagines in conversation and telling the truth to one another are prime examples of women acting honorably. More significantly, they also represent the way in which hierarchies of social power within public realms might be influenced by private concerns, relations, and revelations. Rich's essay, as "notes" toward a new morality, suggests an idea of honor springing from the "separate sphere" of women, and this honor, in its origin, bears little relation to the ways in which male honor is defined. Lillian Smith's example of women telling the truth to one another, however, suggests a crucial relation between women's secrets and male honor: women's secrets have the capacity to dishonor men, that is, as secrets become part of the public discourse, they have the power to change the social order.

By reading Smith's description as one that offers the possibility that knowledge previously contained within the private sphere might collide with and rearrange the public order, we are seriously challenging the Hegelian notion that the history of subjectivity, and the development of human consciousness, excludes women. According to Hegel, who is arguing from the example of the ancient Greek *polis* and family, women remain in the private sphere and cannot participate in history. In Simone de Beauvoir's reinterpretation of this divide, "man is the Subject, the Absolute, representing mind, transcendence, and spirit; woman is the object, the Other, the second sex, representing matter, immanence, and the flesh" (Mills, *Feminist Interpretations* 2).[15] Luce Irigaray rereads this othering in psychoanalytic terms to say that "woman is the unconscious; man is the conscious self."[16] Consequently, "woman has the corrosive power of the repressed parts of the self" and, according to Irigaray, "becomes the voice, the accomplice of the people, the slaves, those who only whisper their revolt against their masters secretly" ("Eternal Irony" 49). Beauvoir and Irigaray are both concerned with "woman's exile from subjectivity" (Mills, *Feminist Interpretations* 8). They "share the conviction that within patriarchy the subject is exclusively male; and they share the belief that to challenge patriarchal domination women must move into the position of the subject" (Mills, *Feminist Interpretations* 8). While the question of how—that is, through what mechanisms—women move into the subject position remains one of serious feminist debate,[17] we might take as given that they do and have. If Smith's "white and colored women" have say in questions of honor, they are clearly operating within the public realm. This points, then, to the idea that social orders are not monoliths or closed systems and that slavery may not mean social death so much as participation in an "other" social order.

Following Orlando Patterson's lead, Eric Sundquist focuses on the oppositional moment of conflict between Frederick Douglass and Edward Covey as the prime example of the Hegelian dialectic of master and slave. According to Sundquist, this event, as portrayed in *My Bondage and My Freedom*, is the "the most remarkable event of Douglass's life story" (*Wake* 122). For Sundquist, in addition to advocating physical resistance by slaves, Douglass extends "individual courage into the domain of cultural politics, mastering a tradition of literature and political philosophy as well as the dogma of revolutionary opposition" (124). In other words, he enters the public domain by not only laying claim to a position within the social order, but also to one within the nascent realm of American literary production. By doing so, says Sundquist,

Douglass has redefined the trope of patrimony, and thus "enter[s] into the self-making process of being an American" (125). Absent from Sundquist's account is the emphasis Paul Gilroy places on Douglass's meeting with Sandy, the "genuine African" with magical powers, who gives Douglass a charm that he claims will protect him from Covey (Douglass, *My Bondage* 238). Gilroy sees Douglass's communion with Sandy as further evidence of his break with Christianity, but we might read this scene as a moment of community for Douglass, of the kind that allows him to stand against Covey, or, recalling Melvin Dixon's language, as a representative moment of slaves "converting themselves to each other" (302). As intriguing as it might be to continue to reinterpret the Douglass/Covey moment along these lines, it is also crucial that we forgo our search for distinctively masculinist dialectical moments altogether so that other telling representations of master/slave conflicts can emerge. These other moments, as we would expect, will share with this one a portrayal inclusive of the collective identity of the bondsman, but will not be homosocial.

At this juncture it is important to consider Hegelian self-consciousness in more detail and to invoke aspects of the master/slave moment with which we have not yet been concerned. According to Hegel's model, self-consciousness knows itself as self-consciousness only when it confronts another self-consciousness, and in order to understand why this is so, Kojève's explanation is most helpful. According to Kojève, Hegel introduces contemplative consciousness in an earlier stage, but it proves not to be self-consciousness because contemplative consciousness is not focused on "I"; it is, instead, "absorbed" by the thing "he" contemplates so that "he *forgets himself*, he thinks only about the thing being contemplated" (37). In order "for this word [I] to appear, something other than purely passive contemplation, which only *reveals* Being, must also be present." As Kojève points out, this other thing, according to Hegel, is desire, because when a person feels desire "he necessarily becomes aware of *himself*. Desire is always revealed as *my* desire, and to reveal desire, one must use the word 'I'" (37). Thus, the two self-consciousnesses that meet in the master/slave moment are two desiring self-consciousnesses, and what each desires more than anything is the desire of the other, that is, recognition. Since, for Hegel, mutual recognition is not possible in this moment, force becomes necessary, and there begins the famous fight to the death for recognition. In this fight, when one self-consciousness values life more than recognition, one self-consciousness becomes slave as the other becomes master. As events continue to unfold, of course, the recognition the master gets from the slave proves not enough (since it is only recognition from a slave), and there begins the process by which consciousness continues its development.

Judith Butler's *Subjects of Desire*, a study of "the concept of desire concentrating on Hegel's *Phenomenology of Spirit* and some of the central appropriations of that theme in twentieth-century French philosophy," contributes significantly to our understanding of the ways in which desire is integral to the movement of Hegel's dialectic.[18] In her reading of the life and death struggle of master and slave, Butler sees "an extension of self-consciousness' initial project to gain unity with the Other, and to find its own identity through the Other." She then provides a clear description of how the master/slave dynamic shifts from a desire to kill to a desire to dominate:

> The dynamic of lord and bondsman emerges as an extenuation of the desire to annihilate, but, because annihilation would undermine the project altogether by taking away *life*, this desire is held in check. Domination, the relation that replaces the urge to kill, must be understood as the effort to annihilate within the context of life. The Other must now *live its own death*. Rather than become an indeterminate nothingness through death, the Other must now prove its essential nothingness *in life*. The Other which was at first captivating, now becomes that which must be captured, subdued, contained. (52)

If we now turn to African American narrative literature and allow ourselves to consider the possibility of heterosexual master/slave moments, in many ways Butler's description seems to correlate with the life of slavery that Harriet Jacobs describes. Jacobs characterizes Dr. Flint as a man with "an iron will . . . [who] was determined to keep me and to conquer me" (42). In this context, "conquer" clearly means to convince her to willfully enter into sexual relations with him. In response to Dr. Flint's plan to build Jacobs a small house, "in a secluded place, four miles away from the town," she declares: "I vowed before my Maker that I would never enter it. I had rather toil on the plantation from dawn till dark; I had rather live and die in jail, than drag on, from day to day, *through such a living death*" (53; emphasis added).[19]

According to Peter Kalkavage, "the key to the self-consciousness chapter" of Hegel's *Phenomenology* "is the violence with which self-consciousness first appears. . . . Hegel's technical word for this violence is *negativity*; the experiential word for it is *desire*" (5). Kalkavage continues by pointing out that in the introductory section of the *Phenomenology* entitled "The Truth of Self-Certainty," Hegel says: "Self-consciousness is desire." For Kalkavage, understanding this statement is key to understanding the concept of

Hegelian self-consciousness (5). In Kojève's reading, in order for desire to transform consciousness it must be "directed toward a non-natural object, toward something that goes beyond the given reality," but "the only thing that goes beyond the given reality is Desire itself," and so it is "Desire directed toward another Desire, taken as Desire, [that] will create, by the negating and assimilating action that satisfies it, an I essentially different from the animal 'I'" (Kojève 5). In other words, it is not desire for things, such as food, that can be consumed, that brings about self-consciousness, but the desire for the desire of others, the kind of desire that Dr. Flint exhibits toward Harriet Jacobs, for example. Or, to move from Harriet Jacobs's narrative back to Frederick Douglass's, it is not Douglass's own conflict with Covey, but rather his aunt's torture by Captain Anthony, the very first instance of a slavemaster's brutality that Douglass reports in explicit detail (both in his *Narrative* and *My Bondage*), that better fits the master/slave scenario depicted by Hegel.

Douglass's aunt Esther (Hester in Douglass's *Narrative*; Esther in the later account in *My Bondage*) is repeatedly bound and whipped by her master for preferring the sexual attention of another slave, Ned Roberts, over her master's.[20] In a clearly sadistic and sexually charged scene, Esther is stripped to the waist, her "wrists . . . firmly tied, and the twisted rope . . . fastened to a strong staple in a heavy wooden joist above" (*My Bondage* 87). Douglass describes the master taking pleasure through this torture: "Behind her stood old master, with cowskin in hand, preparing his barbarous work with all manner of harsh, coarse, and tantalizing epithets. The screams of his victim were most piercing. He was cruelly deliberate, and protracted the torture, as one who was delighted with the scene" (87). While numerous critics have read this passage as significant within the construction of Black masculinity, here our focus is on the terms of Hegel's/Kojève's analysis.[21] Captain Anthony, acting out a scene familiar to pornography, desires not just Esther, but Esther's "desire." He, in other words, gives Esther what (he fantasizes) she masochistically "wants." Esther, once "captivating" to Captain Anthony (in Butler's terms) is, in typical sadistic/masochistic fashion, then captured and dominated by him.

In *Subjects of Desire*, Judith Butler points out an important aspect of Kojève's view of the relation between desire and self-consciousness. Butler writes: "For Kojève, desire motivates the formation of a distinct sense of agency. In order to achieve what one desires, one formulates desires in speech or expresses them in some other way, for expression is the instrumental medium through which we appeal to Others" (66). The point, she concludes, is that "subjectivity is unwittingly created and discovered through the concrete expression of desire" (66). In the scene between Esther and Captain Anthony, Douglass makes a clear point of referring to Anthony's speech: he chronicles that Anthony speaks "tantalizing epithets" and reports that, in response to Esther's cries, Anthony produces answers "too coarse and blasphemous" to be repeated by Douglass.[22] This ritual torture, then, portrayed as a regularly repeated occurrence, includes the verbal expression of the master's desire, which brings with it his subjectivity. He is not the only one to speak, however. As Douglass reports, Esther is also verbal: "Have mercy . . . I won't do so no more" (88), she cries. This, too, is the expression of desire, not the fantasized desire for brutalization but the desire that this brutalization cease. Significantly, Esther's words also contain a lie, since, as Douglass relates, Esther continues to see Ned Roberts, which she proclaims she will no longer do. This has ramifications for Esther's "subjectivity": through Esther's lying speech her subject position is significantly elsewhere—lies, like whispers, defer to the master's authority but also align the speaker with that "other" membership group, here tying Esther's identity to slave community, to the group consciousness that operates as the third term within the master/slave moment.

While critics Orlando Patterson, Eric Sundquist, and Paul Gilroy consistently put forward the Douglass/Covey confrontation as a Hegelian master/slave moment, these critics also each make the claim, puzzling in Hegelian terms, that Douglass proves in this moment that he is Covey's equal. Douglass demonstrates his "negation of the condition of slavery," to use Sundquist's words (*Wake* 124), first in his consciousness and then through his actions of physical resistance. The confrontation suggests "the Hegelian impasse" because "each [man] was able to contain the strength of the other without vanquishing him" and so the fight ends in "mutual respect," according to Gilroy (62). From Douglass's biographical writing itself, we see that he says, about this incident, whereas "I was nothing before, I was a man now," which indicates that he is no longer slave within his own consciousness (*Life and Times* 143).[23] In the Douglass/Covey moment as it is interpreted, then, the triumph is that Douglass becomes "master" of himself, and, through resistance, is recognized by Covey as an equal. As important as it is, however, this interpretation does not represent Hegelian transformation. In Hegelian terms, the person in the slave position does not resolve the master/slave conflict by proving himself equal to the master. And while we might claim, as Orlando Patterson does, that Hegel simply misunderstands the dynamics of the master/slave relationship, I would suggest instead a serious reconsideration of the ways that the Douglass/Covey confrontation is not progressive as Hegel envisions the transformation that takes place through the master/slave conflict. If the two combatants simply shift positions so that now Douglass rather than

Covey wins, these two subjects remain locked in a confrontational dynamic such that success, in this struggle, remains defined according to Covey's terms. There are other ways, as we might suspect, to reinterpret Douglass's story such that the Hegelian master/slave conflict indeed becomes transformational for American consciousness writ large; these interpretations would, however, also displace the Douglass/Covey moment as it has been presented by other critics.

In this context, we now reconsider that other moment from Douglass's narrative writing, the disturbing image of Captain Anthony's brutalization of Douglass's aunt Esther. This master/slave image also resonates within American consciousness, and it presents an alternative representation that fully characterizes, in Hegelian terms, the dialectical relationship. The Anthony/ Esther moment is so disturbing, in part, because there is no parallel "fighting back" by Esther of the kind that suggests the masculine impasse between Douglass and Covey. Instead, many critics (see, for example, Maurice Wallace 249) have read Esther's victimization as also one of rape because Douglass's earliest account of the brutality, in *Narrative*, includes the comment, "She now stood fair for his infernal purpose" (52). This remark, together with Douglass's additional comments that he cannot talk of all that he sees, suggests sexual victimization, and his comments also point to the secrets that Douglass keeps, embedded in this scene, all of which adds to the image's disturbing resonance. The moment between Captain Anthony and Esther does portend transformation, however, and, insidiously enough, what is at issue is *her* issue. In later chapters I will examine the ways that African American women writers explore sexual violence, attendant biracial children, and concomitant race and identity issues. Here, however, the question is what, or who, the offspring of Captain Anthony and Douglass's aunt Esther is.[24] However we answer this question, transformative knowledge is implied. Within the trope of race, we say that such children also represent some third term since they are neither white nor Black, both white and Black, and, simultaneously, something else, which I will characterize as *mestizo*, using Gloria Anzaldúa's term.

Readers of Hegel's dialectic within an African American context have difficulty with Hegel's idea that work is necessary to the process through which slaves are transformed, or, as one critic interprets, that "Hegel's dialectic depends on the slave's identification with his forced labor" (Cassuto 241). Orlando Patterson simply rejects this idea (99), while Leonard Cassuto suggests that the work of the slave is, at least in part, the writing of his narrative, which brings with it self-conscious subjectivity on the part of the slave, and the objectification of the master.[25] At this juncture we must realize that the labor of reproduction, as Mary O'Brien has defined it in *The Politics of Repro-duction*, might also be taken into account. One consequence of slavery, then, could be characterized as forced reproductive labor on the part of enslaved women, and a resulting identification with the value of this labor, inherently wrapped up within the birth of a new generation of children, which thus engenders not just a new self-consciousness, but also a new American iden-tity.[26] Here, Hortense Spillers's remarks are apt: "[The] 'threads cable-strong' of an incestuous, interracial genealogy uncover slavery in the United States as one of the richest displays of the psychoanalytic dimensions of culture before the science of European psychoanalysis takes hold" (223). Enslaved women's identification with forced reproductive labor (as a later chapter focused on the fiction of Frances E. W. Harper and Pauline Hopkins will suggest in detail) becomes transformative, and not only within African American communities but also in America's history of consciousness.

By reading Hegel's dialectic through the lens of African American ex-slave narratives we are able to see the clear role that secret community, the community of those enslaved, plays as the "always already" third term of the dialectic. Secrets of paternity, however, the "masters' secrets" of slavery, point to the significance that gender makes in relation not only to slave experience, but also to the way in which that experience is transformed. This is directly tied to what O'Brien calls "reproductive consciousness," and the way in which that consciousness is different for men and women. Paternity, O'Brien argues, is necessarily a concept, that is, it "must be conceptualized because it is not immediate . . . is shot through with an intransigent uncertainty, an uncertainty contingent upon the alienation of the male seed" ("Hegel" 198). Consequently, according to O'Brien, Hegel sees the human race as "'self-developing and self-generative'" but "it is nothing of the kind." Instead it is "developed and sustained by women's labor," a labor through which woman is "mediating her separation from the child, canceling by life-risking activity the self-alienation of *her* seed in the certain conceptualization of the child who is born as hers" (198–99). Whether slave or free, men do not *know* who their children are; women, however, do know their own children and, often, also *know* their children's father. The implication of this is a gendered self-understanding and a distinctive difference between the self-identity of African American sons and African American daughters. While I will explore this difference in detail throughout the remaining chapters of this study, it is also evident in its earliest incarnation through descriptions of secret white paternity in ex-slave narratives.

Additional information about Douglass's relation to the masters' secret fathering is presented in his narratives, for example in the first few pages of his *Narrative*, where he reveals that he will never know the identity of his father, yet within the slave community his father is admitted to be a white man and "whispered" to be Douglass's master (this is, of course, the same Captain Anthony who regularly brutalizes Douglass's aunt Esther). The significance to Douglass of this piece of information, along with information about his mother, changes as Douglass writes his later autobiographies, a clear indication that the identities of his father and mother disturb him.[27] Even in the 1845 *Narrative*, however, Douglass determines that he will never know who his father is because, being separated from his mother as an infant, he has had "the means of knowing" withheld from him. Douglass knows that some people, the people whispering, have an opinion of who fathered him, but this is not a source reliable enough for Douglass to trust. The implication from this version of Douglass's story of his birth is that slave mothers *know* who fathers are; sons do not.

We can compare Douglass's attitude toward the question of who his father is to Harriet Jacobs's clear knowledge that Dr. Flint fathered at least eleven offspring of slaves: "My master was, to my knowledge, the father of eleven slaves" (35). This, too, suggests that there is a gender-based distinction to be made between the relation males and females have to the "masters' secret" of paternity contained within the legacy of slavery. Jacobs *knows;* Douglass does not. Further, Jacobs's knowledge of Dr. Flint's fathering is dependent on a female community in which secrets are told: we presume it is through talk with other women who have themselves had sexual relations with Dr. Flint that Jacobs becomes certain of Flint's fathering of slave children.[28]

The different relation enslaved men and women have to the secret identity of white fathers stems not only from differences in reproductive consciousness, but also from the matrilineal inheritance of slave status as well as from the differing relations to the slavemaster that exist for women and men. One way of thinking about this difference in relations is to realize, as Hortense Spillers points out, why bastard children are always male: "Because the traditional rites and laws of inheritance rarely pertain to the female child, bastard status signals to those who need to know which son of the Father's is the legitimate heir and which one the imposter. For that reason, property seems wholly the business of the male. A "she" cannot, therefore, qualify for bastard, or "natural son" status, and that she cannot provides further insight into the coils and recoils of patriarchal wealth and fortune" (204). While any slave child, male or female, might have been fathered by his or her master, *status* is conferred differently, based on gender: only male slaves might be illegitimate sons, and only sons might be patriarchs. Female slaves, because they are female, might only be illegitimate wives, a role of some distinction but no legal status. The possibility of acknowledgment as an illegitimate son makes men like Douglass interested in sources that "prove," legally, the identity of fathers but not so interested in the "hearsay" evidence that surrounds them. On the other hand women, interested in either avoiding or being able to anticipate and thus manipulate what we would call "sexual harassment" or "sexual abuse," and deeply concerned with forced procreation, are more likely to rely on first-person accounts that document wrongs, but, also, generative identities not ever addressed within the legal system. This suggests, then, male interest in birth*right* but female interest in the preservation of bodily integrity and the development of generative knowledge. That this knowledge is distinct from the "body of knowledge" contained within patriarchal institutions such as the legal system presages the way an alternative female authority, rooted in the institution of slavery, reverberates through late nineteenth- and twentieth-century America.[29] Also, the fact that the female slave has no status as "illegitimate daughter" perhaps makes incestuous acts both more probable and unrecognizable (by the father) as such.

Thomas Nelson Page, the plantation school writer mentioned earlier who denies a rebellious or resistant attitude among slaves through his depictions of the "faithful slave," also writes about fathering. In another story from the collection *In Ole Virginia*, titled "Ole 'Stracted," Page presents a Black husband and his wife and children who are all tenant farmers on a former plantation, now owned by a clearly lower-class white man who undeservedly came into possession of the property just before, or during, the war. This Black tenant family is about to be evicted from the property they are farming because of an unpaid debt. An old man also lives nearby; he is an ex-slave of the place who remembers it in its glory. This man has become mentally unbalanced, "distracted," because of trauma experienced when his old master, long ago, lost all of his property and saw his slaves sold from him. At this time Ole 'Stracted, too, was sold away, although the slave and master had "growed up togerr" (193). Even worse, Ole 'Stracted's wife and son were sold to some other slaveholder, with the consequence that the slave husband and father lost touch with his family completely. Now in the last stages of his life, this old man, who does not even know his real name, is waiting for his master to keep his promise to return and buy him back. Further, Ole 'Stracted has twelve hundred dollars to give to his old master so that his master can also buy back his wife and son.

This story ends with Ole 'Stracted's death, which is meant to be a senti-mental tearjerker, because Ole 'Stracted is finally reunited with the master he has been waiting for all these years. Further, in his dying moments when he hears the tenant farmer's wife call her husband's name, he recognizes it as his own, which reveals that he is the tenant farmer's long-lost father. This wraps up the subplot of the story: Ole 'Stracted's money, saved for the purpose of buying his wife and son, will now be used by the son to pay off his debts and purchase the land he has been farming. The ending is meant to be a happy one all around. For purposes of our focus on paternal secrets, however, the most significant feature of the story is the way that it so determinedly fixes the identities of missing fathers of slaves (or ex-slaves) and white slave mas-ters. They are emphatically not the same person, an example of vehement denial of the kind Toni Morrison makes reference to in "Unspeakable Things Unspoken." In fact, the imagery used to end this story suggests that while a slave's missing father must be another slave, the white master is the Christian godhead, the "Master" who comes, at last, to bring the old slave "home."

In a bizarre twisting of this identification between master and "Master," or slaveholder and God, and in keeping with the nineteenth-century idealization of the written word, James Henry Hammond, a nineteenth-century South Carolina politician, writes diaries he labels "secret and sacred." Hammond is one of the few slaveholders who records, from his own point of view, his sexual relations with female slaves. In his "secret and sacred" personal diaries he documents his long-term relationships with Sally Johnson and, eventu-ally, her twelve-year-old daughter Louisa (whom he did not father). A letter written by Hammond to his son, dated February 19, 1856, and quoted by Carol Bleser in her introduction to *Secret and Sacred: The Diaries of James Henry Hammond, a Southern Slaveholder*, makes clear the perverse attitude of the slaveholder/father toward his offspring:

> My Dear Harry:
> In the last will I made I left to you, over and above my other children Sally Johnson the mother of Louisa and all the children of both. Sally says Hen-derson is my child. It is possible, but I do not believe it. Yet act on her's rather than my opinion. Louisa's first child *may* be mine. I think not. Her second I believe is mine. Take care of her and her children who are both of *your* blood if not of mine and of Henderson. The services of the rest will I think compensate for an indulgence to these. I cannot free these people and send them North. It would be cruelty to them. Nor would I like that any but my own blood should own as Slaves my own blood or Louisa. I leave them to your charge, believing that you will best appreciate and most

independently carry out my wishes in regard to them. Do not let Louisa or any of my children or possible children be slaves of Strangers. Slavery *in the family* will be their happiest earthly condition.

Ever affectionately,

J. H. H.[30]

By labeling his diaries "secret," Hammond indicates that he recognizes that he is writing about personal details of his life forbidden from public discourse. By labeling these diaries "sacred," however, he also makes the claim that his version of these events is to be neither questioned nor contradicted. Not only does Hammond have the right, presumably, to control public discourse, but he also lays claims to the *true* presentation of his own secrets. This, he seems to indicate by calling his diaries "secret and sacred," is the power of the written word.[31] In this context, the claim of Mattie J. Jackson in her as-told-to slave narrative published in 1866 is profound: "Manage your own secrets, and divulge them by the silent language of your own pen," she advises.[32] It seems that slaveholding men and enslaved women realize that their issue, whether literal or figurative and creative, is contested territory. And yet this issue is not simply territory, a "new world" to be appropriated. Often "it" has names, personal names, and an identity inclusive of the full measure of free will that modernity bestows upon human beings.

Thomas Nelson Page's story, "Ole 'Stracted," which attempts to focus on African American characters but in fact presents, in Morrison's terminology, an *Africanist* rendition of the Old South, denies the secret truths about African American existence during slavery that African American narratives present. Specifically, Page denies that a slave's community and identity come from somewhere other than his or her master. Further, he denies that the white master might, himself, be the father of slaves. Page's story bears much in common with the problematic accounts of contented slaves that historian Leon Litwack declares too insistent to be believable. Like those accounts, "Ole 'Stracted" demonstrates the overdetermined insistence that masks feelings of fear and vulnerability. Stories about contented slaves were codified because the institution of slavery was at stake, threatened from within. Page's insistence in this story on the role played and not played by the white master shows, however, that patriarchy itself, not just its manifestation as the institution of slavery, is also threatened. Page's revisionism insists not only that plantation life was idyllic, but also that patriarchy is benevolent. Slavery's secrets, however, prove otherwise. When these secrets are told, the depravity of Southern white men claiming to be American patriarchs is exposed and understood as such. For this reason, one consequence of telling slavery's secrets is that American patriarchy can never be the same.

Understanding modernity, Paul Gilroy argues, "requires a return to and a rethinking of the characteristically modern relationship between the master and the slave" (*Black Atlantic* 45). It is imperative, I am arguing, that in this rethinking we focus on the paradox of the woman who is slave. If we follow Hegel's lead and exclude this figure from our consideration of the meaning of modernity, from our examination of the development of human history or of human consciousness, we also implicitly accept Hegel's belief that patriarchy is natural rather than historical, that the separation of the public and the private is a precondition to history rather than "a working structure of patriarchal hegemony" (O'Brien, "Hegel" 187). Certainly it is true that one operating principle within modernity has been its challenges to patriarchy. We cannot explain this adequately without an understanding of the role, and the authority, of the woman who is also slave. Nor can we adequately understand freedom. In Hegelian terms, within patriarchal history, women are contained (or "exiled" or "confined") within the familial or private realm, yet in this same history slaves share the public stage with masters. Where, then, is the place of women who are slaves? And further, where is the place of these women's children? Perhaps in the end this place is not adequately characterized as either private or public but is something else entirely. To put it in Black Atlantic terms, perhaps subject position hybridity influences hybrid cultures and creates hybrid ideas, which points us toward significant, and signifying, transformation. One final point: the modernity attendant upon all that succeeds the master/slave moment is intimately tied to language acquisition—not, however, the acquisition of new languages, of "foreign tongues," but the acquisition of new ways with language—ways that begin with the telling and the hearing of secrets.

2

Father/Son Relations in African American Abolitionist Fiction

◆◯ς ℥◯◆

My old man's a white old man
And my old mother's black.
If ever I cursed my white old man
I take my curses back.

—Langston Hughes, "Cross"

In antebellum American terms, as corollary to gendering female the slave of the master/slave moment, the truly tragic mulatto becomes male. That is, as antebellum African American fiction demonstrates, African American sons have a particularly difficult, even tragic, relationship to fathers, who are often white, that must be negotiated on the way to discovering their own manhood. By referring to manhood, here, I mean simply to point toward a self-consciousness that is gendered male rather than female, and in this chapter I will develop the idea of gendered self-consciousness as introduced in chapter 1. Thinking through Mary O'Brien's concept of reproductive consciousness and Hortense Spillers's point that for males but not females there is the possibility of bastard status, territorially speaking, manhood (as compared to womanhood) means less certainty of paternal identities but also more possibility of benefits stemming from illegitimate son status. These two sets of problems might be said to inform the earliest fiction by African American male writers, and as this fiction asserts selfhood within a call for the abolition of slavery that also critiques American patriarchy, African American sons demonstrate a psychologically complex need for recognition from fathers, a desire to circumvent the inevitability of tragic endings when recognition is not forthcoming, yet all the while confront the slave masters/fathers that perpetuate slavery as an institution.

In their construction of narrative voices, the earliest fiction by African American male writers asserts selfhood within a critique of American patriarchy dependent upon telling patriarchal secrets, that is, secrets whose tellings condemn the institution of slavery as patriarchal social order. This is true of William Wells Brown's *Clotel; or, The President's Daughter* (1853), Frederick Douglass's *The Heroic Slave* (1853), and Martin Delany's *Blake; or, The Huts of America* (1861), texts I will discuss in detail. I take as my *Ur*-text, however, Victor Séjour's "Le Mulâtre," to date the first known work of fiction published by an African American, but a story that has attracted little critical attention because it was written in French rather than English (and, indeed, it was not published in English until 1997). Séjour, born a *quarteron libre* (free Quadroon) in New Orleans, wrote "Le Mulâtre" after arriving in Paris at age nineteen and first published the story in the *Revue des Colonies* in March 1837.[1]

As psychologically compelling as Sophocles' *Oedipus the King*, this story's power, as Werner Sollors comments, depends upon "Séjour's mythic method of locating the deep tragic themes of the son's search for the name of the father and of the father-son conflict" (167). "Le Mulâtre," told as framed narrative, presents Antoine, "an old negro," who tells the story of his friend Georges, regularly referred to as "the mulatto," to an unnamed narrator. The setting is "a small town in St. Domingue, now known as Haiti," and the most significant details of the plot are as follows. Georges has a mother, Laïas, enslaved, who keeps the identity of Georges's father from him but promises to reveal this identity when Georges becomes an adult, saying, "My son, you shall learn your name only when you reach twenty-five, for then you will be a man; you will be better able to guard its secret" (290). Georges's mother dies, but not before giving Georges a pouch (with a portrait of his father in it) that he promises not to open until he is twenty-five. When Georges's master Alfred is threatened by robbers, Georges saves his master's life but is shot in the process and almost dies. Alfred then becomes enamored of Georges's wife, Zélie, whom he sees as he visits the wounded Georges. Zélie spurns Alfred's sexual advances in such a way that Alfred falls and injures his head and, consequently, Alfred condemns Zélie to be hanged. For this, Georges promises revenge as he escapes with their son to join the Maroons; and three years later, after Alfred has married and become a father, Georges returns to avenge his wife's death.

In the concluding scene of the novel, Georges confronts his master, Alfred, makes clear he has fatally poisoned Alfred's wife, and prepares to behead his master with an ax. Georges is momentarily distracted, however, when Alfred pleads with him in "the name of your father" and Georges, "with tears in

34

his eyes," says, "My father . . . my father" and then says, "Do you know him . . . oh! Tell me his name. . . . What's his name . . . oh! Tell me, tell me his name . . . I'll pardon you . . . I'll bless you" (297). But Georges once again becomes vengeful, and remembers his desire to "settle accounts . . . for his wife's blood." The ax falls as Alfred is saying, "You might as well kill your own fa-,'" and then, we are told, "Alfred's head rolled across the floor, but, as it rolled, the head distinctly pronounced the final syllable, "-ther. . . ." Georges opens "the fateful pouch" and cries out "I'm cursed. . . ." The last sentence of the story reads: "An explosion was heard; and the next day, near the corpse of Alfred, was discovered the corpse of the unhappy Georges. . ." (299). In this tragedy, then, which we might consider the mulatto's tragedy, Georges has killed himself upon discovering the identity of his father, perhaps because he cannot live with the knowledge of who his father is, or perhaps because he cannot live with the knowledge that he has killed his father; combined, these two facts seem to overdetermine his self-annihilation.

While such an abbreviated and telescoped account of this story does not do justice to its emotional power, it does provide us with the details of the son's complex fate. Georges wants to know who his father is in order to know his own "name," but his mother has been forbidden to tell, and is afraid that the young Georges's life will be endangered by the knowledge of his father's identity. Georges's interest in his name suggests his own patriarchal, or at least paternal, desires—he wants to be recognized by his father in order to take his rightful place in society. When this recognition is withheld, mayhem ensues. Alfred, the father, also does not recognize Georges's matrimonial rights, does not recognize Georges's wife as belonging to Georges. Consequently, the struggle between Alfred and Georges over Zélie's fate, a contest that Georges loses, sets the remainder of the tragedy's action in motion, and as is befitting a tragedy, there seems to be no other possible conclusion than the murders and suicide that occur. The question becomes, then, whether or not it is the case when the master/slave struggle is also a father/son struggle that the destruction of both parties is inevitable. This is the question that Antoine asks just before he tells Georges's story to the unnamed narrator. In various forms, it is also the question that William Wells Brown, Frederick Douglass, and Martin Delany explore in their abolitionist fiction.

One way to avoid the father/son death struggle may be through recognition by the father of the son, a recognition that would dramatically shift the father/son confrontation away from a master/slave struggle while also allowing the son to then assume his own patriarchal position. This is the possibility that Brown and Douglass pursue, and in *Clotel* and the *Heroic Slave* each narrator tells secrets in an attempt to validate, even legitimate, African American sons by seeking recognition of African Americans as the progeny of (white) American forebears, as sons (or daughters) of statesmen or of the state. Another possibility, however, is to destroy the master-who-is-father/slave-who-is-son relationship by *overthrowing* the institution of slavery. Presumably, in "Le Mulâtre," by the time of the telling by Antoine of Georges's story, since St. Domingue is "now known as Haiti," the Haitian Revolution has occurred and forms the historical background of the story (Sollors 165). Possibly, too, this revolution, which has not intervened in Georges's tragedy, at least makes Georges's story possible, by allowing the old man Antoine to tell it to the unnamed narrator, whom he calls "Master," and who may even be white. Delany's novel, *Blake*, also focuses on revolutionary possibility, and consequently presents a son who is recognized not by American fathers but by African fathers, as represented through an African diasporic community. Also, Delany uses secrets in his novel to emphasize the significance of this shift from American to African progenitors: the greatest secret of *Blake*, never explicitly told to his antebellum American readers, concerns not American identity at all but rather African American community and African heritage. Another way to avoid tragedy, then, is to turn the son into an abolitionist revolutionary of a different father altogether, who will kill not in the name of vengeance but in the name of freedom, and so has no need to destroy himself as a consequence of his killing of others.

As the son's story, Brown's, Douglass's, and Delany's fiction, even when it makes oblique reference to the master/female slave moment, definitively and carefully focuses elsewhere, an indication that male legitimacy rather than female knowledge is each story's point. African American manhood, as constructed through these texts, attempts to situate itself with regard to white patriarchs and white patriarchal models but define itself differently, "otherly." This other way is not strictly oppositional, not contained within master/slave moments. It is, instead, relational, and specifically, each text constructs African American manhood relationally by constructing its narrative based on the triadic formulation inherent in secrets, where someone speaks to someone and not to someone else.[2] Each text, then, also relies upon a dialectical process inclusive of an already present third term. As the persons from whom secrets are kept, slaveholders are rarely addressed directly by these antebellum African American writers. In Brown's *Clotel*, Douglass's *Heroic Slave*, and Delany's *Blake*, opposition to the patriarchal social order of slavery is narrated to and through a third party or group that serves as an outside agent. In *Clotel* the third party is the British public; in the *Heroic Slave* it is the northern traveler

Listwell combined with the sailor Tom Grant; and in *Blake* it is the Pan-African community gathered in Cuba and united to overthrow white rule. Black male subjectivity is developed in each of these texts in relation to the third parties constructed, much more so than within master/slave relationships. As these texts explore masculine subjectivity by constructing sons, analyze father/son relations, and represent the son's need for recognition, they bring what Houston Baker refers to as "the *sound* of Caliban" into literary history.[3] Here, however, Caliban's vernacular is not represented as an alien tongue but as a loose tongue: it reveals patriarchal secrets. Further, we recognize secret tellings as "the *sound* of Caliban" because narratives constructed as such bring forward that already present third term within the dialectical process, which is, after all, another kind of "triple play," another way to disrupt fixed dualities, including the oppositional duality characterized as the master/slave moment.

Clotel: The Bastard Son's Story

In his 1847 address to the Female Anti-Slavery Society of Salem, at Lyceum Hall, William Wells Brown announces that his "subject for this evening is Slavery as it is, and its influence upon the morals and character of the American people." He follows this statement, however, by declaring that it is not really possible to publicly represent slavery as it is: "Were I about to tell you the evils of Slavery, to represent to you the Slave in his lowest degradation," Brown declares, "I should wish to take you, one at a time, and whisper to you" ("Lecture Delivered" 4). In *Clotel*, Brown determines a narrative strategy and constructs a narrative voice that represents that whisper, a voice by and through which he makes slavery's secrets public. In this earlier address, however, Brown is still grappling with the existential impossibility of the speaking slave, the slave who will speak up, grappling with his knowledge from slavery that "the Slave shall have no right to speak; he shall have nothing to say. The Slave cannot speak for himself; he cannot speak for his wife, or his children. He is a thing" ("Lecture Delivered" 4). Brown follows this statement declaring slaves to be "things" by determining that there is only one way for the speaking *man* to emerge: "If I wish to stand up and say, 'I am a man,'" Brown states, "I must leave the land that gave me birth." Here I will consider in detail how Brown becomes able "to stand up and say, 'I am man,'" that is, how he determines the public, speaking identity with which he narrates his novel *Clotel* and so tells his reading public slavery's secrets.

In *Clotel*, Brown clearly has a secret to tell, and it is partly personal. As he declares in the narrative of his life that prefaces the novel, and again in the opening lines of the novel itself, Brown knows the identities of many white fathers of slave sons and daughters, including his own. In his narrative, he not only declares that "his father was a slaveholder," but also names him as related to both his master, Doctor John Young, and "the Wichlief family, one of the oldest, wealthiest, and most aristocractic of the Kentucky planters" (17). In the opening to *Clotel*, he generalizes his personal story to explain that many of the expanding population of "slaves in the Southern States of America" are "half whites . . . whose fathers are slaveowners, and their mothers slaves" (59). Yet, as a former slave who knows his own identity because he indeed knows his father, Brown also knows that he has been disavowed by that same father, has been made illegitimate. By the way in which he investigates the topic of "the degraded and immoral condition of the relation of master and slave in the United States of America," we might additionally say that Brown is indignant that so many children, including himself, have been born illegitimately. Yet, by writing *Clotel* in order to avert the tragic consequences of "mulatto" birth, Brown, I am suggesting, legitimizes himself, and even, by taking on the identity of professional fugitive, as defined by Paul Gilmore, repaternalizes himself. In his desire for his own patriarchal legitimacy, however, Brown must disassociate himself not only from the land that gave him birth, but also from the person who gave him birth. This disassociation has consequences, and the most serious, as we shall see, is the way this affects Brown's imagination with regard to enslaved women. For Brown, master/female slave relations bring death to the women involved. While this state of affairs has often been read as the tragic mulatto's fate, we should remember that this is the son's version of a story self-determined by its narrator's desire to come into patriarchal manhood.

A novel focusing on the biracial offspring of slaveholders and slaves and subtitled "The President's Daughter" is clearly meant to tell a great secret. Lyrics collected and printed by Brown in his *Anti-Slavery Harp* (1849) put the matter bluntly: "Jefferson's child has been bartered for gold" one line proclaims, with the intent to stir outrage that Jefferson himself has fathered a slave whom he has allowed to be sold.[4] *Clotel* tells this secret about an American statesman less to help save Jefferson's daughter, however, than to validate, even legitimate, African American sons. *Clotel*'s telling of the secret relation between Black and white Americans is a son's critique of American patriarchy, and this is made evident through Brown's focus on African American illegitimacy as the great consequence of the institution of slavery. This illegitimacy is represented as a personal concern for Brown since his own father is a slave-holder. But Brown is also concerned with the illegitimate status of African Americans more generally, and, consequently, with the figurative fathers of such offspring—America's forefathers and statesmen. As Brown proclaims, he wants to "fasten the guilt on those who move in a higher circle" (16); thus, with *Clotel*, Brown signifies on all of these American fathers of African American children.

Paul Gilmore makes a convincing argument that Brown's literary manhood is achieved through Brown's "acquisition of the traits of middle-class manhood—specifically, literacy and economic success" that he achieves "through his ability to put on multiple masks" (42). Since these traits are not exclusively male, however, Gilmore's argument is more about Brown's acquisition of *person*hood than gendered manhood. Ann duCille, also interested in how Brown constructs personhood, points out that *Clotel*'s narrator focuses his opening comments on "the marriage relation," one indication that "coupling conventions" rather than such traditional "'manhood rights' as suffrage, property ownership, or literacy" are Brown's way of defining selfhood, or humanity (*Coupling Convention* 19). This, also, is not a comment about gender construction, however, since Brown's claim about marriage is that both husband and wife become "conscious of complete humanity" through marriage (*Clotel* 62). Brown's focus on marriage relations is noted by other critics, including John Ernest, who argues that marriage, for Brown, is the "practical model for the wheel of culture," the relationship within which "abstract concepts become felt concerns" (38). With regard to gendered constructions of self, however, ultimately, as duCille in some ways suggests, it is *Clotel*'s narrator's ability to focus "the gaze of the world" on slaveholders and slavery that most characterizes the gendered selfhood that we would term his "manhood."

Clotel represents the creation of an authoritative African American narrative voice, and as I have previously indicated, the novel's narrator more than any of its characters is of primary interest here.[5] In order to create this narrator, Brown carefully revises his own earlier *Narrative of William W. Brown, a Fugitive Slave, Written by Himself* (1847) and uses it as an authenticating introduction to *Clotel*. As Robert Stepto argues, by presenting his introductory narrative he establishes his "*access* to the incidents, characters, scenes, and tales which collectively make up *Clotel*" (*Veil* 30). In other words, he establishes his narrative position as an authority who knows slavery from inside the institution; and he establishes that his critique of the institution originates from this unique vantage point, as well. Ultimately, through the careful creation of this authoritative ex-slave voice, Brown's novel suggests the privileging rather than the repression of slave positionality, and his own transformation from the *object of* to the *authority on* slavery.

In his preface to *Clotel*, Brown addresses a British audience and expresses his belief that British public opinion can sway American politics, in part because the British and the Americans have "one language and one literature" (16). Brown intends, himself, to convince the British public to influence American opinion at least in part because his own status as an African American and fugitive slave makes direct dialogue with slaveholders impossible; in his personal situation, as one example, letters to Enoch Price, the man who purportedly owns him, must be written by an intermediary. Even while addressing a British audience, however, Brown's clear concern is American slaveholders, especially those who are influential in American politics. In his preface he states, "The great aim of the true friends of the slave should be to lay bare the institution, so that the gaze of the world may be upon it, and cause the wise, the prudent, and the pious to withdraw their support from it, and leave it to its own fate. It does the cause of emancipation but little good to cry out in tones of execration against the traders, the kidnappers, the hireling overseers, and brutal drivers, so long as nothing is said to fasten the guilt on those who move in a higher circle" (16). This desire to "fasten the guilt" by "lay[ing] bare the institution," Brown's purpose for writing *Clotel*, brings him to enlist the aid of "Englishmen." When he suggests that these same men might wish to atone "for the fact that slavery was introduced into the American colonies while they were under the control of the British Crown," it becomes clear that "the Englishmen" Brown invokes are the forefathers of American forefathers (16).

Brown's concern with the secret guilt of American forefathers, as stated in his preface, reverberates in the opening of his *Narrative of the Life and Escape of William Wells Brown*, which serves as *Clotel's* introduction, and then becomes the topic of the first chapter of *Clotel*. Brown opens his *Narrative* by stating that he was born a slave near the residence of "the late Hon. Henry Clay"; he then declares that his father was a slaveholder "connected with . . . one of the oldest, wealthiest, and most aristocratic [families] of the Kentucky planters" (17). These are the men "in high places," Brown implies, who in his own life bear the guilt of slavery (15). In the first chapter of *Clotel*, Brown turns to the specifics of this guilt. Here, he does not point to the violence of slavery, a common theme for abolitionist writers. Instead, he devotes himself to his treatise on the importance of the "marriage relation" and calls attention to the societally accepted practice of sexual relations between slaveholders and their female slaves. The problem with these liaisons, as Brown sees it, is the consequent number of illegitimate children born to enslaved women; and not only do slaveholders father such children themselves, but they also prohibit marriage among slaves. Thus, all children of slave mothers are deprived of "the fond covenant of love between parents," and without this covenant, all are illegitimate. This is the situation to which Brown wants to bring "the gaze of the world" and for which Brown wants to "fasten the guilt" upon slaveholders.

Brown's telling of the story of *Clotel*, and his intention to bring "the gaze of the world" upon slaveholders, reverses the subjectivity of the slaveholder-to-slave relation. Brown—and the world with him—looks upon the most secret and intimate actions of slaveholders while they, in turn, become the object of "the gaze." The psychology of this gaze is more complex, however. The objectification of the American fathers also occurs through Brown's appeal to his British audience, the fathers of the fathers, so to speak. The psychological dynamic inherent in fathers looking at sons, of fathers "catching sons in the act," brings shame to the American fathers; if we were to use Freudian terms, we might even say that being seen taps into castration anxiety. In other words, within almost any interpretive scenario, when fathers "gaze at" sons the consequence for the sons is diminished phallic power. By contrast, sons who look on their fathers' nakedness do not have the power to shame, to suggest castration. Instead, they are themselves punished, as the myth of Ham suggests, and patriarchal power, however threatened, remains intact.[6] Brown's characterization of himself as a son with special access to the dirty secrets of slavery, then, also allows him to construct a knowledgeable British reading public, that is, a British reading public that is "in the know," and this reading public, embedded as it is in the novel, gives Brown's narrative further credibility and authority. Perhaps even more significant, however, through this process Brown narrates for himself a new paternity, that is, he conceives for himself, as son, another father.

Six years prior to *Clotel*'s publication, when William Wells Brown published the first edition of his *Narrative of William W. Brown, a Fugitive Slave, Written by Himself*, he was writing according to abolitionist formula. In this earlier narrative, Brown adheres to the various conventions James Olney has identified as characteristic of the slave narrative form, and presents an episodic story with virtually no "reference to memory or any sense that memory does anything but make the past facts and events of slavery immediately present to the writer and his reader" (150).[7] Additionally, in a dedicatory preface to Wells Brown of Ohio, the Quaker who helped Brown during his flight from slavery, Brown pays tribute to abolitionist acts of charity and, in a biblical paraphrase, calls the men who perform them true Christians.[8] The next sentences of Brown's dedication, however, reveal the exact nature of his obligation to Wells Brown: "Even a name by which to be known among men, slavery had denied me. You bestowed upon me your own. Base indeed should I be, if I ever forget what I owe to you, or do anything to disgrace that honored name!" (iii). Wells Brown is the paternal figure to whom William Wells Brown owes his life, but even more, his manhood, in the form of patrilineal identity. By taking Wells Brown's name, and writing this narrative "for" him, William Wells Brown defines himself as the grateful "son" of the abolitionist benefactor, the reader of Brown's narrative.

Toward the end of this same *Narrative of William W. Brown*, when Brown tells the story of acquiring his new name from Wells Brown, he makes it clear that he had only a first name until he took Wells Brown's surname.[9] William Wells Brown has rejected the idea of being called by either of his masters' names. He has also rejected his white slaveholding father, about whose name he says, "I would rather have adopted the name of 'Friday,' and been known as the servant of some Robinson Crusoe" (98). When he extends "the privilege of naming" him to "the first man to extend the hand of friendship," he is, in a sense, replacing his Southern father with a Northern abolitionist (105). In keeping with this sensibility, through his writing of the *Narrative of William W. Brown*, Brown claims his identity not so much as a slave or an ex-slave, but as a member of the abolitionist family. For Brown in 1847, leaving the South without a surname meant leaving without an identity; while the experience of slavery bestowed a past, it was not a usable past. It is not until Brown's later *Narrative of the Life and Escape of William Wells Brown*, published in 1853 as the prefatory introduction to *Clotel*, that his relation to his experience as a slave changes, a change facilitated by Brown's departure from the land that gave him birth and by his newly developed relationship to a British reading public.

The *Narrative of the Life and Escape of William Wells Brown*, published in the same volume with *Clotel*, stands in the same prefatory and authorizing relation to the novel as letters from white abolitionists do to slave narratives in general, and, in particular, as the letters from Edmund Quincy and J. C. Hathaway do to Brown's 1847 narrative of his life. As a consequence, in the 1853 edition, Brown's narrative of his life as a slave is no longer the primary story, requiring authentication from abolitionist authority; instead, it is the prefatory material, which itself authenticates from its own, inherent authority, that becomes the focus. As such, we might consider it a significant extrinsic "fictive" element of the story, that is, as William Andrews defines, one of the technical devices used to authorize narrative voice and make fictional worlds believable.[10] This change in the signification of Brown's narrative is highlighted by the most startling difference between Brown's 1847 *Narrative of William W. Brown* and his 1853 *Narrative of the Life and Escape:* the change from first-person to third-person narration. While it might seem that by telling his own story through a third-person narration, Brown rejects his own subjectivity, his own "I" voice, this shift to third-person demonstrates Brown's additional interest in constructing not just his own subjectivity, but a fictive world that includes the point of view that sees and relates his subjectivity. Further, by constructing a first-person narrative of self, Brown and other ex-slaves demonstrate their existence oppositionally, that is, as Brown characterizes in his 1847 address to the Female Anti-Slavery Society of Salem when discussing just how difficult it is to speak at all, he and others demonstrate through an "I" voice that slaves have other than "thing" status. By constructing a third-person narrative of self, however, Brown constructs himself relationally: he constructs himself through another point of view that sees and knows him.

While Brown, in his 1847 *Narrative of William W. Brown,* identifies himself according to his filial relation to Wells Brown and the American abolitionist movement generally, by 1853 his identity is tied to his *fugitive* slave status, which has caused him to be expatriated in Britain. Brown had sailed to England in July of 1849 in order to attend the Peace Congress convening in Paris later that summer (see Farrison). While he had originally intended to remain in Great Britain "no more than a year," the Fugitive Slave Law enacted in September 1850 made it impossible for him to return to the United States.[11] Brown was in exile in London when he published his revised narrative and *Clotel;* documentation of his expatriated status, and the reason for it, were also published as part of his *Narrative.* Consequently, Brown's 1853 narrative ends with a series of letters, the first and last of which are from Enoch Price, the man who claims to own Brown. In the first letter, written by Price after receiving a copy of Brown's 1847 *Narrative of William W. Brown,* Price offers to sell Brown to the Anti-Slavery Society of Boston, or Massachusetts, for $325, which Brown refuses, on principle.[12] By 1852, however, Brown desires to return to the United States and has an agent acting on his behalf offer Price fifty pounds for the necessary emancipation papers. Price's reply is the final letter of Brown's *Narrative of the Life and Escape.* In it, he raises the price for Brown's freedom to one hundred pounds, or five hundred dollars, claiming that since he made his offer of $325, "the laws of the United States are materially changed," a reference to the Fugitive Slave Law. This means,

Price says, "I can now take him [Brown] anywhere in the United States, and I have everything arranged for his arrest if he lands at any port in the United States" (55). William Wells Brown, by concluding his narrative with this letter from Price, confirms his identity as a fugitive, expatriated American slave; and with the voice of a fugitive slave, he begins *Clotel*.

Paul Gilmore makes reference to Brown as a professional fugitive, meaning by the term "those former slaves who supported themselves through abolitionist activity."[13] Brown's status as a fugitive is important to his narrative authority: by fleeing the United States Brown finds the British audience to whom he can tell the American fathers' secrets.[14] Brown's status as a *professional* fugitive, however, is also important to his construction of his narrator's manhood. By turning to his British audience as a professional fugitive, he requests and receives payment enough to support himself and his two daughters. This patrimony, if you will, from these other fathers, in turn helps to re-establish Brown's patrilineal identity and so redefines him.

The professional fugitive writer refers to a U.S. president in his novel's full title, *Clotel; or, The President's Daughter: A Narrative of Slave Life in the United States*, and, of course, that president is Thomas Jefferson. With this title, Brown points to the irony that the author of the Declaration of Independence has a slave daughter, and he includes as epigraph on the original title page the best-known sentiment from the document: "We hold these truths to be self-evident: that all men are created equal; that they are endowed by their Creator with certain inalienable rights, and that among these are LIFE, LIBERTY, and the PURSUIT OF HAPPINESS" (13). But this epigraph also allows Brown to position himself outside of the United States, and he does so, again on the title page, by naming these words by their nationality: they are, he notes, from the *"Declaration of American Independence."*

As William Edward Farrison documents, Brown combines stories he knew either firsthand or through newspaper accounts with rumor that had circulated since at least 1802 about Thomas Jefferson's slave daughters (204–19).[15] Brown knew he was not writing a factual story about Jefferson, nor was his purpose to attack Jefferson's character. As Farrison states, Brown used reports about Jefferson "for their sensational value to illustrate the ironical inconsistencies that existed between the theories and the practices of *soi-disant* democratic American slaveholders" (218). What mattered to Brown was not whether the reports about Jefferson's mistress and daughters were literally true, but that they could well be true, and that similar reports were certainly true of many slaveholders Brown knew personally, including, of course, his own father.[16]

Rumors concerning sexual relations between Thomas Jefferson and Sally Hemings were made public when a journalist, James Thomson Callender, printed information about the affair in the *Richmond Recorder* on September 1 and 22, 1802, during Jefferson's first term as president (Brodie 249). This scandalous story, at the time considered by some newspaper editors to be "filth, blasphemy, lies" and by others to be verifiably true, was such a sensation that Jefferson never escaped it during his public career in politics.[17] At first the story was used by the Federalist party to damage Republicans, generally. Later it was used by abolitionists as evidence of the corrupting influence slavery has even on American leaders. After Jefferson's death in 1826 and that of his son-in-law, Thomas Mann Randolph Jr., in 1828, Monticello was sold and many of Jefferson's slaves were auctioned (Brodie 469). This state of affairs, perhaps coupled with Sally Hemings's death in 1835, created a situation editors of abolitionist newspapers could use to their advantage. Thus, the *Friend of Man* (August 22, 1838, 246) and the *Liberator* (September 21, 1838, 152) ran stories of a report by a white Southerner, heard secondhand, that Thomas Jefferson's daughter had been sold at a slave auction in New Orleans for one thousand dollars.[18]

William Wells Brown became involved with this story of Jefferson's daughter early in his writing career, at least to the point of collecting and reprinting the information. His 1849 *Anti-Slavery Harp: Collection of Songs for Anti-Slavery Meetings* includes a satirical poem, published previously in *Tait's Edinburgh Magazine* (July 1839) and the *Liberator* (May 26, 1848, 84), titled "Jefferson's Daughter," which is based on the story of the New Orleans sale.[19] William Edward Farrison, Brown's biographer, considers this poem to be the sensational piece of Brown's songbook, and notes that it "seems to have been included in no other antislavery songbook" (125). Although Brown never claims to have met any of Jefferson's offspring personally, he does construct himself as someone who may have better information about their fates than most people. In the narrative that prefaces *Clotel*, Brown deletes many of his experiences in slavery in order to focus on his situation while working for James Walker, a slavetrader. These experiences, Brown suggests, contributed greatly to his knowledge of slavery: "After being let out to a steamer as an under-steward, William was hired by James Walker, a slave-trader. Here the subject of our memoir was made superintendent of the gangs of slaves that were taken to the New Orleans market. In this capacity, William had opportunities, far greater than most slaves, of acquiring knowledge of the different phases of the '*peculiar institution*'" (19). By establishing himself as someone who knows slavery and has met slaves through the slave trading that occurs on the New Orleans market, Brown leaves his readers with the fictive possibility that this is how he learned of the story of Jefferson's daughter.[20]

As I remarked at the beginning of this discussion of *Clotel*, Brown's interest in re-establishing his status as son of another father means that he leaves, as he knows he must, "the land that gave him birth" and the person who gave him birth ("Lecture Delivered" 4). In the *Narrative of the Life and Escape of William Wells Brown*, Brown includes the poignant scene in which he sees his mother for the last time (28–30). Later, in his imagination, he has a vision of his mother, "in the cotton-field, followed by a monster task-master, and no one speaking a consoling word to her," and also his sister, "in the hands of the slave-driver, compelled to submit to his cruelty, or, what was unutterably worse, his lust" (31). Ultimately, Brown must give up these women. Further, as if to say that no woman can continue to live within or past the master/ female slave moment, the enslaved female characters in *Clotel*, too—particularly those confronted with a master's lust—die. Currer, Clotel's mother, and Althesa, Clotel's sister, both die of "yellow fever," a fate worse in its irony for two such "mulatto" characters (167, 206). When Althesa's daughters by the white Henry Morton are remanded into slavery, both die rather than submit to their new masters' sexual desires (208–10). Clotel herself, of course, escapes from a master whose sexual advances she refuses, and then jumps into the Potomac River rather than be recaptured and brought back into slavery.

In the end, however, *Clotel* is not really the story of any of the daughters of Thomas Jefferson, fictional or otherwise. When Clotel jumps into the Potomac River, she drowns "within plain sight of the President's house and the capitol of the Union" (219), and even at her death the narrator's focus is slaveholding fathers and the hypocritical American patriarchal system. In order to further highlight his focus, Brown, the professional fugitive, again emphasizes his own point of view as British and, after presenting Clotel's death, refers to "the Declaration of *American* Independence" written by "one of the first statesmen of *that* country" (220; emphasis added). While, then, Brown's authority as a fugitive slave renders *Clotel* believable to his British audience, that audience, in turn, is enjoined to "gaze" at all those in America "who move in a higher circle" and bear the guilt of slavery (16). This very public gaze is itself structured by Brown to add to his effectiveness with American readers who might ordinarily reject his views about slavery. Thus, Brown turns his British audience into his intermediary with the American public, and they see what he sees. Even so, however, *Clotel* does not end here. The last four chapters of the novel that succeed Clotel's death focus on Clotel's daughter, Mary. Through many twists and turns, these chapters bring with them the marriage plot, so that Thomas Jefferson's granddaughter marries the heroic mulatto, George, a participant in Nat Turner's rebellion, and in the conclusion, both are living happily ever after—in France. While critics have assumed that Brown includes these scenes to add another element from popular nineteenth-century fiction, or to take advantage of readers' familiarity with *Uncle Tom's Cabin* or with "woman's fiction," there may be another motive.[21] Perhaps Brown also wants to uncouple mulatto life from tragedy. Since this novel ends not in death but in marriage it thereby formally marks itself as tragedy's opposite, as comedy. By rewriting this ending with such dramatic purpose, Brown also regenerates mulatto possibilities—and thereby twists fate.

Son of a Virgin Mother: "The Heroic Slave"

While not "mulatto" in the usual way, Madison Washington,[22] the hero of Douglass's novella *The Heroic Slave*, is an illegitimate son of the state described as "the mother of statesmen," that is, Virginia, and as such he carries a hybrid identity (25). Racially, Madison Washington is "black, but comely" (28), and Douglass seems to insist on the representational aspect of this character's identity as specifically African American (and handsome). However, Madison Washington's African American identity does not preclude his qualification as an American hero, and this point, as Maggie Montesinos Sale argues, means that Douglass is making two incendiary claims simultaneously: that enslaved African American men are the equals of "the patriots of the U.S. Revolution," and that slave rebellions are in spirit akin to American Revolutionary fervor (173–97). Madison Washington is not transformed by Douglass from an African American slave into an American hero, however, but instead takes on both identities simultaneously. Consequently, Douglass transforms definitions of American heroism in order to include this African American. Presenting Madison Washington's story, then, is Douglass's tactic for changing the course of American history, and while it may not be as overtly threatening to American patriarchy as the revolution suggested by Martin Delany in *Blake*, there is still great possibility in Douglass's suggestion that acts of African American heroism that rewrite American history will also redefine American male identity.

Frederick Douglass is as much concerned as William Wells Brown with African American illegitimacy, defined as the disavowal of African America as part of America. In *The Heroic Slave*, however, Douglass turns his attention to a figure who is not the secret child of a statesman, as is Clotel, the president's daughter, but the secret son of the state of Virginia. Douglass's narrator opens *The Heroic Slave* by pointing to Virginia as "famous in American annals for the multitudinous array of her statesmen and heroes" (25). "Yet," continues the narrator, "not all the great ones of the Old Dominion have, by the fact of their birth-place, escaped undeserved obscurity." One such unsung hero is Madison Washington, "who loved liberty as well as did Patrick Henry,—who deserved it as much as Thomas Jefferson,—and who fought for it with a valor as high, an arm as strong, and against odds as great, as he who led all the armies of the American colonies through the great war for freedom and independence" (25). In spite of having these qualities, the narrator continues, this son of Virginia "lives only in the chattel records of his native state" (25). With no historical record of Madison Washington's life, we are limited to "glimpses of this great character . . . brought to view only by a few transient incidents." Madison Washington is considered by the narrator to be "like a guiding star on a stormy night," but he is seen only "through the parted clouds" or "by the quivering flash of angry lightning." Then he disappears once again, "covered with mystery" (25–26).

Virginia is the mother of statesmen, including Patrick Henry, Thomas Jefferson, and Douglass's Madison Washington, yet no father of any of these heroes is mentioned by Douglass, and, I would claim, for Douglass no father exists. As Eric Sundquist argues, Douglass is a self-made man who, by the 1850s, sees himself as a "self-fathered subject" ("Frederick Douglass" 128). Partly, this is because Douglass has no relationship with his own father, but also, this is Douglass's rhetorical strategy, a point also made by Sundquist.[23] In *The Heroic Slave*, Madison Washington's identity is formed relationally rather than oppositionally; because neither fathers nor masters figure into the story in any significant way, there are virtually no master/slave moments, a feat, indeed, in a narrative whose hero leads a slave rebellion on board a slave ship, wherein both the slavemaster and the ship captain are killed. And yet, Madison Washington's illegitimacy is tied to the way in which he is not claimed by what we might term "the father," is treated with "some strange neglect," according to the text, even though he is one of "the truest, manliest, and bravest" of Virginia's children. By one way of thinking, then, Madison Washington has no father, just as other American heroes have no father, and Virginia, true to her name, is the virgin mother of statesmen; but by another line of metaphorical reasoning, Madison Washington does have a father because he is the illegitimate child—of American history. In this sense, then, American history is the father who will not claim Madison Washington and the father from whom, through *The Heroic Slave*, Douglass demands his hero's recognition.

Douglass's narrative challenge, in writing *The Heroic Slave*, is how to rewrite history, how to present this secret son of Virginia so that he will be perceived as the son of this mother state, and, thus, a hero. Part of the difficulty is that the slave revolt that Madison Washington led aboard the *Creole* as it sailed from Hampton, Virginia, to New Orleans is itself a historic event that had occurred within recent memory, just twelve years prior to the publication of Douglass's novella. Information about the revolt, in the form of depositions made by the captain and crew of the ship, and by the passengers involved in the transportation of the slaves, became part of the public domain, entered into the *Senate Documents* of 1842. Newspapers in various locales also reported and interpreted the story.[24] Clearly the depositions should not be considered the whole story, as there is no documentation from the slaves' points of view—nor could there be, since according to United States law they were part of the property with which the case was concerned. Nevertheless, no additional information from the slaves' points of view or about Madison Washington was ever uncovered. On June 10, 1842, the *Liberator* ran a story, "Madison Washington: Another Chapter in His History," which purported to have additional details about Madison Washington's life prior to his leading the revolt on the *Creole* (89). The source for this information is not named, however, and the article ends by asking for help from British abolitionists who might have access to Washington and could get the story from his "own lips."

In this void of information, then, Frederick Douglass creates his version of the story of the *Creole* rebellion, which includes, as Sale remarks, "a personal history of Madison Washington" (180). Douglass's *The Heroic Slave* means to present Madison Washington as an American hero, but to do so means also presenting American acceptance of this hero. Thus, as in *Clotel*, with Brown's creation of a British readership for his text, Douglass, too, creates an audience for the story of Madison Washington. In *The Heroic Slave*, however, this audience is modeled through actual characters that Douglass creates and presents within the text of his novel. Taken together, two characters, who each know different parts of Madison Washington's story, confirm Washington's American heroism. In *Clotel*, William Wells Brown creates a bond between his narrator's and the British reading public's point of view: narrator and audience come together by looking at, by seeing, the same sight—the private, sexual behavior of slaveholders. In that text, the secrets being told are those of the master, and at least part of the point is public humiliation. In the first part of *The Heroic Slave*, however, it is the slave's secret, the secret longing for freedom combined with a consciousness of self, that Douglass tells, and with this telling Douglass means to rewrite history. Here Douglass presents not an image but a voice, and his expectation from his audience is not, like Brown, that they see as his narrator sees, but rather that they hear, truly hear, Madison Washington. As Robert Stepto has observed, however, unreliable readers are a problem Douglass must consider. Stepto thus characterizes *The Heroic Slave* as "storytelling *about* storytelling," that is, as storytelling focused on how to tell the story of Madison Washington, including how to tell readers how to hear him (see Stepto "Storytelling").

Douglass responds to the problems inherent in presenting Madison Washington's heroism in two ways. First, as William Andrews has observed, "he made the lack of knowledge about Washington, as opposed to the wealth of historical information about other champions of liberty from Virginia, the gambit of his text" ("Novelization" 29). By doing so, he calls the authority of history into question, thus allowing this fictive narration based on "marks, traces, possibilities, and probabilities" to stand in the place of a full historical record (*Heroic Slave* 26). Second, Douglass introduces two white characters into his novella, one a Northerner named Mr. Listwell and the other a Virginian named Tom Grant. No men who might match these characters figure in the depositions collected in the *Senate Documents*, nor are they characters who strike the imagination of any other writer who tries his or her hand with this tale.[25] Douglass's story requires these two characters, however, as links to the legitimacy he wants to claim for Madison Washington. Together, these two figures characterize Washington as an unmistakable son of Virginia, that is, as a freedom-loving American infused with the "principles of 1776" (68); and significantly, they do this, together, without taking from him what we would characterize as his African American identity.

In his analysis of *The Heroic Slave*, Robert Stepto states that Mr. Listwell "is possibly the most important polemical and literary achievement of the novella" ("Storytelling" 115). Stepto's analysis of the character of Mr. Listwell is rooted in his understanding of the conflicts between Douglass and white abolitionists, in particular William Lloyd Garrison, occurring at the time *The Heroic Slave* was written and published. According to Stepto, Mr. Listwell becomes the model abolitionist whom Douglass needed, because his relations with Garrison were so problematic. Appropriately named, Listwell "*enlists* as an abolitionist and does *well* by the cause" (115). Even more important, Stepto says, is the fact that he *listens* well: "he is, in the context of his relations with Madison Washington and in accord with the aesthetics of storytelling, a model story-listener and hence an agent, in many senses of the term, for the continuing performance of the story he and Washington increasingly share and 'tell' together" (115). Douglass includes Listwell in his story, Stepto says, in order to deliver a message to Garrison and those like him: "One cannot be a good abolitionist without being a good listener, with the reverse often being true as well" (115).

There is more to Douglass's message of listening than Stepto states, however. Listwell is not only a *good* listener, but he is also a *secret* listener. When we first meet him, Listwell is traveling through Virginia and has stopped to let his horse drink "at a sparkling brook, near the edge of a dark pine forest" (26). He hears someone speaking and, curious, ties his horse some distance away and conceals himself "by the side of a huge fallen tree" in order that he may secretly listen and "know what thoughts and feelings, or, it might be, high aspirations, guided those rich and mellow accents" that had initially struck his curiosity (27). What he hears is a soliloquy on the meaning of manhood and life by Madison Washington, who knows he is to be sold away from his wife the next day. This soliloquy ends with Washington's determination, at any cost, to be free. When Listwell realizes what he is witnessing, he becomes frightened "at the thought of his dangerous intrusion" but cannot leave the place because "he had long desired to sound the mysterious depths of the thoughts and feelings of a slave" (28). Unwilling to lose the opportunity, he stays in his hiding place, listening to everything Washington pours from his burdened heart, and not moving until long after Washington leaves him by walking further into "the wildering woods" (29). Here, Douglass's presentation of the hiding Listwell, who hears Washington's story and thus serves as mediator with Douglass's readers, suggests how white Northerners might gain access to the truths, the secrets, of slavery, but it also does more. With Listwell's secret listening to Madison Washington's soliloquy, Douglass also presents a slave's coming-to-consciousness process that differs significantly from the dialectical model. Specifically, the Listwell/Washington moment is not a master/slave moment, although when Listwell realizes his "dangerous intrusion" it seems that he fears being mistakenly identified as someone who desires to engage in the master/slave struggle.

In Douglass's story, Madison Washington, the emerging hero, does not appear to converse with anyone but himself about his desire to be free. Nor is there any suggestion of discussion among the captives on board the *Creole* about what to do and how to proceed; unlike Martin Delany's *Blake*, Douglass's *The Heroic Slave* does not present the communication that would necessarily precede a slave revolt. It may be that Douglass excludes this detail because he does not want to intimidate a white audience, or because he wants to protect

Black insurrectionists. The consequence, however, is that Douglass does not present developed community among slaves, community we know to exist historically and also theoretically, within the master/slave dialectic as the already present third term. Yet, it is not only the already present slave community that is absent from Douglass's presentation of his hero's will toward freedom; Madison Washington's self-made origins, his extraordinary individualism, also bring him to the consciousness of freedom through his own speech act rather than in the usual way, through conflict, as Douglass has earlier described in the Covey/Douglass confrontation.[26] By creating a scenario wherein Madison Washington voices his desire for freedom such that a white man in hiding hears him, Douglass establishes Madison Washington's personhood relationally, rather than oppositionally, and also presents the possibility of community across the line that separates Black from white, enslaved from free. This new community, literally established between Washington and Listwell, presumably includes all others who can hear Madison Washington's secret.

Douglass's concept of secret listening, and the possibility for understanding that it engenders, is not new to *The Heroic Slave*. Douglass had previously, in his *Narrative* published in 1845, expressed a similar idea. In what may be his earliest conception of Mr. Listwell, he suggests secret listening as a way for any of his readers to "understand the deep meaning of those rude and apparently incoherent songs" that slaves sing. These songs are important to Douglass because he traces his "first glimmering conception of the dehumanizing character of slavery" to the hearing of them (37). He tells his readers: "If any one wishes to be impressed with the soul-killing effects of slavery, let him go to Colonel Lloyd's plantation, and, on allowance-day, place himself in the deep pine woods, and there let him, in silence, analyze the sounds that shall pass through the chambers of his soul,—and if he is not thus impressed, it will only be because 'there is no flesh in his obdurate heart'" (37–38).

The idea here expressed is that Douglass's white readers can also understand the true significance of the "sorrow songs"; they need only hide and listen in order to feel the human truths about slavery that the songs express. In *The Heroic Slave*, however, Douglass develops this idea of readers listening in secret in order to understand, so that this becomes his narrative strategy. In this later text, by including Listwell, Douglass does not just give his readers the suggestion to listen in secret, as in his *Narrative*, but instead places them in a position where they cannot help but do so.

By creating Listwell, Douglass also fixes his readers' secret so that what could not conceivably be overheard is as significant as what is heard. Because Listwell's presence on the scene specifically rewrites as heroic a slave's coming to consciousness, Douglass establishes a relational rather than oppositional moment whereby readers know, through Listwell's agency, as listener, that Madison Washington is a man. All of this is to say that Listwell's secret listening is *not* the other secret listening that Douglass mentions in his *Narrative* but better details in *My Bondage and My Freedom:* the son's initiation into sexuality, and in this case pornographic sexuality, as represented by the master/female slave (Anthony/Esther) moment. Douglass states clearly in *My Bondage* that we come to know the master/female slave moment through secret listening: "My sleeping place was the floor of a little, rough closet, which opened into the kitchen; and through the cracks of its unplaned boards, I could distinctly see and hear what was going on, without being seen by old master" (87).[27] As we have explored in the previous chapter, this gendered, sexualized moment resonates within the American consciousness; and, as we will soon investigate, this moment is central to the fiction of Frances Harper and Pauline Hopkins. Douglass's fiction, however, displaces this moment. In a celebration of liberal political thought, Douglass posits Madison Washington, the slave, as also a free-willed individual, and thus implies that the will to freedom is an innate characteristic of personhood rather than a development of consciousness.

We now turn to the other white character created by Douglass in *The Heroic Slave*, the sailor, Tom Grant, who, in Douglass's story, had been on board the *Creole* when the revolt took place. While Listwell figures into parts 2–3 of *The Heroic Slave*, witnessing to Madison Washington's personhood while also giving us the background to the revolt on the slave ship *Creole*, Tom Grant is introduced in part IV in order to tell the details of the revolt itself. Significantly, this second act of telling Madison Washington's heroism is done by a white man who addresses other white men, the *"ocean birds"* assembled at the marine coffeehouse in Richmond (60). Some critics have seen the inclusion of Grant as a narrative flaw and have argued that his telling of the slave revolt takes away from the story of Madison Washington's heroism. Richard Yarborough, for example, argues that by "rendering the *Creole* revolt through the recollections of a white sailor, Douglass cuts us off not just from Washington's heroic violence but from his emotional responses to the dramatic events" (182). Even more problematic, according to Yarborough, is a further consequence of Tom Grant's telling of the revolt: "At the end of the novella Washington stands not as the embodiment of expressive, forceful self-determination, but as an object of white discourse, a figure whose self-assertive drive to tell his own story—to reclaim, in a sense, his own subjectivity—is ultimately subordinated by Douglass to a secondhand rendition by a white sailor who did not even witness the full range of Washington's heroic action" (182). However, this criticism mistakes Grant's purposeful role as a flaw in Douglass's work. Tom Grant makes Madison Washington the object of white discourse, but this is not an unfortunate, unforeseen consequence of his role in the novel. Madison Washington is purposely the object of Tom Grant's discourse because by being so he is thereby masculinized, that is, he is favorably compared to the patriots of the American revolution; in Maggie Sale's terms, he becomes a "revolutionary republican subject," a subject whose "most fundamental feature" is "masculine gender" (185). As such a subject, Madison Washington can achieve Douglass's goal: he can be written into history.

For Douglass, the ultimate measure of his success in rendering Madison Washington an American hero is for a white Virginian to declare him so while other Americans agree. Such brotherly recognition legitimizes Washington so that he is no longer a *secret* son of the great commonwealth. Consequently, Douglass has Tom Grant make a public proclamation of Washington's heroism: Grant states, to other Virginians, that Madison Washington had such a presence that it "seemed as if the souls of both the great dead (whose names he bore) had entered him" (66). Additionally, Grant ends his rendition of Madison Washington's story by calling him a triumphant leader and "heroic chief and deliverer" of the other slaves on board the *Creole* (69). Since these are the final words of the novel, we hear no replies from the men who form Grant's immediate audience in the Richmond marine coffeehouse, but our own agreement, as readers, implies their approval.

Because Tom Grant acknowledges Madison Washington as a man who acts in accordance with "the principles of 1776" (68), he demonstrates that his sailor-audience will find Washington's "display of masculinity compelling," to use Sale's words (185), and in doing so implies that this audience will, consequently, no longer see racial difference. Grant says, specifically, that because of Madison Washington's demeanor, because of his dignity, he "forgot his blackness" (66). For readers, however, Listwell's earlier presence in the narrative fortuitously complicates this erasure of race. When Listwell hears Washington and witnesses his desire for freedom, he does so as a white man who knows the racial difference between Madison Washington and himself, as a white man committing a "dangerous intrusion" by secretly listening to this Black man, as a white man who realizes the potential for conflict if his hiding place is discovered. As a consequence of hearing Washington's soliloquy, Listwell becomes a determined abolitionist, and as such, Listwell functions to convert readers of *The Heroic Slave* to a "true" understanding of slavery. While Grant serves as a white authenticator of Washington, a Virginian who declares Washington "one of us," Listwell does not. Instead, Listwell becomes "one of them," and this standpoint distinction is important. Listwell models a white reading of Madison Washington through which he identifies with Washington but does not turn Washington "white." This, in turn, helps even unreliable readers to do the same.

Listwell and Grant establish Madison Washington as a gendered and racialized subject, then, but at the same time that Grant shows Black men to be very much like white men, Listwell shows that free Americans, given the right opportunity, will feel about slavery in much the same way enslaved peoples do. By including these two complementary responses to Madison Washington, Douglass assures that his readers see Washington as an exceptional American but not an exceptional African American—since his desire for freedom is no greater than that of the other "men and women . . . chained and fettered" and bound for the slave market (52).[28] If Douglass has succeeded in writing Madison Washington into history, then, he has written him in as both an American hero and an African American ex-slave—in other words, as Virginia's Black son. Here, we might pause to consider the implication, racially speaking, for this son's mother. Under any genealogical figuration imaginable, there's signifying going on, since a Black son calls into question either Virginia's own racial identity or the racial identity of her paramour.

Blake's Redemption Song

In one of the most poignant passages from Ernest Gaines's *The Autobiography of Miss Jane Pittman* (1971), Miss Jane talks of the community, wondering about each child when he is born whether he is "the One." In the final section of Gaines's novel, Miss Jane repeats two distinct but related questions about one of the young men of the quarters destined to be a leader: "You the one, Jimmy? You the One?" and then, "The people, Jimmy? The People?" (199–200, 234–35). These passages represent twentieth-century versions of what Theophus H. Smith calls "the figural vision" of emancipation that "provides the paradigm for subsequent strategies and acts of political imagination" (63). In a very suggestive section of *Conjuring Culture: Biblical Formations of Black America*, Smith analyzes the uses and meaning of the biblical passage Albert Raboteau has described as "probably the most widely quoted verse in Afro-American religious history": "Princes shall come out of Egypt; Ethiopia shall soon stretch out her hands to God" (Psalm 68:31, qtd. in T. Smith 58). This passage is the foundation of Ethiopianism, according to Smith, which is a literary-religious tradition that "spanned the late eighteenth and early twentieth centuries, and engaged black communities on both the African and American continents" and that focused on the resurgence of Africa "against the background of the slave trade and Africa's nineteenth century humiliation by European colonialism" (65). Martin Delany also works with this biblical passage in his novel, *Blake*, and in his figuration of Ethiopianism he connects the ethnogenesis of a Pan-African communal identity with the construction of revolutionary Black masculine subjectivity. Thus, Delany's revolutionary son is born of the Father-land rather than any mother, is "pure" Africa, and has no relation to Americans or Europeans involved in the slave trade or the practice of slavery, except, in the position of "General-in-Chief of the army of emancipation," as their sworn enemy.

In *The Autobiography of Miss Jane Pittman*, when Miss Jane schools Jimmy about not forgetting the people, she is molding him into an Exodus figure. As such a leader, he may not get to "freedom land," but, as is the point, his people will. Indeed, in Gaines's novel, Jimmy is killed but other members of his community go ahead to the courthouse. Delany's *Blake* also presents an Exodus figure in the form of Henry Blake, otherwise known as Carolus Henrico Blacus, its main protagonist. Critics have pointed out the Moses-like characterization of Blake, and with that characterization both the Black nationalist and messianic implications (see R. Levine 180). But it is as equally important in *Blake* as in *The Autobiography of Miss Jane Pittman* to also remember "the people." In part 1 of Delany's novel, the people who form community with Blake are slaves in various parts of the South and Southwest whom he visits in seclusion so as to make preparation for insurrection. In part 2, set in Cuba, community is formed by a transnational group of men and women who will become the leaders of the emancipation of enslaved men and women throughout the world. This Pan-African community formed of people from throughout the diaspora is crucial to Blake's identity, as Delany characterizes it. Here we once again see masculine subjectivity defined relationally rather than strictly oppositionally, so that even as a Black revolutionary on the verge of waging "war upon the whites" (290), Delany's protagonist, like Douglass's heroic slave, is as representative of the people as he is exceptional.

Like William Wells Brown's *Clotel* and Frederick Douglass's *The Heroic Slave*, Martin Delany's *Blake* concerns itself with the validation of African American sons and the telling of slavery's secrets. *Blake*'s protagonist, however, seeks validation from neither the British nor from Americans but instead from the African diasporic community; further, the great secret of Delany's novel is never explicitly told to his American readers, and it concerns African American and then Pan-African community rather than American identity. As one critic has observed, "what is finally most striking about the work is its air of mystery, of secrets suggested but untold, and of an organization powerful because it is, in fact, and will remain, a secret" (Earnest 112). While Blake proceeds to spread his secret in front of us, because readers are never let in on this secret the community comprised of those who know the secret, the in-group being constructed before our eyes, very definitely does not include us. This narrative strategy is in marked contrast to Douglass's in *The Heroic Slave*, where the audience is purposely included as secret listeners who then turn the secret son of the state into a publicly acknowledged American hero. For Delany, one might say, distrust of the reader is so much a part of the point that not even an exemplary "hearer" will show the reader the way.

In part 1 of *Blake*, Blake travels the southern and southwestern United States, telling trusted members of each slave community he visits of a secret "scheme . . . for a general insurrection of the slaves in every state, and the successful overthrow of slavery" (39). In part 2 of the novel, Blake continues this same kind of organizing in Cuba. All the details of the plan for "general insurrection," and especially by what means slaves will know of the uprising, are secret. In part 1, Blake tells the details, during "seclusions," to those whom he trusts, and he never privileges the reader with them.[29] For example, Andy and Charles, Blake's old friends and fellow slaves, respond to Blake's telling them the secrets of his organization with declarations that they should have thought of such a simple plan themselves, since it is so easy that a child could understand (40). Readers, however, who have not been told the details, are teased by the idea that the plan is "simple" but never privy to it, which positions them with slaveholders, the main group, as we have discussed, from whom secrets are kept. A similar situation reoccurs each time Blake tells a group of slaves the secrets of his organization. Subsequent to his telling they know what to watch or listen for, but readers do not. In this way, by generating the plot's suspense, secrets are crucial to the novel even while its narrative structure continues to keep rather than tell them.

Because *Blake* is not so much an ex-slave narrative as a novel of African nationalism, master/slave moments are not highlighted within the novel. When they are included at all, the slave characters involved are specifically female, or effeminate male children, so that Black male subjectivity is never really presented as subjugated to white slaveholding power.[30] While it may seem in *Blake* that the secret spread by Henry Blake in part 1 of the novel is only for slaves, in fact the community constructed by the sharing of Blake's secret is defined by their African diasporic, or, in the case of the people of the Indian nation in Arkansas, their nonwhite identities, rather than their slave status. Of primary importance is the point that Blake himself is not "really" a slave. Readers discover that Henry Holland is otherwise known as Carolus Henrico Blacus, and later known as Henry Blake, a native Cuban, cousin to the famous poet Placido. As the novel opens, Blake is in the United States because when he "left school and went to sea" as a young man he was subsequently sold into slavery by a vengeful commander (193–94). In the United States, Blake is not truly an American slave but only acting as such in order to be near his wife; as soon as he decides to leave his situation as a slave, he has no difficulty doing so. Additional information that demonstrates Blake's origins as other than American and his status as other than slave is his sailing experience in "the African waters" and from Africa to the Caribbean islands and to North and South America (194). From this experience he identifies himself as a sailor who has "gone through all the grades" and "who on the [African] coast had full command, as no white men manage vessels in the African waters" (194). This very different Middle Passage experience translates, upon his return to Cuba, to his election to the post of "General-in-Chief of the army of emancipation of the oppressed men and women of Cuba" (241). Taken together, these details establish Blake's identity as African or Afro-Cuban but not American and his status as that of sailor and soldier rather than slave.

While Blake is not really a slave, the woman he meets when he is held in the United States against his will is prototypically so. Maggie is the daughter of the slavemaster Colonel Stephen Franks, "the mother being a black slave," as the novel's narrator parenthetically remarks."[31] Part 1 of *Blake* begins with the familiar scenario of a slave sold to another master because of her insubordination, that is, her refusal of her master's sexual advances. Since in this instance the slave sold is Maggie, Blake's wife, this action causes Blake, here known only as the slave Henry Holland, to escape from the plantation of Colonel Franks and begin his tour of the South and Southwest. After helping other slaves from the Franks plantation escape to Canada, Blake then sails to Cuba where Maggie has been taken, buys her freedom, and begins organizing the Black insurrectionary force whose purpose will be to overthrow the Cuban government and then the institution of slavery worldwide. Just as the insurrectionists decide to act, however, this serialized novel breaks off. The last approximately six chapters written by Delany and published in the *Weekly Anglo-African* in 1862 have not yet been discovered.

Maggie, Blake's wife, brings the master/female slave moment into this text, yet while she could easily be its focal character, she is not. Paul Gilroy points out that *Blake* is "a narrative of familial reconstruction" because "the momentum of the book is supplied by the zeal with which its hero strives to reconstruct and regenerate his family life" (26). Events in Maggie's life, then, create the crisis that spurs Blake into acting as the catalyst for organized slave revolt. Because Blake is the center of this action, however, Maggie becomes a peripheral character. This is especially significant since, as a "secret" American, Maggie is the character drawn in the tradition of Brown's *Clotel* and Douglass's *The Heroic Slave:* she is an all-American mulatto slave. Maggie's story, told as backdrop to the plot proper, begins as she is being sold by Colonel Franks of Natchez, Mississippi, to a sadistic Northern woman, who, with her husband the eminent judge, will soon sail to Cuba. Franks's main reason for selling Maggie, despite loud protestation from his own wife, is that Maggie refuses his sexual advances and, worse, tells his wife about his adulterous behavior. For this she is labeled "disobedient and unruly" by Franks (8). In part 1 of *Blake*, it seems as if Maggie is the daughter of Mammy Judy and Daddy Joe; Joe, for example, prays to God to let his "po' chile" come back (11). In part 2, however, the narrator summarizes Maggie's early life by saying: "Goaded and oppressed by a master known to be her own father, under circumstances revolting to humanity, civilization and Christianity, she had been ruthlessly torn from her child, husband and mother, and sold to a foreign land, all because, by the instincts of nature—if by the honor of a wife and womanhood she had not been justified—she repelled him" (190). Maggie, then, is the unacknowledged daughter of Colonel Stephen Franks of Natchez, Mississippi, and is sold for refusing an incestuous sexual relationship with him.

Unlike William Wells Brown's *Clotel*, while *Blake* presents these details about Maggie, the novel does not include her death because of her victimization that results from the sexual perversions of white slaveholders. In *Blake*, it is the men who have sexually abused women held as slaves who pay the consequences, through retaliatory action by men of African origin.[32] Maggie's sale to Madam Ballard precipitates the action of the novel, since as a result Blake becomes a runaway, travels the South with his message of insurrection, guides the rest of his family to Canada, and then goes to Cuba in search of his wife. But Blake is always the primary actor in this novel; his stage, rather than being the United States, is, instead, the African diaspora. Consequently, while the novel sharply critiques slavery and its oppressive social order, the basic premise of this critique is that slavery is an inherently African rather than an American drama that requires an African rather than an American solution.

Delany redirects our attention from the United States to the African diaspora in the opening scene of *Blake*, as well as throughout part 2 of the novel, set primarily in Cuba but also on the coast of Africa as well as on a ship at sea between Africa and the Caribbean islands. The opening scene of the novel presents a meeting between United States and Cuban slavetraders that situates slavery within an economic, transnational context. This meeting points to ways in which the United States is inextricably connected to the Americas generally, as well as to Caribbean and West African nations, a point developed in part 2 as these same slave traders complete their business transaction.[33] A further complicating factor regarding the slave trade, at least according to Delany's portrait of the slave traders, is that they see themselves as above the law of any given country, including the United States. In the first paragraph of the novel, for example, the men are described as "little concerned about the affairs of the general government," because they are "entirely absorbed in an adventure of self-interest" (3). In a later example in part 2, when the traders are trying to determine where to land the slave ship, the most important consideration is where they might sell slaves for the most money, not where the trading is legal (213–14). Because of this attitude on the part of slave traders, Delany suggests, the United States government may not be powerful enough to abolish slavery, and certainly cannot worldwide. Thus, according to Delany's reasoning, in order to accomplish the complete abolition of slavery, Africans themselves must act toward this purpose.

As has been pointed out by other critics, it seems reasonable conjecture that the subtitle of *Blake*, "The Huts of America," is a play on the "Cabin" in *Uncle Tom's Cabin*. Delany also quotes verse by Harriet Beecher Stowe at the beginning of part 1 and again at the beginning of part 2 of *Blake*, further evidence that he had her novel in mind when writing his own.[34] Most convincing, however, are the parallels between the opening scenes of each novel. Close comparison indicates that *Blake* is Delany's deliberate revision of Stowe's understanding of slavery. *Uncle Tom's Cabin* opens as Mr. Shelby, a slaveholder, and Mr. Haley, a slavetrader, discuss business, namely, the sale of some of Mr. Shelby's slaves. Other elements of chapter 1 include Mrs. Shelby's attachment to the female slave, Eliza; the introduction of Eliza's precocious son, Harry; and the actual sale of Tom and Harry. *Blake* also opens as slavetraders discuss business, but rather than focus on the personal business of one slaveholder, Delany focuses on the larger arena of the international slave trade. Business completed, we are then introduced to the family of one of the businessmen, Colonel Stephen Franks. As in *Uncle Tom's Cabin*, the principal actors in the ensuing family drama are the slaveholder's wife, Mrs. Franks; her close female slave, in this case Maggie; and Maggie's son, Tony. These similarities between the openings of *Uncle Tom's Cabin* and *Blake* force readers to notice the differences, as well, primarily the difference between Uncle Tom and Henry Blake. By revising *Uncle Tom's Cabin* in this way, Delany focuses his readers' attention on this very different kind of man, whose identity is African rather than American, and whose response to slavery is a determined organization of insurrection.

The first two chapters of *Blake* present, first, the business meeting among American and Cuban slavetraders, and then a conversation among the colonel and Mrs. Franks and Madam Ballard about selling Maggie. Although the topic of conversation in both instances is slavery, it is never directly mentioned as such. The narrator, in relaying the conversation between American and Cuban slavetraders, uses euphemism to make the type of business they are engaged in understood: reference is made, for example, to "the place best suited to the completion of their arrangements," to the place which might provide "the greatest facilities," and to the question of which nation has shown itself most committed to "the encouragement and protection of the trade" (3). With this language, the slave trade is talked about just as any other business venture, and the businessmen's concerns are presented as ordinary. The narrator uses similar euphemistic language again to report the family discussion of the next chapter, mentioning that "the conversation, as is customary on the meeting of Americans residing in such distant latitudes, readily turned on the general policy of the country" (4). Further, when the colonel notices that his wife seems unlike her usual self, she replies that her "spirit is heavy," refuses to discuss her concern regarding the sale of her slave, Maggie, yet still makes her disapproval known to her husband.

Delany couples this careful use of euphemism in reporting the business discussions and family conversations of white Americans with instance upon instance of coded speech by Black American slaves. Taken together, these obfuscations indicate an aura of secrecy among both white and Black Americans regarding the specifics of the slave trade as business and slavery as social order. It is particularly striking, in *Blake*, how much is understood through what is *not* said. When Mrs. Franks refuses to talk about her heavy spirit, for example, Delany's narrator describes Franks's response: "Giving his head an unconscious scratch accompanied with a slight twitch of the corner of the mouth, Franks seemed to comprehend the whole of it" (6). These involuntary body movements are just the sort of sign that slaves learn to read well. According to the narrator: "Not unfrequently the mere countenance, a look, a word, or laugh of the master, is an unerring foreboding of misfortune to the slave. Ever on the watch for these things, they learn to read them with astonishing precision" (11). Through this type of "reading," Maggie's foster father, Daddy Joe, knows before he is told that something is wrong with his family. Further, because there is a coded method among slaves of referring to other slaves who have recently been sold, and because such references become part of the salutation as slaves meet, Daddy Joe first hears of Maggie's fate while he is walking to town. Delany explains: "In the lower part of the town, bordering on the river there is a depot or receptacle for the slave gangs brought by professional traders. This part of the town is known as 'Natchez-under-the-Hill.' It is customary among the slaves when any of their number are sold, to say that they are gone 'under the hill,' and their common salutation through the day was that 'Franks' Mag had gone under the hill'" (11). This detail is an overt indication of the informal yet organized dissemination of information among slaves.

In June 1853, as he was beginning to formulate *Blake*, Delany delivered a treatise before St. Cyprian Lodge in Pittsburgh titled *The Origin and Objects of Ancient Freemasonry; Its Introduction into the United States, and Legitimacy among Colored Men*.[35] In this treatise Delany claims that the "mysteries of Ancient Freemasonry" are African in origin: that the "mysteries of the wise men of the East" are from Africa, that Africa "gave birth to Euclid, the master geometrician of the world," and that the great Pythagoras's twenty-five year residence in Africa enabled him to discover the key problem in ancient geometry.[36] Delany's treatise and his interest in the African origin of freemasonry suggest his considerable knowledge about secret societies, and perhaps even secret societies in Africa. Since Delany is a Mason himself, the question arises as to whether or not he was involved in abolitionist organizing as a Mason, and whether there are connections to be drawn between that activity and the fictional organizing done by the protagonist Blake.[37] If such connections can be made, even hypothetically, then new possibilities for a reading of the secret organizing in *Blake*, based on African retentions and secret societies, also present themselves.

More significant, however, is the refiguration of Egypt expressed through Delany's address on Freemasonry. As Theophus Smith explains, Exodus figuration is all about the negative valuation of Egypt—in other words, in Exodus figuration Egypt is the land of bondage for Moses and his people. In "mature developments of Ethiopianism," however, "ancient Egypt was understood to be a civilization of black rulers instead of a prison house of black slaves" (66). This Egypt is the one celebrated by Delany when he makes reference to Euclid and Pythagoras, and consequently, when Delany makes Ethiopianist references in other works, including *Blake*, it is important to understand these as references to an ancient Egypt representative of the highest order of civilization.

Theophus Smith also suggests that to "designate a deity . . . means also to image a self," which is an appropriate way to characterize the ethnogenesis of communal identity presented in *Blake*. As Smith explains, "when a community or people designates its patron god or deities it simultaneously constitutes or reconstitutes its collective identity" (62). In *Blake*, the communities formed in both part 1 and part 2 of the novel can best be characterized as communities of believers, and the Pan-African community of part 2 is organized around two biblical passages that are its foundation. At a crucial point when the Pan-African council is determining what its policies should be, and is specifically being challenged by one of its members concerning questions of equality between the white and Black races, Blake says: "'Ethiopia shall yet stretch forth her hands unto God; Princes shall come out of Egypt'; 'Your God shall be my God, and your people my people,' should comprehend our whole policy" (285). The collective identity formed from the combination of Psalm 68:31 and Ruth 1:16 suggests the ethnogenesis of a Pan-African communal identity that is based, then, not on slave status nor even in race but on the conceptualization of the deity of the people.

In addition to quoting Psalm 68:31 during this critical moment in *Blake*, Delany also makes reference to this biblical passage in his *Official Report of the Niger Valley Exploring Party* (1861) and in his *Principia of Ethnology: The Origin of Races and Color* (1879). In both the *Official Report* and the *Principia*, however, he quotes the passage as it is presented in Psalm: "Princes shall come out of Egypt; Ethiopia shall soon stretch forth her hands unto God."[38] This indicates that his slight misquotation in *Blake* is purposeful, that there are reasons why he has switched the order of the first and second halves of the verse, and changed "Ethiopia shall *soon* stretch forth her hands" to "Ethiopia shall *yet* stretch forth her hands." Delany's revised verse, with its change in the order of the terms, suggests that "Ethiopia" shall create its deity and then leaders will come from "Egypt," rather than that leaders will bring the Ethiopians to conversion. In other words, switching the order of the terms itself suggests the creation of a new deity rather than the Christian conversion of all Africans. This new, or conjured, version of Psalm 68:31 in *Blake* is then followed by a similarly conjured Ruth 1:16. In the biblical passage, Ruth tells Naomi, "thy people shall be my people, and thy God my God. In *Blake*, however, the terms shift ("Your God shall be my God, and your people my people"), and again this creates a causal connection: because your God is my God, your people are my people. In addition to using these two biblical passages to create a deity and define a people, Delany also seems to be basing his novel's two-part structure on the dual clauses of each passage. If "Ethiopia" is read as the American slave population with whom Delany has entered into community, the people in part I who understand his message and "stand still and see the salvation," thus creating their deity, then according to Delany's revision of the divine scheme, leaders, "Princes," will now come out of Cuba.[39] Or, to put the point in terms of Ruth 1:16, the Pan-African community in Cuba believes in the same God as the American slaves with whom Delany went into seclusion, and so the insurrectionary force will not stop until *all* "the people" are free.

William Wells Brown's *Clotel* and Frederick Douglass's *The Heroic Slave* expose the secrets nestled within American patriarchy in an attempt to redefine the social order, abolish slavery, and incorporate African Americans into the concept of American male identity. Martin Delany's *Blake*, on the other hand, keeps secrets that are concerned with slave insurrection in order to establish the identity of a powerful African diasporic people who will be able to overthrow slavery and the social order engendered by it. In order to do this, Delany turns to Africa, the continent he characterizes as the "fatherland," which, as Paul Gilroy points out, means to him a potentially autonomous, Black nation state (19–29). This is the place, literally in his political writings and symbolically in *Blake*, that will beget the "black soldier citizens" needed for the revolution (Delany, *Official Report* sect. 11, 110–11; Gilroy 23). Consequently, again as Gilroy notes, Delany's "new black citizenship" is represented in *Blake* by people brought together "by the transnational structure of the slave trade itself,"—"Abyssa, a Soudanese slave and former textile merchant, brought from Africa on Blake's second transatlantic trip; Placido, a Cuban revolutionary poet who is also Blake's cousin; Gofer Gondolier, a West Indian cook who has attended a Spanish grandee in Genoa; the wealthy quadroons and octoroons of Cuba; Blake himself; and indeed their white revolutionary supporters constitute something like a rainbow army for the emancipation of the oppressed men and women of the new world" (28–29). It is this group of men and women who will abolish the enslavement of Africans in Cuba and everywhere.

Paul Gilroy also suggests that Blake is the "progenitor of black Atlantic patriarchy," a kind of Black Moses. If he is the "Prince coming out of Egypt," a godly or blessed representative of the collective Pan-African identity of Ethiopianist thought, however, he is a new kind of Black leader: he is both Moses and Christ, both leader and redeemer, but most significantly, he is an African representative of the highest order of civilization. In his conclusion to the *Principia*, where he also quotes Psalm 68:31, Delany states: "We shall boldly advance, singing the sweet songs of redemption, in the regeneration of our race and restoration of our father-land from the gloom and darkness of superstition and ignorance, to the glorious light of a more than pristine brightness—the light of the highest godly civilization" (95). This is the task set before Blake and his compatriots in Cuba; and this holy mission, as Delany defines it, will not only lead to the end of slavery but also to the salvation and redemption of humanity.[40]

Delany's belief in Africa's role in the redemption of humanity, I would suggest, indicates another reason why he refers to Africa as "the Father-land": it is, for him, literally the land of the male Godhead. As such, Blake, one of the princes of Egypt, is also that Godhead's son—the son of Africa. Like William Wells Brown and Frederick Douglass, then, Martin Delany's characterization of African diasporic manhood, which includes African American manhood, also depends on "son" status. As we have seen, Brown and Douglass formulate Black men as sons of America; Delany switches continents to identify his representative Black man as the son of Africa. This does and does not represent a great difference in Delany's vision of Black male subjectivity. To the extent that Delany focuses on Africa, with regard to American patriarchy he is not so interested in issues of illegitimacy as he is in independence and influence. Africa, as he has defined it, is a truly distinct third term to which African American men can turn for the courage and strength to oppose slaveholders. And yet Delany's Blake, like Madison Washington and *Clotel*'s narrator, remains a son. Neither he nor they are defined according to familial relations other than that of father to son. Even while Madison Washington and Henry Blake are married, their wives are barely presented, and we witness no insight stemming from husband-wife relations. Madison Washington has no children; Henry Blake's son Tony exists, but has no interaction with his father at any point in the novel. Consequently, selfhood as presented in all three of these novels is fixed on father/son relations, and, consequently, the genesis of African American or African diasporic identity becomes an exclusively male construct, where son status is what counts.

In the story with which we began this chapter, Victor Sèjour's "Le Mulâtre," Antoine, the storyteller who presents Georges story, asks the pertinent question about appropriate responses to the gross inhumanity of enslavement. First, he characterizes male slavery by saying:

A negro's as vile as a dog; society rejects him; men detest him; the laws curse him. . . . Yes, he's a most unhappy being, who hasn't even the consolation of always being virtuous. . . . He may be born good, noble, and generous; God may grant him a great and loyal soul; but despite all that, he often goes to his grave with bloodstained hands, and a heart hungering after yet more vengeance. For how many times has he seen the dreams of his youth destroyed? How many times has experience taught him that his good deeds count for nothing, and that he should love neither his wife nor his son; for one day the former will be seduced by the master, and his own flesh and blood will be sold and transported away despite his despair. (287–88)

After this description, Antoine presents his question: "What then can you expect him to become?" He then continues by suggesting possible answers. "Shall he smash his skull against the paving stones? Shall he kill his torturer?" As we have seen in William Wells Brown's *Clotel* and Frederick Douglass's *The Heroic Slave*, this tragedy of masculinity that Séjour draws, the mulatto's tragedy, is always lurking yet might be thwarted by creating a significantly different relation between master and male slave, father and son. In Martin Delany's *Blake*, too, this mulatto's tragedy is averted because the story is rewritten as the fatherland's son's righteous warring against colonial power. Antoine continues, however, with an additional alternative scenario: "Or do you believe the human heart can find a way to bear such misfortune?" he asks. But about this possibility he quickly declares: "You'd have to be mad to believe that" (288). Madness might also be a gendered concept, however, since this belief that Séjour's Antoine calls mad is for postbellum writers a significant aspect of women's reality. Sons may not be able to envision the human heart as it bears such misfortunes, but as the next chapter of this study proposes to demonstrate, mothers telling secrets suggest otherwise.

3

Slave Mothers and Colored Consciousness

White men's children spread over the earth—
A rainbow suspending the drawn swords of birth,
Uniting and blending the races in one
The world man—cosmopolite—everyman's son!

He channels the stream of the red blood and blue,
Behold him! A Triton—the peer of the two;
Unriddle this riddle of "outside in"
White men's children in black men's skin.

—Georgia Douglas Johnson, "The Riddle"

Whether American or African, individual or community, the third-term figure or group that serves to construct relational subjectivity and mediate discourse between male ex-slaves and American slaveholders in the abolitionist
novels of William Wells Brown, Frederick Douglass, and Martin Delany also
inhabits the masculine world of the public sphere. As a consequence, these
novels characterize the mediating third term and implied collective identity
of slaves, ex-slaves, or African diasporic peoples in masculinist terms. This
also defines the consequent positional relationship between reader and text
as masculine, which limits narrative possibilities while also displacing mas-
ter/female slave moments as focal points in each text. Not until we turn to a
consideration of postbellum fiction by Black female writers, which also focuses
on patriarchal, and specifically paternal, secrets, do we also see significant
female agency represented.

Perhaps because postbellum writers do not need to make abolitionist arguments but instead represent the experiences of slavery for the purposes of
understanding current situations, in late nineteenth- and early twentieth-
century fiction by African American women, the master/female slave moment

comes back into sharp focus. Here we find an inscribed, perhaps even over-inscribed or reified, brutally sexualized confrontation between master and female slave, or in later generations, white men and Black women in similar power relationships, meant to contextualize a concomitant narrative focus: the coming to identity story of light-skinned sons and daughters of slave mothers. Any confrontation between master and slave disrupts the social order by forcing questions of status quo citizenship and the definition of freedom, but confrontations between masters and *female* slaves also disrupt the neat distinction between public and private realms of existence and influence.[1] Such disruptions, in fact, give this fiction its power. Fiction that presents master/female slave moments from inside the relationship, rather than from the voyeuristic or son's perspective, focuses upon the private behavior of men not simply to bring such behaviors public; this fiction specifically tells secrets about white paternity so as to also very deliberately construct a foundation for race identity defined by a new colored consciousness.

Consider the question at hand, which concerns identity formation, retrospectively, from the vantage point of the 1920s. In the foreword to the 1925 anthology *The New Negro*, Alain Locke declares that the volume's aim is "to document the New Negro culturally and socially,—to register the transformations of the inner and outer life of the Negro in America that have so significantly taken place in the last few years" (xv). Locke claims that "Negro genius" of the 1920s "relies upon the race-gift as a vast spiritual endowment from which our best developments have come and must come" ("Negro Youth Speaks" 47). Yet he also claims that the New Negro is a "changeling" who has not been "swathed" in the formulae of "the Sociologist, the Philanthropist, the Race-leader," the three norns,[2] thereby implying that the New Negro's conception and infancy have not yet been rightly identified ("The New Negro" 3). As I will suggest in this chapter, however, what Locke's sociologist, philanthropist, and race-leader fathers cannot explain, African American mothers can. The "changeling" identity knowledge marked by race pride that defines a new generation of writers and artists is, as Frances E. W. Harper and Pauline Hopkins tell the story, both possessed and passed on by enslaved and ex-slave women.

In Frances E. W. Harper's famous speech at the World's Congress of Representative Women at the Columbian Exposition in 1893, she posits that while "the fifteenth century discovered America to the Old World, the nineteenth century is discovering woman to herself."[3] Calling for "fairer and higher aims than the greed of gold and the lust of power," she declares this moment at the end of the nineteenth century to be "the threshold of women's era" and predicts that "women's work" will be "grandly constructive" ("Woman's Political Future" 433–34). In making this pronouncement about a new era centered on women's work, Harper draws from the collective vision of numerous Black women of the late nineteenth century who formed clubs dedicated to cooperative efforts that would give "causes dear and vital to humanity the valuable aid of organized intelligence" (Hopkins, "Club Life" 273). These club efforts attempted to define a new morality focused on the idea of "uplift," a moral imperative tied both to liberation theology and racial solidarity (see K. Gaines). Most significantly, many of the women involved in uplift work knew that the attention of the world focused on them as women. With this consciousness the Woman's Era Club was formed in Boston in 1873, and a journal titled *The Woman's Era* (ed. Josephine St. Pierre Ruffin) was published during the mid-1890s. Disappointed by the efforts of Black men with regard to racial equality, Black clubwomen felt that they could prevail where Black men had not; and in this regard editorials in *The Woman's Era* portray Black women's efforts as superior to the efforts of Black men, call for "timid men and ignorant men" to stand aside, and criticize Black male organizing as only talk.[4]

If Black women were disappointed with Black men, they were exasperated with white women who attempted to exclude Black clubwomen from the General Federation of Women's Clubs. While early Black women's clubs seem to have grown out of established, predominantly white women's clubs as more specific interests warranted, they were not exclusively Black—the Woman's Era Club, for example, upon its founding, had several white members. When racism within the white women's club movement forced Black women to organize their own federation in 1895, which they called the National Conference of the Colored Women of America (later the National Association of Colored Women), the women who attended the federation's organizing conference refused to define themselves by race or color. As Hazel Carby details, because these women had been excluded from white women's organizations, they would not prohibit from membership anyone "who could share the aims and ideals of the movement." The president of the Woman's Era Club who called the conference, Josephine St. Pierre Ruffin, stated: "We are not drawing the color line; we are women, American women, as intensely interested in all that pertains to us as such as all other American women."[5] Further evidence of this understanding comes in the form of disagreement with Booker T. Washington on the subject of social and political equality. In direct opposition to Washington, with whom the National Association of

Colored Women was indirectly linked,[6] clubwomen "took a stand against the prohibition of interracial marriage," knowing that "such laws made black women all the more vulnerable to sexual exploitation" (Giddings 105).

The National Association of Colored Women determined to call itself "colored" during a time of great argument against the use of this term as too general and not racially specific. Self-identification as "colored" (rather than "Negro" or "Afro-American") at the turn of the twentieth century was sometimes dismissed as the consequence of class bias or intraracial prejudice against darker African Americans, an unjustified simplification of the term's mediative use, particularly with regard to Black female experience. "Colored" suggests that Black women leaders at the turn of the century understood their mission and their collective identity to be integrally connected to both Black and white life, to be, in other words, significantly focused on the interconnections between the races. Pauline E. Hopkins, who edited and wrote for the *Colored American Magazine*, is at the center of these formations of colored identity. Through the *Colored American Magazine*, Hopkins develops a female-centered colored consciousness that in and of itself is a complex and fascinating precursor to the turn of the twenty-first century *mestiza*, or borderland, transformative identity described by Gloria Anzaldúa and now paradigmatic in American and women's studies (see Anzaldúa; see also Pryse, "Critical"). While her career with the *Colored American Magazine* was cut short by a change in publishers and a new editorial mission influenced by Booker T. Washington's ideology, Hopkins's work nevertheless represents a significant contribution to theoretical explorations of race and racial identity. Further, what might be termed Hopkins's new colored consciousness, to parallel Anzaldúa's concept of new *mestiza* consciousness, also plays a significant role in the development of new Negro identity, particularly as it is manifest in literary production of the 1920s and 1930s and characterized by Alain Locke as a new race pride ("The New Negro" 3–16). Specifically, Hopkins's fiction continues a literary tradition established by Frances Harper that transforms slavery's stories of female victimization into the foundation of strong and positive mother identity at once both racialized and racially transcendent.[7] This identity, while not located as such by Locke as he characterizes the "New Negro," might be seen as the changeling's missing story of origin.

At the center of postbellum novels by African American women are moments of confrontation between white male slaveholders and female slaves. These moments are charged with a violence whose implication, at least, is sexual. In *Iola Leroy*, Iola's treatment at the hands of her master is narrated by the slave Tom Anderson, who says that "Marse Tom . . . meant to break her in" (38).

Through Tom Anderson's efforts she is brought by the Union army to its field hospital, salvation described as Iola "taken as a trembling dove from the gory vulture's nest and given a place of security" (39). Later, Anderson reports the confrontation he saw between his master and Iola: "He chucked her under de chin, an' tried to put his arm roun' her waist. But she jis' frew it off like a chunk ob fire. She looked like a snake had bit her. Her eyes fairly spit fire. Her face got red ez blood, an' den she turned so pale I thought she war gwine to faint, but she didn't, an' I yered her say, 'I'll die first'" (41). For her impudence, her master vows to have Iola whipped, although the novel implies that she is saved before this occurs. Not so in Pauline Hopkins's *Contending Forces:* that novel's prehistory, focused on the lives of Charles and Grace Montfort and their children, culminates in the brutal whipping of Grace by two ignorant and low-class white men. Grace is not a slave, but she takes on slave status because of a rumor that she is of African descent. Her lashing with rawhide (the "snaky leather thong") by "the two strong, savage men" is repeated until "fainting fit followed fainting fit" and "the blood stood in a pool about her feet." As Hazel Carby and others argue, this scene represents Grace Montfort's rape, and there is no question as to the significance of this scene to the novel (see Carby, *Reconstructing Womanhood* 32; Bernardi 214). The moment is illustrated, highlighted, and printed as the frontispiece, with a caption and reference to the page where the violence is described. Despite the inclusion of these moments of violence, however, Black women prevail in both novels. The point, in both texts, is not that specific characters have fallen, but that Black or colored women "still" rise: through the values which they embody or impart to future generations, their very survival is triumphant.[8] And this idea is, of course, replayed again and again within the trajectory of twentieth-century characterizations of slavery in African American narratives written by women.[9]

It is no coincidence that postbellum African American fiction, developing as race politics establishes a firm color line between Black and white, focuses on the presentation of biracial characters within the context of these master/female slave moments. While the earliest readings of the "tragic mulatto" see this character's near-whiteness as a device with which to arouse white readers' sympathies (Christian 26; McDowell, "'Changing Same'" 284–85), Hazel Carby's important refiguration allows that the "dominance of the mulatto figure in Afro-American fiction . . . has too often been dismissed as politically unacceptable without a detailed analysis of its historical and narrative function." Consequently, Carby presents the mulatto "as a vehicle for an exploration of the relationship between the races," taking place during a time when politics insists no such relationship exists (*Reconstructing Womanhood* 89). I would also argue that such characters function as affirmations of race consciousness because when these characters are light enough to pass for white they often choose not to, thus rejecting whiteness (and white fathers) and affirming a distinctive racial identity. It is most significant that the post-Reconstruction South focused its efforts on legal segregation, and that the U.S. Supreme Court established the doctrine of "separate but equal" through the 1896 *Plessy v. Ferguson* case, while at the same time the number of "mulattoes" dramatically increased from 11.2 percent of the Black population in 1859 to 20.9 percent in 1910 (F. Davis 54).[10] Consequently, the very existence of biracial peoples contradicts the claim made by Booker T. Washington in his 1895 Atlanta Exposition Address that in all things "purely social we can be as separate as the fingers" (*Up From Slavery* 221–22). Or, as the strongly worded "Furnace Blasts: Black or White—Which Should Be the Young Afro-American's Choice in Marriage" from Pauline Hopkins's *Colored American Magazine* remarks, "Shall the Anglo-Saxon and the Afro-American mix? They have mixed" (6.5: 349).

Plessy v. Ferguson was also responsible for making the so-called one-drop rule the law of the land, thus attempting to replace a complicated question of race consciousness that combines questions of personal identity, history, and memory, with a strictly dichotomous legal definition. As social historians who focus on Black life within the African diaspora have shown, the legal rules of race with regard to citizenship privilege as constructed in the United States are unique: in no other country is the status of the racially mixed population the same as the lower-status parent group (F. Davis 82). When Homer Plessy sued for the right to ride on a train in Louisiana in seats reserved for whites, he argued that because he was only one-eighth Negro and could pass for white he was entitled to consideration as a white man. As part of the argument against this position, the Supreme Court took judicial notice that a person is considered a Negro, or Black, as a consequence of any Black ancestry (F. Davis 8). This superstructure of racial definition constructed by the judiciary system has held as precedent to this day; thus, in modern American life the category "white" implies racial purity while "Black" means everyone else. Historically, then, Black families incorporate within them people of various racial genealogies, and, as we might expect, ideals of domesticity presented by African American writers reflect this multiracial reality.

Claudia Tate makes the point that, unlike their twentieth-century readers, Frances Harper and Pauline Hopkins "regard *mulatto* as a generic term for designating the emancipated population and their heirs" (146). Neither author, in Tate's words, intended to present "racially ambivalent African Americans who rely on their light skin color to bolster their self-esteem and bourgeois ambitions," a common late twentieth-century reading of these authors' texts (146). As I will argue in detail, Frances Harper's novels *Minnie's Sacrifice* and *Iola Leroy; or, Shadows Uplifted* present white-skinned biracial characters as affirmations of race (that is, "colored") consciousness; only because Harper's characters are able to pass for white can they choose not to do so, thus rejecting whiteness and affirming their own racial identity. Harper presents stories of very light-skinned protagonists who grow up believing they are white, until some event occurs that forces them to realize their true identities, yet these stories are more than melodrama. In both *Minnie's Sacrifice* and *Iola Leroy*, these events allow Harper to make connections between matrifocal knowledge, racial identity, and a higher or "new" consciousness. Harper's *Iola Leroy* returns again and again to the figure of the slave mother because race consciousness is born of slave mothers: characters identify with the race in direct proportion to the extent with which they refuse to forsake their mothers. By choosing formerly enslaved mothers over white, often powerful fathers, these characters demonstrate a system of values in deep contrast with, yet clearly superior to, dominant America's. As Harper presents it, first-generation freed men and women endowed with a potentially world-transforming new consciousness comprise the African American community formed from the choice to stand in opposition to America's "arrogance, aggressiveness, and indomitable power" (*Iola Leroy* 260). Further, Pauline Hopkins both acknowledges the vision of Frances Harper and further refines Harper's work into a new definition of turn-of-the-century African American consciousness. Through the *Colored American Magazine* and her own fiction, Hopkins suggests that positionality demands of "colored" mothers an understanding of a blended rather than doubled racialized self, which produces a truly new colored consciousness dependent upon a colored mother's standpoint. This new consciousness, as I will argue, in turn generates that nascent identity known as "New Negro."

Unforsaken Mothers in *Minnie's Sacrifice* and *Iola Leroy; or, Shadows Uplifted*

Following the lead of Frances Smith Foster, critics recognize *Minnie's Sacrifice*, the novel that Harper serializes in the *Christian Recorder* in 1869, as the precursor to *Iola Leroy*, which it precedes in publication by more than twenty years. *Minnie's Sacrifice* tells two stories about young African Americans who grow up believing they are white but subsequently realize they are Black.

The first story, which opens the novel, focuses upon Louis Le Croix, son of a wealthy white planter and a slave mother who dies in childbirth. The second story, which ultimately eclipses the first, focuses on Minnie Le Grange, also the child of a wealthy white planter and a slave mother. Louis and Minnie, neither of whom know the race of their mothers, are both sent North to school by well-meaning fathers. They meet, fall in love, are estranged while their racial identities are in flux, but marry in the end. After the two move back to the South to do racial uplift work, Minnie is killed, presumably by the Ku Klux Klan (thus, her sacrifice).[11] For the rest of his life, Louis then devotes himself to social justice work in her honor.

As Foster notes in her introduction to *Three Rediscovered Novels*, *Minnie's Sacrifice* is "a deliberate retelling of the Old Testament Moses story" (xxx). Unlike Martin Delany in *Blake*, however, Harper focuses on the Moses child rather than the adult leader of an enslaved people. Significantly, Harper seems to have been writing two versions of the story of Moses at approximately the same time. Her poem *Moses: A Story of the Nile* was perhaps initially published in 1868 (the extant second edition was published in 1869), and yet, as Foster also points out, as early as 1859 Harper demonstrated her interest in Mosaic legend by writing, "I like the character of Moses. He is the first disunionist we read of in the Jewish Scriptures. . . . He would have no union with the slave power of Egypt."[12] Yet even in *Moses: A Story of the Nile*, meant to follow closely the story of Moses in Exodus, Harper's interpretation includes, as another critic notes, the "radical presentation of Moses's mother as the key molder of his political and religious consciousness" (Boyd 80). This Moses, precisely because of his mother's influence, cannot help but identify himself as a son of Israel; and because he knows, again from his mother, the stories of his forefathers, he obeys destiny to join his people in order to lead them to freedom. In *Minnie's Sacrifice*, a companion piece of sorts to *Moses: A Story of the Nile*, the young Louis Le Croix's early life imitates that of Moses in that a white slaveholder's daughter claims him as her own in order to save him. But in this version of the Mosaic legend, strong maternal guidance is unavailable to Louis and, consequently, he is not able to understand his own identity—until, that is, he can join with Minnie Le Grange and become sure of himself through his union with her.

Harper begins *Minnie's Sacrifice* by presenting the retelling of "Moses in the Bulrushes." Camilla, young daughter of the slavemaster Bernard Le Croix, is fascinated by a baby recently born in the slave quarters to a woman, Agnes, who has died in childbirth. "I wonder," Camilla says to herself, "if I couldn't save him from being a slave" (5). She had been reading just the day before, she tells the baby's grandmother, "the beautiful story in the Bible about a wicked king, who wanted to kill all the little boys of a people who were enslaved in his land," and how the king's daughter, she said, "found him and saved his life" (5). Camilla means to follow the example of "that good princess," and so convinces her father that the baby, who looks white, should be brought up as his son. Le Croix agrees to this plan, in large part because the baby *is* his son, and this relieves his conscience without adding the necessity that he acknowledge his relationship with the baby's mother. Consequently, Louis is raised as a wealthy Southerner, and sent to school in the North.

Unlike Harper's Moses in *Moses: A Story of the Nile*, Louis does not know his heritage and so cannot choose "his people" over the Southern aristocratic class in which he is being raised. Instead, as a young man in the North, even with Abolitionists as friends, he identifies as a Southerner and feels "a sense of honor in defending the South" (36). At this juncture, Harper strays from the emphasis of the Biblical story that perhaps had been her first inspiration in order to focus on what happens when a young man does not know his own background. Louis believes he knows who he is, and based on that identity he feels a strong loyalty to the South, which develops into a loyalty to the Secessionists. As Harper makes very clear, however, Louis makes his mistake of allegiance because he has never known his mother and never, from her lips, heard tell of "the grand traditions" of his race.[13] In Louis's case, without matrifocal knowledge to guide him, he can only act according to chivalric principle: the South is his mother, he says, "and that man is an ingrate who will not stand by his mother and defend her when she is in peril" (36). Unlike Madison Washington in his relation to Virginia in Frederick Douglass's *The Heroic Slave*, Louis receives no gift of character from his motherland—this Southland—but instead displays a false heroism based on faulty self knowledge.

Louis does have matriarchal figures in his life, however, and they finally tell him his true identity when they hear he is scheduled to march with the Secessionist army. Louis tells his sister, Camilla, and his maternal grandmother, Miriam (whom he thinks of as "Mammy," the housekeeper) that "his country" calls him because "she" is in danger.[14] As a Unionist, Camilla is incensed. "Your country! Louis," she says, "Where is your country?" (58). She then attempts to argue politics with her brother. He is not swayed, however, and when Camilla hesitates to say more, Miriam picks up an unfinished sentence and tells her grandson that "to join the secesh is to raise your hands agin your own race" (59). This pronouncement understandably captures Louis's attention, and the "free papers" he is shown prove to him the validity of the statement. Louis then immediately declares that he can never raise his hand against his "mother's race," but has no understanding of any other implications of his new self-knowledge.

Louis's story, then, which began as a retelling of the Biblical story of Moses, has changed to depict a confused man who has lost his way. This shift away from depicting Louis as a Mosaic leader further emphasizes the other story, representative of Harper's strong belief in the importance of mothers, which becomes dominant for her. Consequently, in *Minnie's Sacrifice*, it seems Harper's interest in a racial discovery of identity overwhelms her African American retelling of the story of Moses, and forces her to forego the idea of a leader ever cognizant of his identity and his destiny. Harper turns the loss of this primary element of the Moses story to her advantage, however, and uses it to complement her portrayal of a different kind of leader. In *Moses: A Story of the Nile*, the people whom Moses leads, as characterized by Harper, are in body free but in soul still enslaved.[15] In *Minnie's Sacrifice*, Harper's other protagonist, Minnie Le Grange, recognizes this problem and becomes the leader who works for the soul's freedom, that is, the moral progress of her people.

Louis's life and story gain meaning again only after he reconnects with Minnie Le Grange, who has herself been transformed through her re-established connection with her own mother. Minnie's story ultimately preempts Louis's own, which demonstrates the depths of Harper's interest in the connection between matrifocal knowledge and racial identity. Minnie grows up in a Northern Quaker household, believes strongly in the abolition of slavery, and feels that prejudice is "wicked." Yet she also states, just before her identity is revealed to her, that she "should hate to be colored!" because of society's prejudice (48). When Minnie and her mother meet on the street, however, and Minnie's mother immediately recognizes Minnie as her daughter, Minnie does not seem so much surprised as relieved: she feels that the "mystery which enshrouded her young life" will soon be solved (50–51). Minnie's attitude suggests that she has, in some way, suspected her racial identity, and that her mother's presence has simply confirmed it for her. Later, as she is recovering from the "nervous affection" to which she succumbs after understanding that she is "colored," Minnie declares that her early life comes back to her "like a dream," and that she has "a faint recollection of having seen" her mother before (53).

Once Minnie reconciles herself to who she is, her future and her reasons for choosing to devote herself to the betterment of "her" people become clear to her. She also becomes Louis's inspiration, telling him that in the future "they should clasp hands . . . and find their duty and their pleasure in living for the welfare and happiness of [their] race" (67). Further, when asked about this hard choice she has made, and given the suggestion that she and Louis might live as members of the white race rather than the colored, Minnie is quite clear: "The prejudices of society are so strong against the people with whom I am connected on my mother's side," she says, "that I could not associate with white people on equal terms, without concealing my origin, and that I scorned to do" (72). While Harper more fully develops the connection between matrifocal knowledge, racial identity, and, ultimately, a higher or "new" consciousness in *Iola Leroy*, she suggests this connection in *Minnie's Sacrifice* by pointing to Minnie's dedication to the work of uplifting the race made hers through matrilineal connection. More significantly, in *Minnie's Sacrifice* Harper delineates the significance of what she terms "standpoint" and suggests a relation between it and the higher state of consciousness that she names "blessed." As an epistemological model, Harper's characterization of the way in which "standpoint" becomes the precondition for the state of "blessedness" prefigures feminist standpoint theory and Black feminist epistemology as defined by Sandra Harding (*Whose Science?*) and Patricia Hill Collins (*Black Feminist Thought*), respectively.

Harper first introduces her conceptual "standpoint of observation" with regard to Camilla, to explain her earliest understanding of slavery's human toll. According to the narrator of *Minnie's Sacrifice*, Camilla "had lived so much among the slaves, and had heard so many tales of sorrow breathed confidentially into her ears, that she had unconsciously imbibed their view of the matter; and without comprehending the injustice of the system, she had learned to view it from their standpoint of observation" (15). Camilla's "standpoint of observation" that allows her to "see the old system [of slavery] under a new light" also becomes, for the narrator, a "good seed" planted, which "was yet to yield its harvest of blessed deeds" (15). In some ways akin to Harriet Beecher Stowe's little Eva (*Uncle Tom's Cabin*), or, more tellingly, Toni Morrison's Amy Denver (*Beloved*), this white girl Camilla, through compassion and perhaps empathy, is able to know slavery from the position of those oppressed by it and understand, as well, the subjugated aspect of such knowledge, marked as secret, and "breathed confidentially into her ears." While Harper does not go so far as to portray Camilla as having reinvented herself as "Other" (Harding chap. 11), this is precisely how she portrays Minnie Le Grange, and later, Iola Leroy, both of whom achieve a state that Harper calls "blessedness," indicative of wisdom and life work that, to use Patricia Hill Collins's language, demonstrates an ethic of caring and personal accountability (*Black Feminist Thought* chap. 11).

Minnie makes reference to her own transformation in conversation with Camilla. The two meet not quite as social equals, yet "mutually . . . attracted to each other" (69). After stating that she refuses to conceal her origin, Minnie explains: "there are lessons of life that we never learn in the bowers of ease. They must be learned in the fire. . . . But now, when I look back upon those days of gloom and suffering, I think they were among the most fruitful of my life, for in those days of pain and sorrow my resolution was formed to join the fortunes of my mother's race, and I resolved to brighten her old age with a joy, with a gladness she had never known in her youth" (72). Minnie recognizes that her new societal position gives her the vantage of being "Other" and allows her to "do for my race, as a colored woman, what I never could accomplish as a white woman" (72), or, as Camilla paraphrases, allows Minnie "to live out the earnest purpose" of her life (73). According to the narrator, Minnie works with the newly freed people as a "labor of love" (75), teaching more than "mere knowledge of books" but also "how to make their homes happy and bright" (74), how, in other words, to locate themselves, make themselves home in the world, and recognize this location as the foundation of self—and race—knowledge. After Minnie's death and as Louis pictures "her shining robes and the radiant light of her glorified face" (89), he, in memory of Minnie, continues the work they began together. Like the characters in *Iola Leroy*, who, "blessed themselves . . . are a blessing to others," he is declared, in the novel's final line, "blessed in his labors of love and faith" (90). Harper's narrator implies, then, that having lived through the ordeal of her death, Louis, like Minnie before him, has reached a new level of consciousness.

While we do not yet know the details of Minnie Le Grange's death because of missing pages or issues of the *Christian Recorder*, later references indicate Minnie's crucifixion at the hands of the Ku Klux Klan. This suggests a moment of confrontation (albeit lost) between Minnie and her white male tormenters, a version of the master/female slave moment.[16] In *Minnie's Sacrifice*, according to Harper, this moment presages a later time of "peace and justice . . . reign[ing] triumphant where violence and slavery had held their fearful carnival of shame and crime for ages" (90). In other words, in *Minnie's Sacrifice*, even as Minnie herself dies, this moment brings about the birth of a new *national* consciousness. Harper continues to develop this idea of a new national consciousness in *Iola Leroy* and, as we shall see, she attempts to make images of Iola's moments of confrontation with male slaveowners central to the story while at the same time refusing to present Iola as a powerless victim. For this reason, the narrative of Iola's past is not presented until chapter nine, after Iola is established as a woman of great moral character and just at the point where she has received a proposal of marriage from the white Dr. Gresham. Gresham's proposal recasts the possibilities for relationships between white men and Black women; it suggests, in other words, potential for something other than master/female slave moments. Iola rejects this relationship, however, specifically because it poses a future that would contradict her potential as mother; and in *Iola Leroy*, Harper develops her idea of a new race consciousness through a reconceptualization of the place of mothers and the role of motherhood.

As both the bedrock of postbellum African American community and the key to a transformed and transformative new identity, Harper's *Iola Leroy* returns again and again to the figure of the slave mother. As I have previously suggested, Harper does this not in acquiescence to the sentimentality of the age, nor as an appeal to a sympathetic white female readership, but because race consciousness is born of slave mothers. According to law, of course, status as free or slave depends upon the status of one's mother. Yet this negative association with slave mothers is, in turn, and particularly for the daughters of slave women, transformed into positive identity. In *Iola Leroy*, it bears repeating, characters identify with the race in direct proportion to the extent with which they refuse to forsake their mothers. This is true of Robert Johnson, who can never forget that his mother was sold away from him. It is true of Ben Tunnel, who will remain a slave for as long as his mother remains a slave, because he cannot leave her. It is most significantly true for the three young biracial characters in the novel: Iola herself; Harry, her brother; and Dr. Frank Latimer, the man who becomes Iola's husband.

The opening chapters of *Iola Leroy*, set during the Civil War, establish a slave community that identifies itself *as* a community. The novel's first chapter, titled "Mystery of Market Speech and Prayer-Meeting," opens with a conversation between two men, Robert Johnson and Thomas Anderson, both slaves, which demonstrates their interest in and knowledge of the events of the war, as well as the coded speech they use to communicate with one another. The next three chapters of the novel focus on the secret gatherings, termed "prayer-meetings," held within the slave community for the purpose of determining whether or not and when members of the community should leave their situations in order to join the Union army. These opening chapters serve the purpose not only of establishing the community's informed attitude toward the war, but also of introducing Iola Leroy within the context of that community and identifying her as someone who has experienced the Christian slave conversion characterized by Melvin Dixon as a conversion not to God but to "each other," the collective slave community.

79

Tom Anderson, double to the slavemaster bearing the same name, becomes Iola Leroy's hero. His intervention on Iola's behalf frees her from "Marse Tom's" clutches, thus enabling her to remember her friend and seek community with his kind. Unlike the Christ-like Uncle Tom of an earlier era, however, Tom Anderson's motives for helping Iola as a woman in distress are clear: he loves Iola "as a Pagan might worship a distant star and wish to call it his own" (40). For this reason, Tom will do anything in his power for the Union soldiers who rescued Iola—and this willingness, in fact, brings him to his death. At the same time, however, Tom, who is "just as black as black can be" (44) is also Iola's best friend, named so by her as she ministers to him on his death bed, called by her "the best friend I have had since I was torn from my mother" (54). Her farewell kiss, and her tears upon his death, perplex the white Dr. Gresham and mark her, for him, other than white; and upon questioning Col. Robinson about Iola's intimacy with Tom Anderson, Dr. Gresham—and Harper's readers—hear, for the first time, her secret history.

In the early chapters of *Iola Leroy*, Iola's confrontations with white slave-masters are narrated primarily by Tom Anderson. It is from him that we hear of Iola's response to "Marse Tom's" sexual overtures, including her remark, "I'll die fust" (41). Here, Harper highlights his role, and his feeling that "it does me good to know dat Marse Tom ain't got her" (42). Later in the narrative, however, Iola states her own understanding of her situation: "I was sold from State to State as an article of merchandise. I had outrages heaped on me which might well crimson the cheek of honest womanhood with shame, but I never fell into the clutches of an owner for whom I did not feel the utmost loathing and intensest horror" (115). Even later, she tells her mother that she "passed through a fiery ordeal of suffering" (195). It is her ultimate triumph over suffering, the "path she had trodden with bleeding feet" which she transforms "to lines of living light" that during a speech entrances her audience (257). If Frederick Douglass's confrontation with Edward Covey "makes him a man" thus demonstrating his coming-to-consciousness of his humanity, then Iola Leroy's ordeal at the hands of "Marse" Tom Anderson and other slaveholding men is as pronounced a demonstration of *her* coming-to-consciousness of her humanity. Iola's experiences within master/female slave moments also bring about, as Harper claims, a necessary and beneficial transformation of standpoint that produces significant access to self-knowledge. "I would not change the Iola of then for the Iola of now," (273) our title character proclaims, saying further that "fearful as the awakening was, it was better than to have slept through life" (274). As further testament to the significance of this state of newly realized human consciousness, in response to Iola's new understanding of herself her future husband reminds her—and her readers—that those who "miss the deepest pain . . . also lose the highest joy" (274).

Both *Minnie's Sacrifice* and *Iola Leroy* demonstrate the inability of African American women to enter into sustained marriage relations with white men. Iola Leroy's past is similar to Minnie Le Grange's and Louis Le Croix's in that Iola, too, is the child of a wealthy white slaveholder and an African American mother, yet she grows up with no knowledge of her mother's racial identity. Although Iola's mother has been manumitted and her mother and father are married, this makes no difference once her father dies and her father's wicked cousin determines to take possession of the property. At this point, Iola becomes a slave. None of Iola's tragic personal history takes place in the novel's present, however, which is part of Harper's narrative strategy to keep readers from revictimizing her protagonist. Readers are informed of the past events of Iola's life only after Tom Anderson's death and Dr. Gresham's puzzlement at her intimacy with the former slave. When Iola refuses the white Dr. Gresham's offer of marriage, this too highlights the role of African American women and their families within the larger public sphere.

If there is no real possibility of marriage to white men, ex-slave women, even in their relations of "concubinage" rather than marriage, do not quite inhabit the private realm of family. In the end, then, the legal possibility of being remanded to slavery takes precedence over any private relations, even those clearly marked as family relations, and for this reason slave and ex-slave women are not privileged as members of the private sphere. This raises "concubinage" as a dire issue, one Pauline Hopkins names along with lynching as a death threat for African Americans. In terms of the master/female slave moment and the role it plays as race knowledge develops and race relations progress and regress—because even wives, if they are African American or purported to be so, are not immune to the threat of enslavement—slave status, for them, clearly trumps gender identity. This, ironically, keeps enslaved women on the public stage. While Frances Harper does not explore the implications to the larger society of familial relations made and kept public in this way, Pauline Hopkins does, as we will consider in detail through readings of her novels *Contending Forces* and *Of One Blood; or, The Hidden Self.*

In *Minnie's Sacrifice*, Harper explores the meaning of racial identity by presenting protagonists who have their identities revealed to them, thereby focusing on what it means to these protagonists to discover their racial heritage. In *Iola Leroy*, however, because Iola has learned of her racial heritage prior to the novel's opening, that heritage functions quite differently and the master/female slave moment becomes a transcendent signifier. The army field hospital, the public stage with which the novel opens, is the only place where Iola's identity is kept from anyone, and there it is kept from Northern white men by Northern white men—in fact, Dr. Gresham's marriage proposal brings with it the opportunity to "bury her secret in his Northern home" (59–60). Learning Iola Leroy's true identity provokes Dr. Gresham to propose marriage to her, but in response she gently probes his and his family's prejudice. While he claims there would be none toward her, when she asks what might happen if one of their children shows "unmistakable signs of color," his gaze falls and his face flushes, an indication that he had neither thought of this possibility, nor could accept it (117). At this, Iola Leroy rejects Dr. Gresham's marriage proposal. As Claudia Tate comments, for Harper "constructions of identity and community solidarity arise from the politics of family formation and not from platform politics" (86). Here, when Iola looks into her future, she defines herself as the mother of darker children rather than the wife of a white man.

Iola's identity as a potential mother is also clearly tied, for her, to her role as her own mother's daughter. As Iola rejects Dr. Gresham's marriage proposal, she tells him of her plan: "When the war is over I intend to search the country for my mother. . . . Oh, you do not know how hungry my heart is for my mother!" (116). Again, in conversation with Robert Johnson when the war is finally over, Iola proclaims: "Now, that freedom has come, I intend to search for my mother until I find her" (142). In this context, the reconstructed family becomes the precondition for the transformed community, and the melodrama of family reunion central to the middle plot of *Iola Leroy* serves as marker for this transformation. After Iola does search and is successfully reunited with her mother, Dr. Gresham meets her once again, and again offers marriage. At this point Iola says: "My life work is planned. I intend spending my future among the colored people of the South" (234). In response to the doctor's plea that she not give her life to an ungrateful people, Iola explains that she is not acting upon "wholly unselfish" motives: "My dear grandmother is one of the excellent of the earth, and we all love her too much to ignore our relationship with her" (235). Through this series of statements about her relationship to her mother and her mother's mother, Iola clearly identifies herself matrilineally. Further, she embraces this identity that ties her to her formerly enslaved grandmother, and through this act she comes to know not only herself, but also the future work to which she will dedicate herself.

Iola Leroy is not the only biracial character in Harper's novel to focus on matrilineal identification. Harry, Iola's brother, although never remanded into slavery, also identifies himself as colored, and for reasons similar to those of his sister when she rejects Dr. Gresham's marriage proposal. Harry joins the colored regiment of the Union army because he believes this will allow him his best chance to find his mother and sister. He says, in determining that he will take this step, that "to find my mother and sister I call no task too heavy, no sacrifice too great" (126). Harry later explains his choice and the matrilineal identification which motivates it: "I confess at first I felt a shrinking from taking the step, but love for my mother overcame all repugnance on my part" (203). He continues this sentiment by explaining that he has accepted himself as a colored man and intends to remain committed to his race: "Now that I have linked my fortunes to the race I intend to do all I can for its elevation" (203). In the end, by marrying the "very dark" Lucille, Harry links his fate to that of his race in a most permanent way, through the children that the two will presumably produce.

Dr. Latimer, the final biracial character to whom Harper introduces us, is yet another man who refuses to forsake his mother and her people. We first hear of Latimer's history from a friend of his: "He belongs to that Negro race both by blood and choice. His father's mother made overtones to receive him as her grandson and heir, but he has nobly refused to forsake his mother's people and has cast his lot with them" (238). He has, in other words, chosen his mother over his patrimony. Later, in conversation with Iola, Dr. Latimer describes his actions using similar words. He explains that he only did his duty in refusing his paternal grandmother's offer and asks rhetorically, "My mother . . . faithful and true, belongs to that [colored] race. Where else should I be?" (263). Through this conversation, Iola realizes that she and Latimer are soul mates, and she becomes enamored of him. In a later discussion with her uncle Robert Johnson, Iola compares Latimer with Moses, not as a future leader of a new nation, but as a man "willing to put aside [his] own advantages for . . . race and country." That, according to Iola, is "high, heroic manhood" (265).

In *Iola Leroy*, then, through the examples of Iola Leroy, Harry Leroy, and Frank Latimer, Harper demonstrates that embracing an African American identity means choosing to identify with—or more specifically, not to forsake—an African American mother. This, however, is only one of the novel's statements about African American motherhood, a topic to which Iola Leroy is specifically devoted. At the meeting attended by the intellectual elite, Iola gives a paper on the "Education of Mothers" (253). Further, her future life's work, at the end of the novel, is "for the especial benefit of mothers and children" (278). According to the narrator, "Little children love her. Old age turns to her for comfort, young girls for guidance, and mothers for counsel" (279). As further testament to her belief in the significance of the institution of motherhood, Harper presents Iola Leroy as having a very special role within the group of young intellectuals representative of the possibilities of the Black community. In the novel's conclusion, Harper presents Iola not as a teacher like her brother Harry and his wife Lucille, nor as a doctor like her husband. Instead, Harper presents her title character as a Sunday school helper who works with mothers and children in order to provide moral instruction, and who in that role leads a life "full of blessedness" (279). Harper has foreshadowed this pronouncement of Iola's "blessedness" by descriptions of her as "angelic"; in one instance, the novel's narrator describes her as a speaker whose tones are "like benedictions of peace" and whose words are "a call to higher service and nobler life" (257). Through the character of Iola Leroy, then, Harper suggests not only that daughters see slave or ex-slave mothers as the origin of race consciousness, but also that motherhood as an institution developed by daughters with such insight will be the vehicle that transports African Americans into a new era of consciousness.

When Iola Leroy was thrown from a comfortable, upper-class, white life into slavery, she was not only displaced but also transformed. After she agrees to marry Frank Latimer, she talks about the transformation that occurred during her confrontations with slavemasters, confrontations that bring with them knowledge of white patriarchy's basest secrets, and characterizes this transformation as her soul's "awakening" (273–74). By this, and through the use of Christian imagery, Harper presents a woman with a new consciousness. Here, as we consider Iola in her Christian context, we might again reconsider Melvin Dixon's definition of Christian slaves who convert themselves not to God but to each other. This Christian conversion, an apt way of characterizing Iola's immersion into her identity as slave, also signifies her embodiment of the transformed collective consciousness of the group.

Further, however, Iola Leroy's new consciousness is something akin to Gloria Anzaldúa's *mestiza* consciousness: using Anzaldúa's formulations, Iola has been "jarred out of ambivalence by an intense . . . painful, emotional event" and now seeks not simply to bring "severed or separated pieces" of her life together or to balance "opposing powers," but instead is "attempting to work out a synthesis . . . greater than the sum of [the self's] severed parts" by synthesizing her white and "colored" identities, her free, slave, and ex-slave identities, in order to lead women in "grandly constructive" work, to use Harper's phrase.[17] Iola Leroy talks to Latimer about her past:

84

she remembers the terrors and indignities of being enslaved as well as the privileges and pleasures of being upper class and white. As a consequence of her shifted circumstance and standpoint, she says, her life now "has a much grander significance" (274). Through her characterization of Iola Leroy as "blessed," then, Harper creates a consciousness of conversion and presents Iola Leroy as someone with this expanded consciousness, someone whose work is, as Anzaldúa characterizes, "to break down the subject-object duality that keeps her a prisoner and to show in the flesh . . . how duality is transcended" (102), someone who is otherly conscious rather than doubly conscious.[18] This new consciousness, as Harper presents it, has the potential to become the guiding force in the formations of African American communities that are comprised of the newly freed people.

In her eloquent "Address Delivered at the Centennial Anniversary of the Pennsylvania Society for Promoting the Abolition of Slavery" (1875), Harper uses vivid imagery to describe the "upbuilding" work which she envisions in the future: "The most important question before us colored people," she says, is "what are we going to do for ourselves?" ("An Address" 64–65). The context of this question is Harper's realistic assessment of the political climate of the day and the values of the larger society. She does acknowledge that the abolition of slavery indicates some progress: "One hundred years ago and Africa was the privileged hunting-ground of Europe and America, and the flag of different nations hung a sign of death on the coasts of Congo and Guinea. . . . Less than twenty-five years ago slavery clasped hands with King Cotton, and said slavery fights and cotton conquers for American slavery. Since then slavery is dead, the colored man has exchanged the fetters on his wrist for the ballot in his hand. Freedom is king, and Cotton a subject." ("An Address" 65) Her intent, however, is not to express gratitude. She castigates American society for the lack of humanity that allows the lawless to lynch Black citizens with impunity: "I do not believe there is another civilized nation under Heaven where there are half so many people who have been brutally and shamefully murdered, with or without impunity, as in this Republic within the last ten years. And who cares? . . . . Sheridan lifts up the vail [*sic*] from Southern society, and behind it is the smell of blood, and our bones scattered at the grave's mouth; murdered people; a White League with its 'covenant of death and agreement with hell.' And who cares?" ("An Address" 65–66). Harper's criticism of American values, her scorn for a society basking in "wonderful material prosperity" yet lacking a sense of justice, forms the background to the question, "What are we going to do for ourselves?" that she asks in this "Address." In the work of upbuilding the race, Harper's goal is not integrationist; she does not believe in accepting white society's values without scrutiny. Instead, Harper emphasizes the possibility that the larger society might be transformed by the values held by a new African American community; and this, too, is part of the potential she sees in the new colored consciousness that she presents in *Iola Leroy*.

In her "Address," Harper speaks of the work before the nation as "grandly constructive." It is "noble" work filled with "glorious opportunities" to save rather than destroy. Harper sees African Americans engaged in "moral warfare" consisting of "a battle against ignorance, poverty, and low social condition." A significant component of this "conflict of moral and spiritual progress" is that "in fighting truly and nobly for others you win the victory for yourselves." Most important, "in the great work of upbuilding there is room for woman's work and woman's heart." It is to African American women that Harper appeals when she asks that "the weaker and less favored" not be dismissed. It is to women that she entreats, "If you have ampler gifts, hold them as larger opportunities with which you can benefit others." It is from women that she expects a response when she reasons, "Oh, it is better to feel that the weaker and feebler our race the closer we will cling to them, than it is to isolate ourselves from them in selfish, or careless unconcern, saying there is a lion without" ("An Address" 67). The willingness and ability to act according to this ethic of caring, to use Patricia Hill Collins's phrase for one aspect of Black feminist standpoint knowledge, is precisely the example Harper means to offer by creating her protagonist Iola Leroy.

Frances Harper's vision of women's roles in society reflects her personal experiences and the experiences of many African American women like her. When she declares, in "Woman's Political Future," that "if the fifteenth century discovered America to the Old World, the nineteenth is discovering woman to herself," her point is that while women did not have the opportunity of discovering new worlds, they do have the opportunity of "filling this old world with fairer and higher aims than the greed of gold and the lust of power" (433). Harper sees women's right to vote as imminent; but she feels that political power is not as important, in itself, as rightly informed political judgment. For that, Harper believes, the nation must rely on women, whose duty it is to build character. Her closing appeal in this speech is: "Let the hearts of the women of the world respond to the song of the herald angels of peace on earth and good will to men. Let them throb as one heart unified by the grand and holy purpose of uplifting the human race, and humanity will breathe freer, and the world grow brighter. With such a purpose Eden would spring up in our path, and Paradise be around our way" (437). By following the example of African American women, Harper sees the women of the world involved in reforming the world.

In *Iola Leroy*, Harper has Iola express a sentiment taken from Harper's own "Woman's Political Future" address. From Iola's speech, we can gain a better understanding of the role Harper expects her exemplar to play: "But beyond the shadows I see the coruscation of a brighter day; and we can help usher it in, not by answering hate with hate, or giving scorn for scorn, but by striving to be more generous, noble, and just. It seems as if all creation travels to respond to the song of the Herald angels, 'Peace on earth, good-will toward men'" (249). Uplift is a moral concept which means rising above hatred and injustice; and, as Harper sees it, uplift comes to stand for the value system inherent in a new colored consciousness. During the same meeting where Iola speaks, Harper also presents the Rev. Carmicle extolling his audience to realize that their greatest need is for a religion "replete with life and glowing with love," especially in a world where the values of the dominant race seem to be "arrogance, aggressiveness, and indomitable power" (260). Here, the reverend defines the new collective consciousness of the people as a matrifocal sensibility that will, ultimately, displace patriarchal values in the larger society. This love, he declares, will also "broaden" the African American community's sympathies from "mere racial questions" to "humanity's wider issues," and thus, this new consciousness will also transform America.

The conclusion of *Iola Leroy* brings with it final portraits of Iola Leroy's family and presents a positive and idealistic view of the future for each of them. This is not because Harper lacks the nerve to imagine the violence and disappointment of the late nineteenth century—she has already presented that picture through Minnie Le Grange's death at the hands of the Ku Klux Klan in *Minnie's Sacrifice*. Harper does not claim that life for this family will now be blissful. Her conclusion is: "The shadows have been lifted from all their lives; and peace, like bright dew, has descended upon their paths. Blessed themselves, their lives are a blessing to others" (281). It is, to use a key phrase of Harper's, "the inner life that develops the outer" ("An Address" 103). She lays the foundation of a new race consciousness by creating a first-generation community of "blessed" freed men and women whose value system is uplift. The new consciousness of this community, inherited matrilineally, is the legacy Black foremothers like the fictitious Iola Leroy have inherited and passed down in place of birthright. Harper would have us believe that given this new foundation of identity dependent upon respect for and identification with enslaved or freed mothers, everything else of importance will follow. This is her message for African America, and it is also her message for America.

The New Colored Consciousness in
Pauline Hopkins's Fiction

Just after a reorganization of the Colored Co-Operative Publishing Company, the October 1900 issue of its *Colored American Magazine* published as frontispiece a photogravure of "The Young Colored American." Placed on a pedestal and, consequently, higher than the viewer's eye, with an American flag draped to one side, is a young child of indeterminate gender, right arm outstretched with forefinger in air, smiling and looking upward. This illustration, I will argue, is the embodiment of Pauline Hopkins's idea of "uplift" and representative of an ideal that, according to later advertisements for reproductions, "makes a picture that should be in every home in this land"(75). The frontispiece of the next issue of the *Colored American Magazine*, also telling, is an illustration of that moment in *Contending Forces* when Grace Montfort is brutally whipped by her would-be overseer. According to the caption, printed in capital letters, "When Hank Davis had satiated his vengeful thirst, he cut the ropes which bound her, and she sank upon the ground again." This advertisement for the novel, also published by the Colored Co-Operative Publishing Company, demonstrates the power of the master/female slave moment, crucial to understanding Hopkins's turn-of-the-century new colored consciousness. Taken together, these images, I will argue, suggest the birth of a "New Negro," to borrow common terminology, based in the history of female triumph over sexual degradation at the hands of white men.

The best evidence suggesting the acceptance by early twentieth-century Black women of a racially mixed heritage as the basis of African American identity comes in the form of Pauline Hopkins's fiction. As Hazel Carby has argued, Hopkins's work with the *Colored American Magazine* fulfilled the call by Black women intellectuals for "race literature" that would establish "good, helpful, and stimulating" examples of African American values and achievements (*Reconstructing Womanhood* 120). An editorial in the first issue (May 1900) of the *Colored American Magazine* states that the magazine proposes "to offer the colored people of the United States, a medium through which they can demonstrate their ability and tastes, in fiction, poetry, and art, as well as in the arena of historical, social and economical literature" (60). As the first "general purpose" African American magazine, the *Colored American Magazine* seems to have been under Hopkins's control from its inception until June 1904, and as such it seems particularly focused on a reading audi-

Frontispiece, *Colored American Magazine*, November 1900. This image was advertised in the magazine as a poster for sale through February 1902.

ence inclusive of African American women. During the first four years of its existence, Hopkins's imprint on the magazine is undeniable, and her own writing dominates many of the magazine's issues. The first issue notes that Hopkins will be the editor of a "department devoted exclusively to the interest of women and the home" beginning in the next issue, but her influence seems to quickly expand. The second issue presents the promised "Woman's Department," presumably written by Hopkins, that reports news from Black women's clubs, but by the third issue (August 1900) this function has been folded into the editorial column "Here and There" and the magazine as a whole is very obviously gender-inclusive: photographic images present professional Black women, and three works of fiction by women are included (works by Angelina Grimké and, it seems, Anne Spencer).[19] By September 1900, the magazine advertises Hopkins's own novel, *Contending Forces*, with a two-page spread including an order form (195–96). In addition to writing *Contending Forces*, published by the same publishing company but separately from the magazine, and her editorial work, Hopkins also wrote prodigiously for the magazine; under her own name or the pseudonym Sarah A. Allen she published three serialized novels, seven short stories, the series "Famous Men of the Negro Race" in twelve parts, the series "Famous Women of the Negro Race" in eleven parts, and twelve additional articles.[20] The photogravure of the "Young Colored American" appears in the same issue of the magazine as Hopkins's story "Talma Gordon," and the offer for its reprint is bundled with a year's subscription to the magazine—both for $1.50—suggesting that the magazine's editorial vision and the representative Young Colored American are congruous.

The magazine's opening editorial also states, after naming its purpose in terms of demonstrating the colored American's "ability and tastes" in "fiction, poetry, and art," that its mission is to "above all . . . [aspire] to develop and intensify the bonds of that racial brotherhood, which alone can enable a people, to assert their racial rights as men, and demand their privileges as citizens" (1.1: 60). Advertisements in the magazine for *Contending Forces* use similar language and make it clear that the publication seeks, in particular, to strengthen "brotherhood" through the fiction it presents. In the September 1900 prospectus of *Contending Forces*, for example, after asking the question, "Of what use is fiction to the colored race at the present crisis in its history?" the text states that "it is the simple, homely tale told in an unassuming manner which cements the bond of brotherhood among all classes and all complexions." Again, according to this prospectus and additional advertisements for *Contending Forces*, the novel presents incidents that "have actually occurred,"

Frontispiece, *Contending Forces*. Boston: The Colored Co-Operative Publishing Co., 1900. This illustration also advertised the novel in the *Colored American Magazine*. Reprinted by permission of the Manuscripts, Archives and Rare Books Division, Schomburg Center for Research in Black Culture, the New York Public Library, Astor, Lenox and Tilden Foundations.

and while the story is told impartially, "both sides of the dark picture—lynching and concubinage" are included. "Lynching" and "concubinage" are, as Hopkins presents them, both intertwined with issues of racial mixing—the latter as dangerous to African Americans as the former.

Within our turn to the language of Hegel's dialectic, and specifically the rise of self-consciousness contained in the confrontation between master and female slave as reinterpreted through the lens of African American women writers, it is "concubinage" that must be highlighted. Concubinage specifically is not marriage, and so, as a relation, it does not remove women from the public realm and into the family, does not make them "wives." Significantly, concubinage often tends to be a "secret" relationship, that is, a relationship not made public, but when secrets are told it becomes so. While Pauline Hopkins and earlier African American writers, including William Wells Brown, view the concubinage relation as a major problem in African American life, ironically, however, it is also a source of power, as Hopkins recognizes. In particular, children born outside of the marriage relation, even children born into slavery, are not "socially dead," to use Orlando Patterson's term, but socially "other." That such an "other" exists is the very source of the power that African American mothers and their children fathered by white men outside the marriage relation can claim through telling. While this "other" society is very much in keeping with Frances Harper's community of first-generation freed men and women whose value system is uplift, its central act of defiance, for Hopkins, is not the way in which children opt to claim enslaved or formerly enslaved mothers, but the way in which mothers claim their children, and in the most extreme case, the way in which a mother, Sappho Clark in *Contending Forces*, claims her child conceived through her rape by her white uncle. If we return, once again, to the *Colored American Magazine*'s illustration of the "Young Colored American" placed on the pedestal, we might say that this is Hopkins's way of representing, and claiming, *all* children of colored mothers.

In *Contending Forces* there are two female characters who are, presumably, victims of rape. The first, Grace Montfort, figures into the history of the Smith family as the mother of Jesse Montfort, and her brutal treatment by Hank Davis and Bill Sampson forms the pornographic moment illustrated as the frontispiece within the novel itself as well as the advertisement for the novel as printed as frontispiece in the November 1900 issue of *Colored American Magazine*. The second, Sappho Clark, is the mother who keeps secret her child conceived in rape, Alphonso, but then lays claim to him. Here the details of the fate of Grace Montfort, particularly in contrast to Sappho, are significant. Grace Montfort is freeborn; she may be "tainted" by some African blood, but the novel treats this assertion by the few as both unproved and unfounded. Causal responsibility for her misery lies within her marriage to Bermuda planter Charles Montfort, whose desire to "retain my patrimony and free my slaves, too" brings him to the United States, and specifically North Carolina (28). As a consequence of his unwillingness to forgo his wealth, his "patrimony," "nature avenges herself" (65). In North Carolina, this same marriage can be called into question, and it is. Grace's husband pointedly cannot protect her from her fate: she calls upon him to save her, to no avail. In the situation of female slave, however, Grace Montfort does not do well, does not, in fact, survive: she "destroys herself" by drowning in the waters of Pamlico Sound (71). That she does so is testament to the horrors of slavery for women which, when juxtaposed against other female slaves' desires not only to live but also to claim children born from the sexual violation of the master/female slave moment, makes these latter acts all the more remarkable. No child issues from the sexual violence Grace experiences, and perhaps her very suicide prevents such a birth. She is the mother, however, of two boys who witness their father's murder and their mother's violation and subsequent suicide. In the context of Pauline Hopkins's story, then, the child Jesse, witness as Frederick Douglass was witness to his aunt Esther's sadistic treatment by Captain Anthony, becomes the patriarch of the Smith family. By marrying an African American woman he is "absorbed into that unfortunate race, of whom it is said that a man had better be born dead than to come into the world as part and parcel of it" (79), thereby setting in motion the events of the story that follows.

Contending Forces ranges over some four hundred pages and presents a complexly interwoven storyline. In order to demonstrate the significance of the multiracial roots of African American families for Hopkins, however, we need only focus on the subplot that presents the story of Sappho Clark—where Hopkins addresses "accusations that miscegenation was the inmost desire of the darker races of the earth" by reconstructing miscegenation "as white male rape" (Carby 141)—and juxtapose the contemporary Sappho Clark against the historic Grace Montfort. Sappho Clark is herself, as the daughter of parents who are each biracial, the product of miscegenation. We discover through Luke Sawyer, public speaker at a forum on lynching, that when she was a fourteen-year old girl known as Mabelle Beaubean, Sappho's white uncle abducted her from her Catholic private school in New Orleans, raped her, and kept her imprisoned in a house of prostitution for three weeks until her family managed to rescue her. Further, when a mob burns her family's house, Luke himself, motivated as Tom Anderson was toward Iola Leroy, carries her to the safety of a convent in New Orleans. He, however, believes "Mabelle" has died in childbirth. And even as he tells Sappho's past, we as readers are not sure that Mabelle and Sappho are the same person. Sappho has kept this past as her secret, but leaves trace of it in the form of a son, Alphonse, until forced through blackmail into public acknowledgment, which she finally enacts through a letter to her intended, Will Smith. In the chapter titled "Mother-Love," Sappho has run from the present but decides to no longer run from her past, and weeps bitter tears yet feels peace. Looking on her sleeping child, she "fold[s] him in her arms" and when he awakes she feels "new-found ecstacy [*sic*] at the rosy face." According to the narrator, while "her feeling of degradation had made her ashamed of the joys of motherhood, of pride of possession in her child . . . all that feeling was swept away" (345). For the first time, Sappho tells the child that she is his mother and promises him that she will always be with him. Thus, with this reunion Hopkins demonstrates that the significant miscegenation issue in American society is the way in which mothers lift and carry into the Black community their biracial children conceived through acts of white male rape.

By acknowledging her son Alphonse, which Hazel Carby argues is the "necessary transition" that precedes "the final transformation into wifehood and marriage," Sappho becomes, in a sense, sanctified (Carby 143). Like her predecessor, the title character in Frances Harper's novel *Iola Leroy*, the psychic pain Sappho experiences brings her to a new consciousness. By accepting her son as her own, however, Sappho literally overcomes the basest form of white male aggression, transforming it into an object worthy of love. At this point, Sappho begins to see herself and her suffering as part of a larger purpose and, says the narrator, will in the future learn "to value the strong, chastening influence of her present sorrow, and the force of character it developed, fitting her perfectly for the place she was to occupy in carrying comfort and hope to the women of the race" (347). As she is spiritually transformed, Sappho also becomes psychologically ready for the work of racial uplift, and ready, as well, to marry her intended, Will Smith. When the two meet again, they are quickly reunited. They marry, and together plan "to bring joy to hearts crushed by despair," presumably by speaking from their own experiences (401). At the conclusion of the novel the reconstructed African American family stands on the deck of a ship bound for Europe. They have become rich through reparations paid as a consequence of a lawsuit against the United States, and these riches will be shared with all the family's members, including Sappho and her son, Alphonse, who is accepted as one of their own.

When we reconsider the claim made by the advertisements for (and preface to) *Contending Forces* that its story will "cement the bond of brotherhood among all classes and complexions" while keeping this concluding image in mind, we discover a new image of the racially subscribed subject. Sappho, our exemplar, clearly demonstrates that her choice of mother-love, her choice to claim her child, plays the significant role in establishing race consciousness. Further, the family does not move forward, cannot form itself anew, until its members revisit and reconstruct the trauma buried in consciousness. All Black women, Hopkins implies, no matter their past experiences, make the claim of the racial subject and so define the race. In this context, Anna Julia Cooper's famous statement, "Only the Black Woman can say, 'When and where I enter, in the quiet, undisputed dignity of my womanhood, without violence and without suing or special patronage, then and there the whole *Negro race enters with me*'" applies not to the privileged few but to each and every Black woman (31). This image of inclusion correlates with the mission of the Black women's club movement in its intent to reach out to all women regardless of their pasts; further, traditional judgments concerning women's morality become clearly inappropriate. When family is defined matrilineally, and uplift is defined through a mother's choice to hold her child in her arms, as Sappho's claiming of her son Alphonse suggests, the bond of brotherhood depends upon embracing and being embraced by a common mother.

In June 1904 the *Colored American Magazine* announced for the second time that it was "under new management" and became editorially controlled by Fred R. Moore, acting in the interest of Booker T. Washington. Historical scholarship published as early as 1928 suggests that Hopkins's editorial stance was incompatible with Washington's views. Under Hopkins's editorship the masthead proclaimed, "Devoted to Literature, Science, Music, Art, Religion, Facts, Fiction and Traditions of the Negro Race" and then, still under Hopkins's editorship, simply "Devoted to the Interests of the Colored Race." Under new management, Moore explains, the magazine now "seeks to publish articles showing the advancement of our people along material lines, believing that the people generally are more interested in having information of the doings of the members of the race, rather [than] the writings of dreamers or theorists" (7.9: 693). By extending Arnold Rampersad's argument in "Slavery and the Literary Imagination" about the nature of the disagreement between W. E. B. Du Bois and Washington to Hopkins, we can see that more than the role of imaginative work is at stake. In *Up from Slavery*, according to Rampersad, Washington treats the institution of slavery as something whose "evils, insofar as they existed, were to be acknowledged briefly and then forgotten" (106). Relying on a vision of the African American as a Black Adam, Rampersad explains, Washington refigures slavery as the fortunate fall whereby "Africans gained the skills and the knowledge needed for the modern world." In Washington's view, then, no one should blame white America for slavery's debilitating effects; further, as with all Adamic stories, the point is that the individual himself must, as Washington has, build himself up into a "powerful, fully realized human being" (Rampersad 110). While we, along with Rampersad, might see this vision of slavery as obviously problematic on many levels, it becomes even more so when we consider the role of women. Rampersad suggests that, for Washington, the slave himself must be responsible for his fall, but Adamic myth would place that blame on enslaved women. This Adamic mythologizing of slavery, then, is particularly pernicious in its effects on women because it twists Black female experience so that, for example, white male rape becomes Black female seduction. Given Washington's presentation of slavery in this manner, his ideology is clearly incompatible with Pauline Hopkins's fiction, with its focus on female experiences of victimization, and it is therefore not surprising that the consequence of Washington's influence on the magazine is Hopkins's release from editorial responsibilities.

According to most accounts, Hopkins was released as editor because she was too outspoken. In the November 1904 issue, however, the "Publishers' Announcements" said only "on account of ill-health Miss Pauline Hopkins has found it necessary to sever her relations with this Magazine" (7.9: 700). By this time, the aim of the magazine had completely changed. It was no longer a cooperative venture asking for a member's contribution of one dollar, but instead incorporated and selling stock at five dollars a share. In addition to its focus on "the doings of the race along material lines," it had become much more exclusively male, adding, for example, a "Masonic Department." Nevertheless, reports that Hopkins parted company with the magazine for other than health reasons persisted. In a 1912 issue of *The Crisis*, W. E. B. Du Bois explains that Hopkins was not "conciliatory enough" for the new management. Further, in a 1928 article on African American magazines, Charles S. Johnson notes that because Hopkins made "no attempt to modify the magazine's expressions out of consideration for the white persons from whom most . . . support was obtained," she was removed by people who believed "that there was greater usefulness in a more conciliatory policy" (see Du Bois; see also Charles S. Johnson).[21] Combined, these comments point to a particular conflict that occurred in 1903 between Hopkins and

Cornelia Condict, a white subscriber to the magazine, recorded through the letters to the editor of the magazine.

Referring to Hopkins's serialized novels *Hagar's Daughter: A Story of Southern Caste Prejudice; Winona: A Tale of Negro Life in the South and Southwest;* and *Of One Blood; or, The Hidden Self,* Cornelia Condict wrote to complain that "without exception [the serialized novels] have been of love between colored and whites." Furthermore, she states, "the stories of these tragic mixed loves will not commend themselves to your white readers and will not elevate the colored readers" (6.5: 399). In her response published with Condict's letter in the March 1903 issue of the magazine, Hopkins boldly replies:

> My stories are definitely planned to show the obstacles persistently placed in our paths by a dominant race to subjugate us spiritually. Marriage is made illegal between the races and yet the mulattoes increase. Thus the shadow of corruption falls on the blacks and on the whites, without whose aid the mulattoes would not exist. And then the hue and cry goes abroad of the immorality of the Negro and the disgrace that the mulattoes are to this nation. Amalgamation is an institution designed by God for some wise purpose, and mixed bloods have always exercised a great influence on the progress of human affairs. (399)

After making this statement, Hopkins continues by claiming that the letter shows that "white people don't understand *what pleases Negroes,*" thereby suggesting that these stories of relationships that cross color lines are profoundly important to her African American audience. While Condict has misread the stories' purposes as insinuating that sexual relations with whites are advantageous in the progress of the race, Hopkins instead focuses on the spiritual crisis her characters face through sexual victimization and implies that her fiction speaks to needs springing from group trauma.

Hopkins's attitude toward "amalgamation," that is, consensual marriage by people of different races, is presented in detail in an earlier short story, "Talma Gordon," published in the October 1900 issue of the magazine. In that story, during a discussion among the most elite class of men in Boston, members of the Canterbury Club, the renowned doctor at whose home these twenty-five men are dining takes the surprising position of believing in the inevitability of intermarriage among people of different races. In order to make his "meaning clearer with illustration," Dr. Thornton tells the story of the Gordon family, one of the founding families of New England (274). Through various twists in the narrative we discover that none of the family is who they appear to be: the patriarch of the family is really a pirate who has made his fortune at the expense of others; the mother who died after childbirth is proven by her dark-skinned child to be an "octoroon" herself; and the daughter, Talma Gordon, who has been accused of the murder of her father, stepmother, and half-brother is innocent of any crime.[22] While Dr. Thornton's story of the Gordon family, in itself, presents a common story of accidental racial intermarriage, the flourish of "Talma Gordon" occurs as Dr. Thornton finishes his tale. "But what became of Talma Gordon?" one of the listeners asks. In answer to that question, Hopkins adds the final line of her own story: "Gentlemen," says Dr. Thornton, "I shall have much pleasure in introducing you to my wife—*nee* Talma Gordon" (290). This racial intermarriage, clearly no accident, is presented as the deliberate action of a most sophisticated and brilliant man of social position. With this statement, Hopkins counters the more popular opinion expressed earlier by one of the members of the Canterbury Club, that intermarriage, if it takes place at all, will only take place "among the lower classes."[23]

Hopkins's final novel, *Of One Blood; or, The Hidden Self*, which was being serialized as Cornelia Condict wrote her complaint about the preponderance of stories in the *Colored American Magazine* focused on "tragic mixed loves," also presents a racially tangled familial lineage. This novel's point, however, is in its title phrase, repeated throughout the text: "His promises stand, and He will prove His words, 'Of one blood have I made all races of men.'"[24] Going much further than even "Talma Gordon"'s claim of the inevitability of racial intermarriage, *Of One Blood*, with its focus on the "Africentric" roots of Egyptian civilization, strikes at the heart of Eurocentric claims of racial superiority. Hopkins, in this novel of race pride, attempts to write the supernatural into reality in order to show America's racial problems as foreshadowing the world's future. She begins with her claim: there is a real yet hidden city in Ethiopia whose riches prove it the true birthplace of "all the arts and cunning inventions that make . . . modern glory" (560). It is to this civilization that the African American Reuel Briggs returns as the long-awaited king. This Pan-African vision does not, however, mean that Hopkins was making a Black nationalist argument.[25] In the final image of the novel, Reuel is waiting in the Hidden City "with serious apprehension, the advance of mighty nations penetrating the dark, mysterious forests of his native land."[26] Given that the conversation about the inevitability of amalgamation presented in Hopkins's "Talma Gordon" began as discussion of the subject: "Expansion; Its Effects upon the Future Development of the Anglo-Saxon throughout the World," we can safely assume that racial purity will have no place in the modern future that Hopkins envisions ("Talma Gordon" 49).

In *Of One Blood*, as in Frances Harper's novels *Minnie's Sacrifice* and *Iola Leroy*, transformative knowledge is passed matrilineally, from Aunt Hannah to her granddaughter, Dianthe Lusk.[27] Jennie Kassanoff points out that "Aunt Hannah administers the healing antidote of narrative of decoded genealogies [and] descriptive histories" (176). Aunt Hannah's knowledge of true identities springing from events of slavery is disruptive yet restorative; while sharing her knowledge ends some lives and changes others, it is necessary to a true preparation for the possibilities of the future. For readers, believing her means acknowledging the authority of the woman known as "the most noted 'voodoo' doctor or witch in the country" (*Of One Blood* 603). Further, this authority is matriarchal: Aunt Hannah knows, through her own sexual experiences, the patrimony of her own daughter; and presumably, through her daughter's confidences, she knows who has fathered her grandchildren. But Aunt Hannah has acted to obscure identity, as well. It is through an act of her own deception that one of her grandchildren thinks of himself as a white man when this is not true. Judging from this tangled genealogy, then, in general we might say that Hopkins wants us to understand that full knowledge of identity can be obtained only after consultation with Black matriarchs; and this would be as true for "white" men as for Black women.

In *Contending Forces*, as a consequence of the brutal confrontation with Hank Davis and Bill Sampson, Grace Montfort commits suicide, thus indicating, in this case, the choice of death rather than enslavement, contrary to Hegel's notion of the master/slave dialectical moment which would have the slave choose life above all else. Nevertheless, her descendants live and prosper. While the evil Anson Pollock is haunted by his past deeds, in ways reminiscent of Simon Legree, he also lives. His descendent, however, who seems to carry with him his forebear's character traits, ruins himself by his own hand (339). At the end of the novel John Langely is the last survivor among a group of men who have set out for the Klondike gold fields, and he perishes, as a fortune teller has predicted, on a "field of ice and snow which had been shown to him stretched before him in dreary, unbroken silence," (400) an image we might read as deathly white silence, with all its racial implications. This suggests that through the generations, as the conflict between slavemaster and slave becomes the legacy of both, it is the slave's consciousness, now writ into the African American community, that has synthesized and transcended past experience. *Of One Blood* suggests a similar story: the evil white man, Aubrey Livingston,[28] is hypnotized so that he commits suicide. This is done in keeping with the "ancient laws of the inhabitants of Telassar," which demanded that "members of the royal family in direct line to the throne became their own executioners when guilty of the crime of murder" (620). In *Of One Blood*, then, Hopkins's vision shows white men who are guilty of the basest crimes writ off the world stage by their own hand—not subdued or overcome by the ex-slave's power as the consequence of a master/slave confrontation but removed from the history of consciousness by their own will, even if that will has been influenced by a mesmerizing ancient African power. Thus, Hopkins suggests, justice demands the ultimate concession from white men, that their own subject position, insofar as it embodies the legacy of the slavemaster's relation to slave, be removed from both the world stage and next stages of human consciousness.

In August, 1904, just after Fred R. Moore had taken control of the *Colored American Magazine*, the magazine ran an essay by T. Thomas Fortune, editor of the *New York Age*. Fortune's essay, titled "False Theory of Education Cause of Race Demoralization," stressed as ridiculous an education that focused students' attention on "building up . . . the character and material well-being of . . . the race, as the first rule of action" (7.6: 473). According to Fortune, students should be building up "individual character and material well-being," following the example of Booker T. Washington. "The Negro and Indian are the only race elements of the American citizenship who are taught that their chief mission in life is to lift up their race," he notes, while continuing by suggesting that success lies in "individual initiative and selfishness, with no conscious thought of benefitting the race or nation, as the case may be" (474–75). Fortune's philosophy could not be more antithetical to the prevailing ideal of the colored women's club movement, focused on women as they define themselves through racial subjectivity. This concern for the individual as expressed by Fortune entirely disregards Black women's experiences at the turn of the century. At the center of Fortune's criticism of the education he received at Howard University, for example, is the charge that it did not offer "the proper sort of education in manliness and self-respect and self-interest" that would make "strong and useful men" (476). Here the "race" is the men, born of themselves or their own will to power. This vision of Black manhood allows no room for any reminder of the crucible of slavery, nor for Black matriarchs or mother-love. And yet, read against the ethos of Pauline Hopkins's *Colored American Magazine*, Fortune's position is overdetermined in its emphasis on Black masculinity, and his revisionist definition of the race points to the significance of Hopkins's colored vision.

Thomas Fortune's "strong and useful men," following the exemplary Booker T. Washington, must ignore the "race-gift" conveyed by Black women in order to become Black "individuals" rather than "race men." As individuals, they are the ideological, if not literal, children of white fathers. Yet Georgia Douglas Johnson's 1922 poem "The Riddle," the epigraph to this chapter, speaks of these men who claim individual rather than race identity: men who are "white men's children in black men's skins" but, when so posited as children, also identified as children of "other" mothers, of colored mothers. Johnson's "cosmopolite" is the modern everyman, here characterized as the son of white male aggression and empire building "over the earth." Yet he is not Locke's "changeling," not a child switched at birth, not adopted as white. The metaphor Johnson uses in place of "changeling" is "Triton," creature of two identities, literally both/ and—in Johnson's words "peer of the two," in Hopkins's work, "colored." In this light, then, women's colored experience lends itself to a subjectivity that blends rather than doubles the racialized selves. The riddle of "outside in" thus re-characterizes Frances Harper's claim that "the inner life . . . develops the outer" and makes a claim for self-consciousness based on race consciousness rather than ethics. Yet this race consciousness, tied as it is to the underside of empire and conquest, represents not the victor but the vanquished who also becomes in the twist of "the rainbow suspending the drawn swords of birth" the "world man," the subjective rather than objective universal, an imaginary with epistemic privilege.[29] As one of Frances Harper's character's states, "The world . . . is fast becoming a vast whispering gallery, and lips once sealed can now state their own grievances" (225). Pauline Hopkins's new colored consciousness is this vast whispering gallery's antecedent, then, perhaps only aspirational, but nevertheless a consciousness conscious of itself as representative of new human potential indicative of a more fully communicative, and representative, world history.

4

Narrative Fathering and the Epistemology of Secret Knowing

◆◦§ ९◦◆

> Let's face it. It's in our faces already, anyway. Whose child are you? What's your name? American history can be read as a long paternity suit, or series of suits. If the suit fits . . . .
>
> —John Edgar Wideman, *Fatheralong*

While antebellum male writers of African American fiction in the mid-nineteenth century critique white patriarchy by telling secrets, the colored consciousness developed by postbellum African American women is not accessible to them, and consequently, manhood remains defined, relationally more than oppositionally, in white patriarchal terms. By the early twentieth century, however, male writers create male characters who are vexed by their relation to "colored" mothers, who explore definitions of masculinity in relation to the epistemology of the secret knowing that engenders colored consciousness, and who begin to understand the need for, if not the contours of, a racial subjectivity that is not solely masculine in origin. Further, for these next generation writers, coming to terms with the master/female slave moment means coming to terms with issues of origin. In the early twentieth-century male imagination, however, this moment is tellingly not one of sexual violence. Instead, "colored" women and men have the capacity to love across the color line and thereby engage in intimate relations that produce children who then form intimate and procreative relationships themselves. Against this mixed-race heritage as backdrop, and with the knowledge that racial consciousness is tied to mother identity, the question becomes how to father in racially conscious ways. Charles Chesnutt's *The Marrow of Tradition* and James Weldon Johnson's *The Autobiography of an Ex-Coloured Man* explore questions related to the subjectivity of fatherhood—what fathers might know as fathers—and in this exploration present secret knowers who are both epistemologically privileged and gender transgressive, thus suggesting that the new race consciousness defined through the standpoint of colored mothers also represents a subjectivity with new possibilities for Black men.

There is no question but that African American thinking at the turn of the twentieth century became influenced by patriarchal gender conventions that competed with racial consciousness as defined by "colored" mothers. If we return to T. Thomas Fortune and his belief in individualism, we are reminded that there is no racial imperative in his call for "strong and useful men" (476). As in Booker T. Washington's philosophy of "self-help" as a replacement for political agency, which stresses individual rather than group identity, racial consciousness as such really has no place. This is not to say that the construct of race is absent from Washington's way of thinking, but rather to make a distinction between racial strife as a social and political problem and racial consciousness as a basis for group identity. Kevin Gaines points out, in *Uplifting the Race*, that the early twentieth century brought with it a complex and often contested ideology of uplift. In this arena, as Gaines says, "black women . . . were contributing their own visions of racial uplift, calling for women's leadership as vital to race progress, a view that clashed with a male-dominated vision of race progress within a patriarchal political culture" (4). As we have seen in the preceding chapter, Frances Harper's and Pauline Hopkins's vision of uplift is characterized through the psychological work of mothers who claim and "uplift" racially mixed children. This vision, however, competes with the pull to fulfill "majority society's normative gender conventions" that create "uplift ideology's romance of the patriarchal family" and a sense of respectability reliant upon "denouncing nonconformity to patriarchal gender conventions and bourgeois morality" (Gaines 5). The promotion of bourgeois selfhood, then, combines with a focus on home and the patriarchal family because of "the respectability supposedly conferred by patriarchal gender conventions" (12). According to the terms of family life as characterized by Frances Harper and developed by Pauline Hopkins, of course, this patriarchal family is not recognizably African American. Further, while it is true that an ideology focused on Black patriarchal power elevates men, it also relegates Black women to the family in imitation of bourgeois gender conventions and thus confers on them the "respectable" status of wife, but also buries the revolutionary aspect of "colored" consciousness as legacy of the master/female slave conflict. The most famous image of this ideology of bourgeois uplift, Charles Keck's 1922 monument of Booker T. Washington "lifting the veil of ignorance" from the crouching ex-slave depicted with a plow by his side and a book on his lap, reminds us that this inherently masculinist vision of uplift is also a masculinist version of slavery since this ex-slave is obviously male; in both the past and the future represented by this image, then, women are written off the public stage.

In striking ways, however, the colored mother's legacy is central to early twentieth-century literary texts that explore male agency, and particularly to those texts that explore the subjectivity of African American men in the modern moment. These texts are not so focused on bourgeois respectability that they redefine the family strictly in terms of patriarchal gender conventions that erase the "colored" mother's consciousness. Even the rigidly masculinist *The Souls of Black Folk*, as Hazel Carby makes clear in her feminist interrogation of the theme of race men, presents the figure of the African American mother as central to Black consciousness. While for W. E. B. Du Bois, as Carby argues, this mother indicates the "'hereditary weight' . . . imposed on Black men by history because they could not control the sexual reproduction of black women," and is thereby dismissed by him, Carby implies the necessity of reckoning with this woman (Carby 33; Du Bois 6). In the second chapter of *The Souls of Black Folk*, Du Bois introduces two figures meant to represent the "present-past" moment of the slave's "dawn of freedom," the title Du Bois gives his chapter. The slave himself is Charles Keck's crouching, bewildered, newly freed slave (21). The two figures who "stand to typify that day [of freedom] to coming ages" are, first, "a gray-haired gentleman, whose fathers had quit themselves like men, whose sons lay in nameless graves; who bowed to the evil of slavery because its abolition threatened untold ill to all" and, second, "a form hovering dark and motherlike . . . [who] had aforetime quailed at that white master's command . . . at his behest had laid herself low to his lust, and borne a tawny man-child to the world" (21). These two figures standing at Du Bois's "dawn of freedom," or moment of self-consciousness, are, then, the familiar master and female slave of our revised Hegelian dialectic. In Du Bois's depiction, however, the two are passing figures who cannot be brought together ("no man clasped the hands of these two passing figures" [22]), who, "hating, they went to their long home, and, hating, their children's children live today" (22). Further, they indicate, as Carby argues, the masculine gendering implicit in both Du Bois's concept of a double-consciousness and his expression of desire for "true self-consciousness"; the "tawny man-child" born of the white master and the "form hovering dark and motherlike" is Du Bois's doubly conscious American Negro, "longing to attain self-conscious manhood" (3). While Du Bois is clearly right in focusing

Booker T. Washington monument, "Lifting the Veil." Courtesy of the
Tuskegee University Archives.

on these two figures as the key to African American, and ultimately American, consciousness, his presentation of these figures living segregated and hate-filled lives does not accurately represent literary history—or living history.

In *Race Men*, Carby demonstrates the need as well as the desire of some African American men for an alternative masculinity that is not modeled on the family romance of white bourgeois patriarchy. By interrogating "the hege-mony of . . . assumptions about black masculinity and . . . the consensus of a dominant society that 'conceives African American society in terms of a peren-nial "crisis" of black masculinity whose imagined solution is a proper affirma-tion of black male authority'" (6)[1] she makes clear the stakes in acknowledging or denying African American male writers' explorations of male agency within the construct of racial subjectivity. While her project, *Race Men*, focuses on ideologies of masculinity in dialectical relation to "discourses of race and nation in American culture" (2) and often exposes the inherent masculinity in constructs that claim to be racialized but not gendered, her work also points to alternative forms of masculinity as well as alternative constructs of race. Her close reading of Du Bois's *The Souls of Black Folk*, in particular, as a text that establishes a genealogy for an "imagined community" as Benedict Anderson has defined the term,[2] informs the structure of the analysis in this chapter of Charles Chesnutt's *The Marrow of Tradition* and James Weldon Johnson's *The Autobiography of an Ex-Coloured Man* as alternative texts to Du Bois's *Souls*. As Carby observes, Du Bois's concern is "the continuity of intellectual genera-tions," what she calls "the reproduction of Race Men" (*Race Men* 25). While both Chesnutt and Johnson create fathers who take quite seriously their gen-erative roles, and while both authors also create a "narrative fathering," that is, a narrative voice formed and informed by male procreative positionality, Du Bois's concern is not their concern. Chesnutt's *Marrow* anticipates *Souls* in its focus on Old and New Negroes, its consideration of the material con-dition of Blacks in the South as well as the obstacle of post-Reconstruction white Southern ideology, and its interest in a father's emotional response to the death of a firstborn son. Johnson's *Ex-Coloured Man* works directly with Du Bois's ideas of double consciousness and the "waste of double aims" (4), and also with Du Bois's depiction of life "within and without the Veil" (xxxi). Yet these texts are also deeply suspicious of and conflicted about the ideology Carby terms Du Bois's "reproduction of Race Men," and in their suspicion and conflict they demonstrate their authors' desire to locate a subjectivity, albeit male, that is ironically more racialized, in the vein of "colored" moth-ers, than masculinized according to white patriarchal values.

Secrets of Paternity and Inheritance in
The Marrow of Tradition

New understanding of Charles Chesnutt's literary career that takes into account his unpublished novels of the 1920s, *Paul Marchand F.M.C.* and *The Quarry*, makes clear Chesnutt's continued interest in the complexity of life along the color line. Both *The Quarry* and *Paul Marchand F.M.C.* present male protagonists who grow up believing they are African American men, only to find out during early adulthood that they are instead white. *The Quarry*'s Donald Glover and Paul Marchand reject their white identity, and this suggests that Chesnutt's thinking about whiteness is similar to James Baldwin's presenting white identity as an ontological choice.[3] Here standpoint theory would suggest that Chesnutt's protagonists have been privileged with a worldview that sees severe limitations in white male identity, and, significantly, also sees identity as relative to consciousness rather than essential, in "the blood." This seems to have been consistently Chesnutt's position, iterated in his first published essay, "What Is a White Man?" (1889), which argues that "racial identity is man-created, not divinely appointed" (Andrews, *Literary Career* 140). This position, however, also suggests a reading of *The Marrow of Tradition*, the novel to which Chesnutt pinned his greatest hopes, that focuses on questions concerning the construction of whiteness. Specifically, and borrowing Baldwin's terminology once again, I will argue here for a reading of *The Marrow of Tradition* that centers on the novel's concluding presentation of "Dodie," the surviving son of Major Carteret, as perhaps the boy who will become "a new white man." With such an ending, Chesnutt's novel offers a narrative fathering of the only remaining son in the text, thus raising the possibility of cross-racial regeneration.

In a letter to Booker T. Washington, Chesnutt characterized *The Marrow of Tradition* as "by far the best thing I have done," in part for its appeal to "popular sympathies" in its representation of "our side of the Negro question" ("*To Be an Author*" 159–60). Chesnutt hoped that his novel, which he characterized as "a comprehensive study of racial conditions in the South," would change public opinion in the North, thereby putting pressure upon Southern whites, whose "tolerance . . . is necessary to the progress of the colored race, and . . . [whose] friendship desirable" (159–60). In this regard, the point, as other critics have noted, is "not so much the elevation of the colored people as the elevation of the whites," which Chesnutt declared in 1880 as his general reason for wanting to write a novel (*Journals* 139).[4] And even though he focuses on white Americans, Chesnutt's idea of "elevation" should be read as a kind of "uplift." *The Marrow of Tradition* presents the Carterets, a prominent white Wellington family, in crisis, precisely because of an unacknowledged family secret. The interracial family drama that unfolds concurrently with the town's politically charged race riot finally concludes through a confrontation between sisters that results in the telling of all the family secrets. These tellings transform the white Olivia Carteret, who vows to maintain the newly established relationship with her sister, and follows this vow with a symbol-laden long walk home on the arm of the African American Dr. Miller. If, the novel implies in its final paragraphs, Olivia Carteret is truly transformed, then her barely alive son might also be rescued through the intervention of the doctor from the two threats to his life—literally the croup that threatens his very breath, and metaphorically the myth of white supremacy that has forbidden the doctor's involvement in the "operation" of saving his young life.

In imagining a Northern audience as the readers of his novel, and imagining the novel's influence on segregated Southern life as mediated through these Northern readers, we see Chesnutt's conscious strategy of talking indirectly to Southern perpetrators of violence through Northern third parties. He employs, in other words, as in earlier novels written by William Wells Brown and Frederick Douglass, the triadic formulation inherent in secret telling. As Chesnutt is aware, direct address to Southern whites is not allowed; Chesnutt's character Captain McBane declares about an editorial on lynching and its causes, "'Truth or not, no damn nigger has any right to say it'" (86). This world of segregated telling, which produces segregated knowing, is the common legacy the South promises to the young Dodie Carteret—until his constructed world as imagined and presented by Chesnutt threatens his young life, and Dr. Miller intervenes. With Miller's intervention, however, the world that the Carteret child inhabits allows for the possibility of transformative knowledge, even, Chesnutt implies, for white men. While this may at first seem far fetched, we need only consider that even the very racist Major Carteret is allowed a moment when "the veil of race prejudice was rent in twain, and he saw things as they were, in their correct proportions and relations,—saw clearly and convincingly that he had no standing here" (319). A world that even Major Carteret is able to glimpse has been constructed such that in this world white men like him have "no standing." While the possibility of Carteret's own transformation is only barely imaginable, Chesnutt does work with the idea implied, that is, with the idea of transgressing "white" as an identity category, in his unpublished 1920s novels, *Paul Marchand, F.M.C.* and *The*

Quarry. Turning to these novels will give us a better sense of the possibilities imaginable by Chesnutt.

In *Paul Marchand F.M.C.*, a historical novel set within Creole society of the 1820s, the title character "becomes" a white man through his father's, Pierre Beaurepas's, deathbed claim that Paul is his legitimate son and heir. As a consequence, Paul is also presented with the girl—the beautiful Josephine Morales, daughter of Pierre Beaurepas's best friend. Through a series of events connected to a subplot involving desperate runaway slaves, or perhaps free men of color mistaken for runaways, Paul finds himself in a distinctively white man's position: he needs to save "his" girl from the "huge mulatto" who has thrown her "limp form across his shoulder," presumably intending to ravish her in an act of revenge (158). Paul, however, does not see the situation as a white man would, and pauses rather than rushes toward the man who has a knife at Josephine's neck:

> Here for the first time, in an emergency, Paul's quadroon training pushed itself to the front. The ordinary white man at such a juncture would have seen nothing but a white woman, in the grasp of a black brute. Paul Beaurepas— for the moment Paul Marchand—saw, beyond the evil countenance of the man who had faced him the long night of crime which had produced this fruit—the midnight foray in the forest, the slave coffle, the middle passage, the years of toil beneath the lash, the steady process of inbrutement which the careless endowment of white blood had intensified by just so much vigor and energy as the blood of the master brought with it. He must save the woman, but he pitied, even while he condemned, the ravisher. (159)

Seeing, for a moment, *not* as a white man allows him a different insight, and one he cannot in the end renounce. Instead, he renounces his white father and his father's wealth, saying, "Monsieur Pierre Beaurepas has bequeathed me a pair of seven league boots which do not fit, and which I cannot wear" (178). In so saying, he acknowledges that while he may by blood be a Beaurepas and thus a white man, in point of view, or standpoint, he is not. Because he cannot play the part of a white man, but by law is defined as such, he recognizes that there is no place for him in Louisiana and moves with his Black family to France.

The ironic ending of *Paul Marchand F.M.C.* echoes the conclusion of *The Marrow of Tradition* with a focus upon future generations and their racial attitudes. In *The Marrow of Tradition*, the jury is out on Dodie Carteret's future positioning of himself and his understanding of his interracial family, depending on whether or not we believe his mother when she declares that she will maintain contact with her African American half-sister—depending, in other words, on whether or not we believe that she will tell rather than keep the family secrets. *Paul Marchand F.M.C.*'s ending is darker, focused on the "willful naiveté"[5] of the family members who do not wish to know which of them is of quadroon birth, and the racist legacy that these families continue to build as they *keep* their interracial secrets. All of them were "ever in the forefront of any agitation to limit the rights or restrict the privileges of their darker fellow citizens"—for example, they fought for slavery in the Civil War and led the activities of the Ku Klux Klan (184–85). One descendant, Chesnutt's narrator mentions with clear condescension, even introduces to the Louisiana legislature "an amendment to the criminal code, making marriage a felony between a white person and person of colored blood to the thirty-second degree." This virulent racism, Chesnutt implies, is produced within families who refuse to know their own secrets. But of course, as Chesnutt also demonstrates, the joke is on them. Presumably these Beaurepas descendants have married and if so, such a law would redefine their own marriages as felonies.

In *Paul Marchand F.M.C.*, then, Chesnutt suggests that white men who know themselves as colored choose to renounce their whiteness, and white men who do not know themselves as colored do not know themselves well or truly. The daring possibility raised here, of course, is that whiteness as a constructed identity is of diminishing value—and some white men (particularly those not raised as such) know it. In *The Quarry*, set in 1920s Harlem rather than 1820s New Orleans, Chesnutt is once again signifying about race—in this instance, however, focusing not only on the construction of whiteness but also on the construction of the New Negro "race man." Donald Glover is just such a man, destined to become "the intellectual leader of our people," according to the African American lawyer involved in Donald's adoption (284). Within the storyline that Chesnutt develops, however, Glover discovers that he is biologically white, and not racially mixed.[6] Nevertheless, when given the choice to re-identify himself, he decides to "let things stand as they are" because

circumstances had made him one of a certain group. He had been reared as one of them. He had been taught to see things as they saw them, he had shared their joys, their griefs, their hopes and their fears—in fact he had become psychologically and spiritually one of them. He could no more see them with the eyes of the white man of the street than he could make himself over. . . . There might be potential gain in being white, but the game was not worth the candle, the god was not worthy the sacrifice. Manhood and self-respect were more important than race. (278)

Here, then, Chesnutt makes clear a key idea with which we can return to a reading of *The Marrow of Tradition*: "race men," like white men, are constructed but not born as such, and even a white man might become a "race man" by recognizing individual circumstance and making the honorable choice.

In *The Quarry*, Donald Glover has been made the man he is by his mother. According to James L. Brown, the lawyer involved in his adoption, in talking with the white Angus Seaton, who first adopted Glover but then gave him up, it was "the teachings and influence of the woman to whom you [Seaton] gave him, a woman of character with high ideals and a great heart, together with the environment in which he has been reared, [that] have made of him a Negro, devoted to his people, of whom the race is proud and to whom they look for great things" (263). In *The Marrow of Tradition*, too, Dodie Carteret's future depends upon his mother. In effect, however, by the end of the novel he has two mothers, two women concerned with his welfare—and with his elevation or uplift—the white Olivia Carteret and her half-sister Janet Miller. These two are consistently presented as twins. They are characterized as two daughters of the same father, Samuel Merkell: Olivia is born to his first wife, the white Elizabeth Merkell, and Janet to his second, secret wife, formerly his housekeeper, the African American Julia. They are introduced as twins in the first pages of Chesnutt's novel, during the course of the story that Mammy Jane tells Dr. Price in order to explain why Olivia ('Livy) Carteret, the white daughter, has suffered "nervous shock" (2). According to Mammy Jane, "Dis yer Janet, w'at's Mis' 'Livy's half-sister, is ez much like her ez ef dey wuz twins. Folks sometimes takes 'em fer one ernudder,—I s'pose it tickles Janet mos' ter death, but it do make Mis' 'Livy rippin'" (8). Not only does Janet look like Olivia, but she and her physician husband, William Miller, are prosperous, live in the old Carteret mansion, and, much worse for the jealous Olivia, have a "fine-lookin' yaller boy, w'at favors de fam'ly," that is, resembles Olivia's family in physical features (9). At this early point in the novel, the pregnant Olivia goes into a premature childbirth, almost dies, but successfully delivers a son. From here forward in the novel's representations, the twin sisters become twin mothers.

In the conclusion of *The Marrow of Tradition*, the narrative structuring that pairs the two mothers brings them both into maternal relation with the one remaining son, Dodie Carteret, and this saves his life. In the last chapter of

the novel, the Millers are at home grieving over their own son's death from a
stray bullet fired during the racial violence that terrorizes the Black population of Wellington. The Carterets' young son is ill with the croup and his life
is in danger. When Olivia Carteret realizes that only Dr. Miller can save her
son's life, she rushes to his home to plead for help. As Dr. Miller opens the
door and sees Olivia, he thinks for a moment that he is looking at his own
wife:

> A lady stood there, so near the image of his own wife, whom he had just left,
> that for a moment he was well-nigh startled. A little older, perhaps, a little
> fairer of complexion, but with the same form, the same features, marked by
> the same wild grief. She wore a loose wrapper, which clothed her like the
> drapery of a statue. Her long dark hair, the counterpart of his wife's, had
> fallen down, and hung disheveled about her shoulders. There was blood upon
> her knuckles, where she had beaten with them upon the door. (323)

When the white woman lays her hand on his arm, however, Dr. Miller shrinks
from the contact, clearly seeing her across the great racial divide as an adver-
sary rather than a relative. She in turn maintains the contact, and when Miller
declares his unwillingness to save the child of Major Carteret, the man argu-
ably responsible for Wellington's race riot, Olivia Carteret declares the child
hers, not her husband's, and in a voice described by the narrator as like Dr.
Miller's wife's own voice, begins to convince him through her resemblance
(Olivia Carteret "never knew how much, in that dark hour, she owed to that
resemblance") to his wife Janet (324).

When Olivia Carteret literally supplicates herself at Miller's feet, he is
moved by her request and sends her to his own wife: "'My child lies dead
in the adjoining room, his mother by his side. Go in there, and make your
request of her. I will abide by her decision'" (325). And so Olivia goes to Janet:
"Standing thus face to face, each under the stress of the deepest emotions,
the resemblance between them was even more striking than it had seemed
to Miller when he had admitted Mrs. Carteret to the house" (325–26). Chesnutt presents, in *The Marrow of Tradition*, the historical violence of the 1898
Wilmington, North Carolina, race riots. As Joyce Pettis remarks, however,
"he crystallizes the tragedy of immediate events and outdated attitudes by
dramatizing an unfulfilled relationship between two sisters of different races"
(37). For Chesnutt, after so much racial violence promoted and carried out
by white men, primarily against Black men who, in turn, violently defend
themselves, there is no possibility for peace or reconciliation except through
these mothers and their feelings for their children. With "the body of the

dead child," the Millers' son, as "mute witness of this first meeting between the two children of the same father," Janet finally tells her husband to save Olivia's baby's life (325).

Comparing Chesnutt's depiction of Dr. Miller as the bereaved father with Du Bois's portrait of himself as bereaved in "Of the Passing of the First Born," chapter 11 of *The Souls of Black Folk*, enables us to better understand Chesnutt's cross-racial regenerative impulse. Of particular interest is the way in which both Chesnutt's Dr. Miller and Du Bois's narrator defer to and are guided by their wives, the mothers of these sons. Du Bois's "Of the Passing of the First Born" is by all accounts a moving and eloquent characterization of a father's emotional response to the birth and death of his child. Called by Hazel Carby "one of the most direct and passionate revelations of a male soul in American literature" (23), it is also a racially marked revelation that expresses "the frustrated dreams and fears of an entire people" (24). Born within the veil, this "Negro and a Negro's son" is by the middle of Du Bois's musings "'Not dead, not dead, but escaped; not bond, but free'" (147, 150). Through death he is removed from the "living death," the "taunt" of prejudice, and finally, perhaps in some better place "above the Veil" (150–51). Du Bois's own faith cannot quite carry him to this place above the veil, however; he gets here only through that "childless mother" who "in simple clearness of vision sees beyond the stars [and] said when he had flown 'He will be happy There; he ever loved beautiful things'" (149). As Carby makes clear, despite how he responds to his wife's vision of their son in heavenly rest, Du Bois also responds to the death of his son as a man with no heir, and the father's question of literal inheritance becomes the race leader's figurative question of intellectual inheritance—the concern about what Carby names "the reproduction of Race Men" (25).

Within the context of Du Bois's depiction of a father's grief, Chesnutt's presentation and pairing of the Millers and the Carterets is striking. Dr. Miller and Major Carteret, the first to confront one another, do so man to man, father to father: "'Ah!' replied [Dr. Miller], 'as a father whose only child's life is in danger, you implore *me*, of all men in the world, to come and save it!'" When Carteret is then presented with the scene inside Miller's own house, where "on the white cover of a low cot lay a childish form in the rigidity of death, and by it knelt, with her back to the door, a woman whose shoulders were shaken by the violence of her sobs," he sees that in these circumstances "he could not expect, could not ask, this father to leave his own household at such a moment" (319–21). Locked within the logic of fatherhood as defined by white bourgeois patriarchy and represented by Major Carteret, there seems to be no hope for the Carteret's own child. And yet, Olivia Carteret's plea to

Dr. Miller for the life of *her* child, and Miller's consequent deferral to his own wife for a decision about whether or not to save the young Carteret child's life, brings about a family reconciliation that actually redefines the family in something other than patriarchal terms, and in doing so establishes the baby Carteret, potentially or figuratively, as heir to them all.

In order to understand the full significance of Janet Miller's decision to send her husband to help Olivia's baby, we also need to expose the interconnections among the many layers of secrets in the novel. Most important, there is the secret interracial marriage between Samuel and Julia Merkell, insisted upon by Julia and carried out in another town during the military occupation of North Carolina just after the Civil War. Despite insisting on marriage in order to continue their cohabitation, Julia is quite as willing as Samuel Merkell to keep their marriage a secret. According to Samuel's letter to Delamere:

> And then, old friend, my weakness kept to the fore. I was ashamed of this marriage, and my new wife saw it. Moreover, she loved me,—too well, indeed, to wish to make me unhappy. The ceremony had satisfied her conscience, had set her right, she said, with God; for the opinions of men she did not care, since I loved her. . . . It was her own proposition that nothing be said of this marriage. If any shame should fall on her, it would fall lightly, for it would be undeserved. When the child came, she still kept silence. No one, she argued, could blame an innocent child for the accident of birth, and in the sight of God this child had every right to exist; while among her own people illegitimacy would involve but little stigma. (261)

In Chesnutt's version of the relations between ex-slave master and ex-slave after the war, then, the two figures that represent the South in both its promise and predicament are much like Du Bois's, but where Du Bois sees only hate in "these two passing figures of the present-past" and a legacy of hate among "their children's children" (22), Chesnutt sees love. Further, Chesnutt's two figures are not transient in the history of Wellington as Chesnutt tells it. The marriage they create forms a bond that has deep implications for the community, as does the decision to keep the marriage a secret.

In Chesnutt's coupling of Wellington's racial violence with the Merkell-Carteret-Miller interracial family romance, it is as if the public denial of love between Samuel and Julia wreaks havoc on the community. Let us consider the consequences of keeping this marriage a secret for the descendants and families of Julia and Samuel, now leading separate, "split at the root" existences in Wellington.[7] Julia and her daughter are tricked out of their rightful inheritance by Olivia's aunt, Polly Ochiltree, who steals and suppresses both the marriage certificate and the will that bequests property to them. Subsequently, Julia dies "of want" and Janet is raised "by the hand of charity" (328). While Janet marries Dr. Miller and lives an adult life as financially stable as is possible for an African American family in the South, she cannot be satisfied with her life because of a secret desire to be recognized by her sister. Meanwhile, within the Carteret family, Julia *is* recognized by her sister Olivia as someone with illegitimate ties to her father, but this recognition is filled with an abhorrence that has an extremely negative effect on Olivia's family. In particular, there are negative consequences for Olivia's young son, who is born prematurely because of the nervous shock his mother suffered because of her feelings toward Janet. Within this scenario, then, healing the rift between the two sisters means also acknowledging the legitimacy, both legally and emotionally, of the relationship between Samuel and Julia Merkell.

While Samuel Merkell intended to keep his marriage a secret, and hoped that Julia would do so even upon his death, on his deathbed he also made clear to Julia his intention to ensure her recognition as his lawful wife and heir, and also his desire to assure their daughter Janet, if it should matter to her, that she was not born out of wedlock. Here, however, Polly Ochiltree becomes involved in the plot. Polly is worth considering in some detail, not only because she steals the documents that Samuel intends for Julia to present to his lawyer and keeps them hidden for so many years, but also because by keeping this secret she poisons herself and her family. After telling Olivia the story of the secret marriage and will, her own theft of the papers that would prove both, and her confrontation with Julia over these matters of inheritance, Polly is a changed woman, not free of her burden but completely defeated by it. With eyes "half closed" she begins "muttering incoherently," as if the burden of keeping this secret for all these years has affected the old woman's mind and has finally done her in (139).[8]

Polly keeps the secret marriage certificate and will, along with a considerable sum of money, in a cedar chest in her house. Much is made of this cedar chest by Aunt Polly's nieces and nephews; as they remember, it is the source of great childhood gifts. The chest is referred to fondly as "like the widow's cruse" by Olivia Carteret and again like "Fortunatus's purse, which was always full" by old Mr. Delamere (23). Both characters might have more accurately compared it to Pandora's box, however. The baby rattle that almost chokes Dodie Carteret is a gift to him from Aunt Polly's cedar box, and this rattle and the baby's choking put into motion the subplot of Dr. Miller's initial insult at the home and hand of Major Carteret. Gold, too, is a gift from Polly's cedar box, and this gift also precipitates a series of tragic events. As a child, Tom Delamere, Polly's nephew, is given gold every year at Christmas, taken from a red silk purse kept in the cedar box. This gold tempts him to steal when he becomes desperate for money to pay his gambling debts. Further, this theft, during which Polly Ochiltree is murdered, causes the agitation of a lynch mob since Tom has carefully set up the faithful family servant, Sandy, to seem the guilty party. In turn, these events and the discovery of Tom's guilt cause old Mr. Delamere to have a fatal stroke. All gifts from the cedar box, we might say, are tainted by the stolen papers that are also hidden there.

In some ways, the secrets of Polly Ochiltree's treasure chest seem to be Chesnutt's way of signifying on white female sexuality and its popular interpretation in Southern society. After Polly is murdered by her nephew, and despite the fact that there is no evidence, Major Carteret's newspaper makes the suggestion that she has been sexually violated, as well as killed, and calls for the "drastic efforts . . . necessary to protect the white women of the South against brutal, lascivious, and murderous assaults at the hands of negro men" (185). This brings Polly's sexuality into focus for Chesnutt's readers and immediately brings to mind the other editorial about white womanhood presented in the novel, from "the local negro paper" (83). There, the suggestion is that Black men are sometimes lynched for their involvement in consensual relationships with white women:[9]

> It denied that most lynchings were for the offense most generally charged as their justification, and declared that, even of those seemingly traced to this cause, many were not for crimes at all, but for voluntary acts which might naturally be expected to follow from the miscegenation laws by which it was sought, in all the Southern States, to destroy liberty of contract, and, for the purpose of maintaining a fanciful purity of race, to make crimes of marriages to which neither nature nor religion nor the laws of other states interposed any insurmountable barrier. (65)

Polly has outlived two husbands. She wanted to become Samuel Merkell's wife when his first wife died, a fate from which Julie saved him, according to Merkell (134, 261). She is vigorous in her pursuit of men, which is but one piece of background evidence Chesnutt provides about her. The second is her reply to Major Carteret when he imagines her being possibly assaulted by "a burly black burglar." As she declares: "'I've proven a match for two husbands, and am not afraid of any man that walks the earth, black or white, by day or night. I have a revolver, and know how to use it. Whoever attempts to rob me will do so at his peril'" (26). Polly Ochiltree, we might surmise, feels that she can guard her own treasure chest quite adequately herself.

Of course, it is no stranger but rather Polly's own nephew who succeeds in robbing and murdering her, presumably because she does not think to defend herself. When Olivia Carteret hears that Polly Ochiltree has been murdered and robbed, she runs to her aunt's house not only out of concern, but also because she wants to be the first to find the secret family papers whose existence Polly has recently mentioned to her. Olivia's initial impulse in taking the papers before the policeman and sheriff's officer arrive is to avoid a scandal. Once they are in her possession, however, she finds herself in a series of emotional predicaments that ultimately lead to a crisis of conscience. After Olivia reads the papers she burns them, and at this point the burden of the family secret is completely on her; no one else alive knows about her father's second marriage and his will. In deliberations that suggest Chesnutt's further signifying on white female sexuality, however, Olivia begins to feel that she has done something wrong—not because she has taken evidence from a murder scene, nor even, at first, because she is continuing the disinheritance of her sister and disregard of her father's will. Where Olivia's conscience first pricks her is in the way in which she has destroyed the certificate of the marriage between her father and Julia. As Chesnutt's narrator declares, to Mrs. Carteret "marriage was a serious thing,—to a right-thinking woman the most serious concern of life" (263). In effect, as she comes to realize, Julia has acted in just the ways a white woman would, by insisting upon marriage rather than simply agreeing to live with Samuel Merkel, and while Olivia protests to herself that "the woman had *not* been white, and the same rule of moral conduct did not, *could* not, in the very nature of things, apply, as between white people," she knows that it does (266). Reconsidering this relationship between her father and Julia brings Olivia into dangerous territory, where she must consider that the very foundation of white Southern society is built on "a great crime against humanity" for which she, too, must atone (266). With this beginning of a new consciousness, then, she prepares to meet her sister.

Olivia Carteret is not the only sister with a family secret. Janet Miller also has a secret, and it is that she "could have loved this white sister, her sole living relative of whom she knew," if she had only received "a kind word, a nod, a smile, the least thing that imagination might have twisted into a recognition of the tie between them" (65). Janet's secret, which "she had never acknowledged, even to her husband, from whom she concealed nothing else," is that she deeply desires a sister's recognition from the white daughter of her father (66). It is, in fact, her "silent grief" that this recognition is denied her; and when her sister finally does recognize her, the emotional impact is so powerful that for a moment she even forgets her son's very recent death (327–28). The meeting of the two sisters at the conclusion of the novel, then, is not only the joining of the two sides of the family, but also the splicing of the two sides of the family secret that each sister keeps. Olivia and Janet tell one another what no one else knows, and this telling is significant, although in very different ways, to each of them. For Olivia, it is the beginning of her atonement for the "great crime against humanity" she now realizes slavery has been; for Janet, it is the renunciation of what she sees as her "slavish" side—that part of her which "would have kissed [her sister's] feet for a word, a nod, a smile" (266, 66, 328). In spite of this reunion, however, the novel's conclusion is not happy. The Millers' son is dead; that fact will not change. In the end, then, nothing is said about the way inherited secrets affect the Black child of the family; random racist violence has already killed him. The white child's life is, however, saved by his mother's and aunt's act of telling family secrets across racial lines.

While Olivia Carteret and Janet Miller confess their secrets to one another only at the conclusion of *The Marrow of Tradition*, readers of the novel have, of course, been privy to this information all along. This prior knowledge of these secrets means that the function of their telling, in the end, is not the actual disclosure of the information to the readers. Instead, this telling of what has been kept secret focuses the readers' attention on the reception of the secret information and the consequent actions that occur after the telling. In other words, the point of the meeting between Olivia Carteret and Janet Miller is not that we learn about these secret sisters—in fact, we already know them as such—but that we learn how each woman responds to her own unburdening. Chesnutt's purpose, then, seems ultimately not to make a point about past race relations; his main concern, instead, is with possibilities for the future.[10] This is why saving young Dodie Carteret's life really is important. A "new" South will require "new" Southern white men, and the young Carteret is a possible prototype in the making.

Numerous critical readings of *The Marrow of Tradition* focus on the novel as a presentation of "two possible black responses to white oppression," one characterized by Dr. William Miller and the other by Josh Green, whose father was killed and mother driven mad by the Ku Klux Klan.[11] The question for these critics then becomes whether moderation, embodied by Miller, or violent retaliation, embodied by Green, is the proper response to oppression. Yet, such readings ignore the significance of the interracial family at the heart of Chesnutt's novel.[12] Dr. Miller acts, we might say, most profoundly when he is within his family's home, not when he is on the streets of Wellington. His love for his wife and his feelings as a father combine to allow him to follow her will with regard to the Carteret child. It is, after all, no small act to agree to his wife's wishes, to walk arm-in-arm with Olivia Carteret to her home, to perform surgery upon the child by cutting the young white throat carefully, delicately, in order to save his life—to act, in other words, in the ways he has been trained as a physician.

Chesnutt's point seems to be, then, that despite the racial animosity stirred by the "Big Three," Major Carteret, General Belmont, and Captain McBane, the set dichotomy between Black and white is a fiction. Here we might return to Hazel Carby's point in *Reconstructing Womanhood* about the important narrative purposes that mulatto characters serve in African American fiction, as vehicles "for an exploration of the relationship between the races" (89). Janet Miller, as a biracial character, not only mediates between the Black and white worlds, but she is the embodied proof that the racial dichotomy insisted upon by Carteret, Belmont, and McBane is a falsehood. Further, her dearly won understanding of her own identity, presented at the end of the novel, serves as resolution of the tension between Black and white. In what might be termed a "psychic conversion," to borrow Cornel West's term, Janet Miller renounces her father's name, her father's wealth, and her sister's recognition.[13] She no longer needs or wants anything belonging to the master class; instead, having become more psychically self-sufficient, she realizes her own gifts and strengths. This self-centering of her identity is rooted in a transformed consciousness that resembles Frances Harper's characters' racial consciousness; Janet Miller, like Iola Leroy and other characters in Harper's fiction, rejects the position and privilege offered to her by her white family, proudly embracing her own nonwhite identity. Further, at least one ethical characteristic of her newly embraced identity is immediately established through her magnanimous gift of her husband's skills as a physician: even as her husband waivers, she chooses to facilitate healing rather than retribution.

Chesnutt proposes "New Negro" identity, then, similar to and predicated on what Locke calls "self-understanding," which occurs when someone has shaken off "the psychology of imitation and implied inferiority" ("New Negro" 4), but also informed by the wisdom of "colored" mothers, as we have characterized this as standpoint knowledge in the previous chapter. This is the understanding that Janet Miller comes to following the death of her son, a loss she experiences not as bereavement that robs her of an heir, but bereavement that resolves her mother love into an ethic of caring, to once again use Patricia Hill Collins's language.[14] She acknowledges the inter-racial family drama that is part of her personal history but now, with new self-understanding, refuses to continue playing the old role in that drama. Instead, she renounces the relationship with her white family and defines herself in relation to her husband and her deceased son. This act, in turn, changes Olivia Carteret as well. In "The New Negro," Locke also states that "the conditions that are molding a New Negro are molding a new American attitude" (10). In *The Marrow of Tradition* Olivia Carteret portrays this new attitude as she responds to her sister. After acknowledging her sister as such, and hearing her statement of identity, Olivia's fear and jealousy of Janet Miller seem to dissipate; further, upon hearing her sister renounce her family tie, Olivia reiterates her pledge to *be* a sister to Janet Miller.

This newly established relationship between the two sisters brings us back to Olivia's son, Dodie Carteret. Here, too, we must acknowledge that Chesnutt is presenting but also signifying on the idea of this "new white man." Chesnutt presents us with another "colored mother," Mammy Jane, who in addition to being servile in an "old Negro" kind of way, also possesses a conjure-woman's knowledge. Mammy Jane is "not entirely at ease concerning the child [Dodie]," because she discovers "under its left ear, a small mole, which led her to fear that the child was born for bad luck," a euphemism meant to imply "born to hang." As the narrator explains: "Had the baby been black, or yellow, or poor-white, Jane would unhesitatingly have named, as his ultimate fate, a not uncommon form of taking off, usually resultant upon the infraction of certain laws, or, in these swift modern days, upon too violent a departure from established social customs" (10). In other words, Mammy Jane sees the sign of lynching upon the child, confusing though the mark is on the baby of white upper-class parents.[15] However, as the possibilities for transgressive consciousness begin to take shape, we see that Dodie Carteret certainly could be hanged for "too violent a departure from established social customs" if he were, for example, in his adult life, to attempt to follow in his grandfather's footsteps and marry, or even live with, a Black woman.[16] Mammy Jane notes the hangman's mark on three separate occasions, and each time she makes or renews efforts to ward off such bad luck through conjure. She buries a good luck charm, reburies it when Dodie seems threatened, and later hides an additional charm in the baby's crib (11, 46–47, 108). We can only speculate about the adult Dodie's life, of course—if he even has such a life—but perhaps the conjuring on Dodie's behalf will avert his fate, although not by influencing the course of his life and his own behavior. After all, he has extended family enough to influence his actions. Perhaps, instead, Mammy Jane's conjure will allow Dodie to avoid the hangman by influencing the mores of the society in which he will live when he gains his majority; then, we might say, that Chesnutt, as the writer of this novel to which he pinned great hope for societal change, is once more doing a conjure-woman's bidding.

"Divulging the Great Secret of My Life": *The Autobiography of an Ex-Coloured Man*

While Chesnutt's Samuel and Julia Merkell, the familiar ex-master and ex-slave of our revised Hegelian dialectic, produce a child who is in some senses a synthesis of both father and mother, and thus representative of a new self-consciousness, this child is also gendered female, a "colored" mother herself, and consequently too often not, or not necessarily, read as a central figure in the intergenerational, interracial drama unfolding at the turn of the twentieth century. The same cannot be said about James Weldon Johnson's unnamed narrator and protagonist, the ex-coloured man of his *The Autobiography of an Ex-Coloured Man*,[17] who is much more recognizably the "tawny man-child" born of the white master and the "form hovering dark and motherlike" of Du Bois's *The Souls of Black Folk*, and also more recognizably the doubly conscious American Negro "longing to attain self-conscious manhood" (Du Bois, *Souls* 3). Unlike Chesnutt's Dr. Miller, in other words, whose quest for "self-conscious manhood" and consequent saving of a young white male life is mediated through his wife, Johnson's ex-coloured man's struggle with male self-consciousness is presented directly as that of a boy and man who attempts to understand himself as the son of a white father and colored mother. Narratively speaking, however, the presentation we receive is autobiographically retrospective, and significantly, the ex-coloured man identifies the position from which he narrates this story of his life as that of single father (his wife has died) of a daughter and a son. As narrator of his story, this father, I will argue here, is a radical model of racially conscious masculinity, decidedly alternative to Du Bois's "reproducing race men."

If Johnson's ex-coloured man were not a narrator, but simply a mixed-race protagonist who "neither disclaim[s] the black race nor claim[s] the white race . . . but raise[s] a moustache, and let[s] the world take . . . [him] for what it would" and consequently becomes a rich businessman (*Ex-Coloured Man* 190), the numerous critical judgments about the character's moral failure might perhaps be apt (Cooke 43–54; Stepto, *Veil* 95–127; V. Smith 44–64). Taking into account the narrative role the ex-coloured man plays, however, means reading past the end of the narrative itself. Johnson's narrator's conclusion, "I cannot repress the thought that, after all, I have chosen the lesser part, that I have sold my birthright for a mess of pottage" (211), points us to his motive in writing the story of his life, particularly when he "knows that the act is likely, even almost certain, to lead to his undoing" (3). In order to answer this question of the narrator's motive for writing the story of his life, we need to return to his concluding dilemma. No longer interested in his own social position, his reason for keeping his past a secret now revolves around his children, for whom "there is nothing" he "would not suffer to keep the brand from being placed upon them" (210) and for whom his love "makes me glad that I am what I am and keeps me from desiring to be otherwise" (211). Nevertheless, as he says, there remains for him "a vague feeling of unsatisfaction, of regret, of almost remorse," from which he seeks relief through the writing of his life story. That is to say, while he has no desire to place the mark of caste upon his children, he nevertheless does feel the imperative to tell the truth about his life and his past, to acknowledge what he calls his "strange longing for my mother's people" (210), and in doing so, he creates something to give to his children in place of the "mother's care" they will never have, creates for them a new legacy.

For the purpose of this study of African American literature as telling narrative, Johnson's novel is not remarkable because of its unreliable narrator, nor even for its unnameable narrator, as Samira Kawash skillfully redefines the ex-coloured man, but rather because the novel marks that moment of self-consciousness when a constructed narrative voice first takes up the task of telling a representative story (the "composite autobiography of the Negro race in the United States in modern times," according to Carl Van Vechten in his introduction to the 1927 edition of the novel) by divulging a secret. While, therefore, many critics have hailed the work as a major moment in African American literature primarily for its place as the "first instance in black fiction of a first-person narrator" (Gates, "Introduction," xvi), in this study this text is notable because the very structure of its first-person narration is that of telling a great secret. Up to this point, African American narrative literature has been riddled with secrets, and the content of what has been kept secret, as well as the way in which secrets are told—by whom, to whom, for what purposes—has played an integral part in both the telling of stories and the construction of self, or racial subjectivity. *The Autobiography of an Ex-Coloured Man*, however, melds narrative structuring and the construction of the racial subject into this one project of "divulging the great secret," and as such it marks the modern moment in African American literature, modern not because it represents alienation but because it integrates subjectivity and *telling*. Johnson's novel is modern, in other words, not because its subject constructs himself as flawed and unreliable, but because he tells his secret, and through telling this secret he claims self-consciousness that he then passes on generationally, both to his progeny and his readers.

In making this argument about *The Autobiography of an Ex-Coloured Man*, I am revising the critical position elaborated by numerous readers of Johnson's novel, namely, that Johnson's narrator is unreliable. This position, which springs from the earliest formalist readings of the novel, focuses on its irony in order to demonstrate that Johnson's text is sophisticated literature rather than mere sociological study of the race question.[18] As Johnson's novel began to be taken seriously in the 1970s as creative fiction, and as Johnson's narrator began to be read less as Johnson himself both in autobiographical detail and in point of view or opinion, numerous critics put forward the idea that "Johnson's treatment of his narrator is essentially ironic," and consequently, as Joseph Skerrett argues in a very influential essay, that "the narrator . . . is a projection of Johnson and of his alter ego" so that "through the duality of the tragic/ironic narrative, Johnson 'outers' and then exorcises the weakness he saw so clearly . . . the temptation to desire and to seek a less heroic, less painful identity than . . . blackness imposed" (540, 558).[19] In keeping with this argument, then, *Ex-Coloured Man*'s narrator is said to "eschew the meaning, burden, and responsibilities of blackness and to live as if he were white," indicating his "refusal to explore and confront the full meaning of his identity," and ultimately to "shirk the responsibility of identity and individuality" (Smith 44–45). And as such a character, he is profoundly unreliable, a bad reader of his own life (Stepto 114), although, as Henry Louis Gates summarizes, also a protagonist who "embodies the alienation characteristic of modernity" and, therefore, "the first flawed character in Afro-American fiction" (Gates, "Introduction" xviii–xix).

Arguments about the unreliability of Johnson's narrator tend to focus on the narrator's "flaws," demonstrated through his views on specific subjects, particularly race, that are then read as exhibiting his bias or desire to perceive life from the vantage point of a white, rather than a Black man. The problem with such arguments concerns the normative assumptions behind determining what "the black" point of view would be on any given subject. For example, Donald Goellnicht argues that the narrator "frequently chooses to adopt the gaze of white society" in the way that he critiques lower-class Southern Blacks and uses stereotyped notions of beauty to characterize the students at Atlanta University (20). And yet, because so many other African American writers of the early twentieth century create characters who make distinctions based on class preference, or who make clear their own "color struck" attitudes toward beauty, we must say that the ex-coloured man's attitudes might just as easily be those of someone thoroughly and decidedly Black rather than white.[20] In fact, in Johnson's own autobiography, *Along This Way*, he exhibits attitudes on these two subjects as questionable as those of his ex-coloured man's. About the Jim Crow car to which a conductor proposed that he remove himself during an 1896 trip from New York to Jacksonville, Johnson says: "I went forward and looked at the car. It was the usual 'Jim Crow' arrangement: one-half of a baggage coach, unkempt, unclean, and ill smelling. . . . After my inspection I went back and told the conductor that I couldn't ride in the forward car" (86–87). And in his description of the girls of Atlanta University and his response to them he muses, "Perhaps, the perfection of the human female is reached in the golden-hued and ivory-toned colored women of the United States, in whom there is a fusion of the fierceness in love of blond women with the responsiveness of black" (75). My point here is neither to criticize nor defend Johnson's own attitudes as classist or racist (or sexist), but rather to show that the ex-coloured man's point of view is no more that of an "outsider" exhibiting "cultural and emotional distance from African Americans" than Johnson's own (Japtok 38). Johnson's narrator is, in fact, as Kawash argues, better understood as unnameable rather than unreliable.[21]

In numerous cases, Johnson uses descriptions of events, places, or cultural phenomena that he has attributed to the ex-coloured man in his later nonfiction writing. Skerrett remarks that Johnson's preface to *The Books of American Negro Spirituals* contains material he used earlier in his novel, a reference to the similar characterizations of Singing Johnson in both texts (see *Ex-Coloured Man* 178–81; *American Negro Spirituals* 22–23). With regard to song, there is also the ex-coloured man's comment about the melody of "Go down, Moses": "I doubt that there is a stronger theme in the whole musical literature of the world" (181), which Johnson also echoes in the preface to *The Books of American Negro Spirituals* ("there is no nobler theme in the whole musical literature of the world" [13]) and repeats verbatim in the preface to the first edition of *The Book of American Negro Poetry* (1921).[22] The ex-coloured man's enumeration of the four artistic creations of which African Americans should be proud— Uncle Remus stories, spirituals, the Cakewalk, and ragtime—is also repeated verbatim in the preface to *The Book of American Negro Poetry* (*Ex-Coloured Man* 87; *Negro Poetry* 10). Further, the ex-coloured man's characterization of the preacher John Brown matches Johnson's own characterization of "the old-time Negro preacher" in his preface to *God's Trombones: Seven Negro*

Sermons in Verse, published in 1927 (*Ex-Coloured Man*, 174–76; *Complete Poems* 8–12), and parts of the "heavenly march" sermon that the ex-coloured man hears John Brown preach become lines of Johnson's own poem "The Judgment Day" (*Ex-Coloured Man* 176–78; *Complete Poems* 42–44). Johnson does distinguish his own life story from that of the ex-coloured man's, remarking that one of the reasons he has written his autobiography, *Along This Way*, is to make clear that the ex-coloured man's story was "not the story of my life" (239). Yet, he never distances himself from the ex-coloured man's narrative point of view, even going so far in *Black Manhattan*, his 1930 history of Black New York, while characterizing "New York's black Bohemia" as "part of the famous old Tenderloin," as to give a description of the "professional club" by saying: "A description of a club—really Ike Hines's—is given in *The Autobiography of an Ex-Coloured Man*. That will furnish, perhaps, a fresher picture of these places and the times than anything I might now write" (*Black Manhattan* 75). He then proceeds to quote six full paragraphs of description of the "Club" from his novel (*Ex-Coloured Man* 103–7). Literary critics castigate *Ex-Coloured Man*'s narrator perhaps most significantly for his response to the lynching he witnesses while collecting music in the South. But this description, too, as I will characterize, matches other presentations of lynching by Johnson. With these and other details of observation from Johnson's later works, it seems clear that Johnson does not maintain an ironic distance between his own point of view and that of his ex-coloured narrator.

"Doing" secrets, as we will recall, always involves a triad, and in the ex-coloured man's case, until he divulges his secret through his narrative, the membership group that shares knowledge of his secret with him comprises all those people who knew him as a child and young man, while the membership group from whom he has been keeping his secret comprises all the people in his life in the "present" tense of the narrative, and most significantly including his children. In this construction, while we might use the metaphor of passing to say that in the ex-coloured man's past he is racially Black, while in the present he is racially white, or passing for white, in terms of his racial secret it is not the case, as it is in so many other narratives of passing, that his secret is kept along racial lines. In other words, here it is not the case that the membership group from whom Johnson's narrator keeps his secret is white while the membership group with whom he shares it is Black. Instead, and in keeping with a narrative that "is intended to establish the fact that" Black and white racial identities "are entirely socially constructed" (Gates, "Introduction" xvi), not only does the ex-coloured man himself move back and forth between Black and white racial identities, but as narrator he also rejects the race-based epistemological construct: that is, as the ex-coloured man moves back and forth across the race line there is no suggestion that *anyone*, Black or white, can "just tell" his racial identity. By excluding any of the tropes that form the basis of identity politics, or that "identity epistemology" relies upon, Johnson's novel places all the more emphasis on the epistemology of secret knowing—and telling. As someone who engenders a coloured consciousness (before he becomes the *ex*-coloured man), Johnson's narrator is the episte-mologically privileged son of his coloured mother and white father, who experiences life from a colored standpoint. While this does not, in the end, turn him into a "race man," I will argue that his position both as coloured and then ex-coloured defines him racially while coincidentally also shaping him according to an alternative masculinity.

Johnson's narrator's psychic conversion to ex-coloured status, if we can use Cornel West's term in this context, can be characterized as occurring by degrees and in stages, and in this way is reminiscent of slave narratives that document the movement toward freedom, toward ex-slave status. For Johnson's narrator, the originating moment for his ex-coloured position occurs when he witnesses a brutal lynching by burning. This moment also marks the point at which he becomes the keeper of secrets, when he decides to "change [his] name, raise a moustache, and let the world take [him] for what it would" (190). As an ex-coloured man, however, at some point during his successful career as a white businessman, he also decides that he does not want the world to have the final word and so begins his own narration of the story of his life. Why he does this he cannot clearly say, but the writing is for him an erotic act, a "playing with fire" that brings "the thrill which accompanies that most fascinating pastime" (3). Rather than giving up all art and turning his back on his creative impulse, as some critics have argued he has done by abandoning his musical ambitions (Skerrett 556; Smith 63), the ex-coloured man has simply exchanged one art form for another. Further, his narration marks his relational shift with regard to secrets. No longer keeping his "great secret," he is instead "divulging" it. By writing his autobiography, however, the narrator is taking the peculiar step of making his life public without disclosing his own identity; names are omitted and details obscured when they might point a reader to the narrator as author. In this regard, as a secret teller, Johnson's narrator is making his life story known to "the public," but because he tells his story as a secret, he continues to keep his life story and his various racial positionalities from, primarily, his children. By bringing his life story into existence, however, Johnson's narrator has created a legacy for his children, one much more complex than that represented by the box of yellowing manuscripts, the remnants of his musical ambition, which he also has kept. Further, we might conjecture that in just the way Johnson first wrote his novel anonymously, without attaching his own name to the text as its author, but then publicly claimed the work with the publication of the 1927 second edition, so too will the narrator follow suit and at some later date align his subjective self with the narrative he has authored.

In *Crossing the Line*, Gayle Wald reads *The Autobiography of an Ex-Coloured Man* as a satire of "the collective fantasy of heroic black masculinity" as promulgated by precursor texts such as Frederick Douglass's *Narrative*, Booker T. Washington's *Up From Slavery*, and W. E. B. Du Bois's *The Souls of Black Folk*, and in doing so she argues that the novel interrogates the project of bourgeois uplift as represented by these texts (35–41). This is a significant point. In no uncertain terms, the ex-coloured man is a failed "race man," and in this way as well we might read his character as seriously flawed. More to the point, however, is the way that the narrative he writes is a critique of the ideology of the reproducing representative race man. The ex-coloured man had made the decision to become a model race man when he determined that he would leave his millionaire benefactor because of his "unselfish desire to voice all the joys and sorrows, the hopes and ambitions, of the American Negro, in classic musical form" (148). His separation from his benefactor is characterized as his moment of racial self-consciousness; at the same time that his benefactor is characterized as his "best friend" and as exerting a great influence on his life, his own mother is invoked as an even better "best friend" who had an even greater influence on his life (148). In some ways, then, we see that the narrator, by choosing his musical work in the South, is also choosing to ally himself with his mother rather than with his white friend. The race work he begins, as indicated through the descriptions included in his narrative (for example those of the "big meeting" that present Singing Johnson and the preacher John Brown), give us clear indications of just how similar the narrator's racial outlook is to Johnson's own in his later work. The task he sets for himself, however, is not to characterize Southern Black culture, but rather to become a Negro composer by writing "classic music" from "modern rag-time" and "the old slave songs" (142–43). It is this specific work that the narrator abandons, and it is the role of career race man that he rejects—but not the racial outlook, or point of view that he has been developing throughout his life. While his narrative, then, critiques the "race man" ideology, it also offers, I am suggesting here, an alternative and alternatively "raced" model of masculine subjectivity.

It strikes many readers of Johnson's text as peculiar that his narrator witnesses a Black man burned alive by a white mob and responds with feelings of shame—and the decision to pass for white himself. Samira Kawash, however, reads the narrator as identifying with the victim, and consequently coming "face to face with the demand, and the violence, of racial discipline" (154).[23] This racial discipline, or violence, Johnson knew firsthand. Later in his career he became involved with the NAACP campaign against lynching,[24] but as a young man in Jacksonville in 1901 he was nearly lynched himself, as he describes in detail in *Along This Way*. Just after a great fire in Jacksonville decimated one hundred and fifty blocks of the city, civil law was suspended and "companies of state militia from central and western counties had been mustered to form a provost guard" (165). These "troops from the backwoods district of the state"(165) were called upon when Johnson was seen in the new Riverside Park with an African American woman so light-skinned that she appears white. Shifting to the present tense in the style of a flashback, Johnson describes his confrontation with the "detachment of troops with guns and dogs" that has been sent to "get" him:

> I lose self-control. But a deeper self springs up and takes command; I follow orders. I take my companion's parasol from her hand; I raise the loose strand of fence wire and gently pass her through; I follow and step into the group. The spell is instantly broken. They surge round me. They seize me. They tear my clothes and bruise my body; all the while calling to their comrades, "Come on, we've got 'im! Come on, we've got 'im!" And from all directions these comrades rush, shouting, "Kill the damned nigger! Kill the black son of a bitch!" I catch a glimpse of my companion; it seems that the blood, the life is gone out of her. There is the truth; but there is no chance to state it; nor would it be believed. As the rushing crowd comes yelling and cursing, I feel that death is bearing in upon me. Not death of the empty sockets, but death with the blazing eyes of a frenzied brute. (167)

Not only is this a moment of terror for Johnson, but it is also a moment of humiliation. Here his experience of racial discipline, dependent as it is upon a misreading that sees him as sexually involved with a white woman, also serves to sexualize him—and, psychologically, to sexually brutalize him.

Black male sexual humiliation at the hands of white men is perhaps most familiarly depicted by Toni Morrison when she characterizes Cholly Breedlove's humiliation when forced by white men to continue, at gunpoint, his sexual activity with Darlene (*Bluest Eye* 147–49). For Johnson, his experience at the hands of the militia troops is profoundly disturbing: "For weeks and months the episode with all of its implications preyed on my mind and disturbed me in my sleep. I would wake often in the night-time, after living through again those few frightful seconds, exhausted by the nightmare of a struggle with a band of murderous, bloodthirsty men in khaki, with loaded rifles and fixed bayonets. It was not until twenty years after, through work I was then engaged in, that I was able to liberate myself completely from this horror complex" (170). In discussing this incident, Johnson is also quite clear about his understanding of his sexualization. "Through it all," he says, "I discerned one clear and certain truth: in the core of the heart of the American race problem the sex factor is rooted, rooted so deeply that it is not always recognized when it shows at the surface" (170). Further, as Johnson sees it, the strength and bitterness of the complex of white racial superiority "are magnified and intensified by the white man's perception, more or less, of the Negro complex of sexual superiority" (170). In other words, according to Johnson, white men engage in racial policing because they feel themselves to be sexually inferior to Black men. If, as Robyn Wiegman argues, lynching is "a grotesquely symbolic, if not literal, sexual encounter between the white mob and its victim" (82), then we might understand Johnson's experience as symbolic gang rape, insofar as, to his own understanding, his body has been threatened by men with the violent desire to prove their sexual superiority over him.

In *The Autobiography of an Ex-Coloured Man*, the ex-coloured man's race work is interrupted by his witnessing the spectacle of a lynching. White members of the Southern community that he was visiting in order to gather slave songs publicly burn alive a Black man, an event that fills the narrator with the humiliation and "shame, unbearable shame" that drives him "out of the Negro race" (191). The scene of this lynching "disrupts his fantasy of recuperating a stable 'black' self through a self-conscious immersion in black musical traditions," as Wald notes (*Crossing the Line* 38), and it does so, I am arguing, by forcing a moment of self-conscious (and racialized) sexualization absent from the "race man" construct. The lynching that the ex-coloured man witnesses is carried out by "fierce, determined men" of a type he has come to know well, "blond, tall, and lean, with ragged moustache and beard, and glittering grey eyes" (185). As the lynching unfolds, the ex-coloured man describes himself as "fixed to the spot where I stood, powerless to take my eyes from what I did not want to see" (187). The ex-coloured man's powerlessness here is reminiscent of the moment when the young Frederick Douglass witnesses his aunt Esther's brutalization at the hands of Captain Anthony, yet his response is very different. As I have argued in chapter 1, Douglass's description of the brutal conflict between his Aunt Esther and Captain Anthony re-character-izes the moment of self-consciousness as it has been transformed within the American consciousness as a gendered master/slave dialectic. In Douglass's *Narrative*, as he transforms himself from slave to man, we might also say that he re-masculinizes himself, and thereby erases his identification with his Aunt Esther from his consciousness. This is what allows him, in Wald's words, to "reconstruct his social subjectivity within the space of his narra-tion" by physically confronting Mr. Covey (38). In comparison, we might say that upon witnessing the brutal lynching, the ex-coloured man does not take this masculine way out. Or, to say it another way, his response to witnessing this lynching as his own psychological sexualization through racial discipline is to give up race work as his career but to live even more transgressively within his own "category crisis"[25] wherein he is paradoxically unnamed, "ex." However transgressive his new identity, however, he is definitively masculine. His notion of letting the world take him for what it would (190)[26] is, more precisely, letting the world take him for whatever kind of *man* it would since the one way he marks his body in response to the lynching is by "raising a moustache."[27]

The ex-coloured man's description of the man that he witnesses being lynched is often read as indicative of the narrator's underlying problems in identifying with his race. In particular, the ex-coloured man describes the lynching victim, standing before the crowd just before he is killed, as "a man only in form and stature, every sign of degeneracy stamped upon his coun-tenance," with eyes "dull and vacant, indicating not a single ray of thought." Lacking pity, these seem to be the comments of a distant and unsympathetic observer.[28] However, these are, once again, words that Johnson also uses when he writes in his own voice, and reading other texts by Johnson gives us context for reading the description of lynching in *The Autobiography of an Ex-Coloured Man*. For example, his poem "Brothers," published in *The Crisis* (1916), opens:

> See! There he stands; not brave, with an air
> Of sullen stupor. Mark him well! Is he
> Not more like brute than man? Look in his eye!
> No light is there, none, save the light that shines
> In the now glaring, and now shifting orbs
> Of some wild animal in the hunter's trap.
> (lines 1–6, Crisis *Reader* 31)[29]

This description of the victim of a lynch mob is presented from the point of view of the mob; as the poem continues, however, the rhetorical point seems to be that a mirroring phenomenon is taking place, and that the degeneracy that the mob sees is a reflection of its own condition. In the poem, the final words are those of the mob who, as they return to their wives and children, repeat in order to puzzle over what the victim could have meant when he said *"Brothers in spirit, brothers in deed are we?"* which suggests Johnson's understanding of an intimate intertwining of the male subjectivity of mob and lynching victim.

As part of the blending of subjectivity of mob and lynching victim, Johnson's poem also attempts to raise and answer an existential question of vital importance to the ex-coloured man. After description of the lynching victim, through the eyes of the mob, as more brute than man, the question is asked: "How came this beast in human shape and form?" (line 7, Crisis *Reader* 31). We should read this as a question of transmogrification, an extreme form of transgression, and as the victim, who also reflects the mob's identity, begins to answer the question, saying "I claim no race, no race claims me; I am/ No more than human dregs; degenerate;/ The monstrous offspring of the monster, Sin;/ I am—just what I am . . .," we begin to hear echoes of the position that the ex-coloured man has taken as he characterizes himself ("I would neither disclaim the black race nor claim the white race . . . but . . . let the world take me for what it would" [190]). The ex-coloured man is no monster, however. He is not the phoenix rising from the ash, but the one who lived to tell the tale, who in response to the existential crisis of belonging to "a people who could with impunity be treated worse than animals" (191) goes on to live, to love, and to tell the fullness of his own story.

We might think of the ex-coloured man's witnessing of the lynching as his moment of crisis that ultimately brings him to the position of impunity from which he can write an account of his life, a position similar, as Houston Baker has noted, to Ralph Ellison's Invisible Man's position underground ("A Forgotten Prototype" 443). Both characters retreat to a place of stasis; both are waiting for the right time and the right way to return to an active life; both turn to the writing of the narratives of their lives, to explanation of who they are, as their way to return to the world.[30] In this context, too, we see the significance of the fathering role to the ex-coloured man's understanding of himself because it is in this role that he so freely loves and tells of love. The ex-coloured man speaks of the love he feels for the white woman who becomes his wife, the love she expresses toward him, and the love that he feels for his children that "makes me glad that I am what I am and keeps me from desiring to be otherwise" (205, 209, 211). This love is an extension of his own (coloured) mother's love for his father, and himself, so that the *ex*-coloured man seems *not* to have negated a most crucial aspect of his "coloured" self. We take seriously the ex-coloured man's expression of love for his wife but especially for his children, I am suggesting, because of the way it is rooted in, and roots the ex-coloured man in, this firm "I am what I am" understanding of himself that on the one hand allows him to let the world take him for what it will, but on the other hand creates his compulsive desire to narrate himself into existence and so solve his existential dilemma.

Yet if it is the ex-coloured man's love for his children that allows him to accept himself as he is, then we should see the ex-coloured man not simply as tragic but also as regenerative; not simply as failed hero but also remarkably successful as his subjective self. He is thoroughly his mother's son interiorly, and in his love for his own children all the more so than if he stayed true to his mother by exterior sign, by performing as race man. As the recognizable "tawny man-child" of Du Bois's *The Souls of Black Folk*, son of the *ex*-master and *ex*-slave, this *ex*-coloured narrator claims slavery's legacy of secrets through telling the "ex," through narrating what is often marked by exclusion. By being what he is rather than what anyone else configures or expects him to be, in other words, by changing his name and raising a moustache (190), he manages to realize the desire that Du Bois names as the "longing to attain self-conscious manhood," such as it is.

5

Queering America's Family:
Jessie Fauset's Modern Novels

◆◦§ ƺ◦◆

> You know, honey, us colored folks is branches without roots and that makes
> things come round in queer ways.
>
> —Zora Neale Hurston, *Their Eyes Were Watching God*

By arguing in the previous two chapters that "New Negro" identity should
be linked to the new consciousness of "colored" mothers and that *The Autobiography of an Ex-Coloured Man* marks a modern moment in African American
literature because of its secret telling, I am also suggesting that we reconcep-
tualize African American literary history by focusing on, rather than margin-
alizing, master/female slave or ex-master/female ex-slave relations. Doing so,
I will suggest, adds to the current reconsideration and reconceptualization of
the literary movement we call the Harlem Renaissance because Jessie Fauset, regularly dismissed as too conventional to write anything really worth-
while, becomes no longer so marginalized herself. Fauset's stories fall outside
better-known paradigms of racialized American life, and some of her more
recent critics even charge that her characters and the lives they lead are not
"representative of the majority of black women in this country" (V. Lewis
376).[1] But reevaluation of early twentieth-century African American letters,
to which this project hopes to contribute, has also included work by other
critics who characterize Fauset's vision of modern African American life as it
contradicts the more masculinist African American modernity characterized
by "New Negro" identity. As Cheryl Wall recently documents, Fauset's reception, both during her own lifetime and during the 1970s rediscovery of the
Harlem Renaissance, has been biased by gender politics.[2] This is particularly
true, I suggest, with regard to the reception of her final two novels published
during her lifetime, *The Chinaberry Tree* (1931) and *Comedy: American Style*

(1933), texts which center upon ideas taboo for modern Black women writers: the love a female ex-slave has for her ex-slave master (*The Chinaberry Tree*) and the fetishized desire to be white that destroys an African American woman and her family (*Comedy: American Style*). Both texts, however, which in many ways extend the questions Fauset raises in her earlier novels, *There is Confusion* (1924) and *Plum Bun: A Novel Without a Moral* (1929), also further expand turn-of-the-century ideas of colored consciousness tied to an epistemology of secret knowing. In these latter two novels, where the focus is family dynamics, Fauset probes the psychological as well as the epistemological dimensions of secret knowing so that her African American families become, coincidentally and peculiarly, "queerly" and consciously, both modern and American. For this reason, all of Fauset's fiction demands renewed critical attention.

As Marcy Knopf observes in the foreword to *The Chinaberry Tree*, "Scholars and critics typically perceive Jessie Fauset to be outside modernist literary circles" (ix). Modernist literary circles have themselves been redrawn, however, and it is in the context of "new modernist studies" and Rita Felski's argument that modernism is "only one aspect of the culture of women's modernity" that I am suggesting a recharacterization of Fauset's work (25; see also Ardis and Lewis). As I hope to show, the turn toward psychological explanation, in connection to the epistemology of secret knowing, itself characterizes Fauset's vision as modern, as does her developed interest in "colored" life as an exploration of issues of hybridity. Like Pauline Hopkins's, however, Fauset's gendered understanding of post-slavery era African American families means that her vision preserves the generational memory of women's experience within slavery. Simply referencing this history is, by some "New Negro" standards, sentimental and therefore distinctly not modern, so that these same standards ironically dismiss Fauset's vision, colored in the ways we have explored "colored consciousness" in Frances Harper's and Pauline Hopkins's fiction, for the very reasons it should be examined. While it may seem intuitively true that the "New Negro" and the "new woman" are parallel descriptors that characterize identity issues within modernity studies, in fact the parallel raises the same realization that 1980s Black feminism brought to academic consciousness: by these configurations it is too often true that "all the Blacks are men, all the women are white" and Black women do not have a place.[3] When neither the construction of "New Negroes" nor the construction of "new women" incorporates significant aspects of Black women's experience, the vision that references the validity of that experience should not be automatically categorized as "old" (or "Rear Guard" as Fauset has specifically been characterized)—in other words, not modern.[4] A much better descriptor, again in keeping with 1980s Black feminism, might be, instead, "brave."

Taken together, Fauset's novels suggest her to be a keen student of psychology,[5] as well as a writer who understands slavery's psychological legacy as it makes itself manifest, first in American society most broadly, but ultimately in the modern Black family. In her novels, Fauset moves back and forth between issues of miscegenation as they are rooted in sexual relationships between a female slave or ex-slave and a male slavemaster or ex-master, and issues of identity involving racial passing by African Americans so light-skinned that one can "tell" only by *their* telling. Judith Butler suggests in "Passing, Queering: Nella Larsen's Psychoanalytic Challenge" that Nella Larsen's novel *Passing* is "in part a theorization of desire, displacement, and jealous rage that has significant implications for rewriting psychoanalytic theory in ways that explicitly come to terms with race" (*Bodies that Matter* 182). Butler's point in "Passing, Queering" is to tease out the way in which sexual difference might be said to be articulated through the convergence of other modalities of power, and specifically race (167–68), in order to argue against the position that sexual difference is more fundamental than racial difference, and to posit that there is no such thing as "a relationship called 'sexual difference' that is itself unmarked by race" (181). Specifically, Butler points to "racial injunctions which operate in part through the taboo on miscegenation" (167), and novels like Larsen's where racial and sexual passing converge, to suggest that because sexual difference and racial difference are not "fully separable axes of social regulation and power" (182), a rethinking of "the psychic force of social regulation" and a rearticulation of "the psyche politically in ways which have consequences for social survival" (182–83) are in order. Here I will suggest that Fauset's novels represent her developing attempts to theorize the relation between life and desire in an inherently racialized and gendered world. In Butler's terms, Fauset's novels articulate the psyche within a fascinating rethinking of the forces of social regulation. Fauset's two novels of the 1920s focus on young people who attempt to understand themselves as American, confusing as this endeavor is because of race, class, and gender dynamics, while her later novels explicitly present the inner workings of family systems as they develop within these same dynamics of power.

As the narrative voice of Fauset's novels becomes more and more self-conscious, Fauset demonstrates her ability to continuously explore the question of "what can and cannot be spoken," to use Butler's words about Larsen. Indeed, much like Butler's characterization of Clare Kendry as "hiding" in her "very flaunting" (169), Fauset's narrators create a "not said" within the very "telling" of their stories. Narrative secrets revealed point to narrative secrets concealed, which, again to use Butler's language characterizing Larsen, demonstrate a "queering" of Fauset's texts: "As a term for betraying what ought to remain concealed, 'queering' works as the exposure within language—an exposure that disrupts the repressive surface of language—of both sexuality and race" (176). Fauset's texts turn on "queer" exposures that tell, discover, and often still keep secrets, and sometimes layers of secrets, so much so that "queering" might be said to characterize Fauset's narrative strategy. And as I will suggest, Fauset's vision itself is very queer. The ways in which she becomes determined to detail the familial—and specifically generational—consequences of Black women's prohibited desires in *The Chinaberry Tree* and *Comedy: American Style* mean that the very point of origin for her stories exposes what "ought to remain concealed." In this regard, it is important to note again that the legacy from colored mothers that Fauset accepts and extends posits an earlier generation of colored women as representing the foundation of race identity and consciousness that directly contradicts Alain Locke's conceptualization of the "New Negro" as the changeling in the laps of sociologists, philanthropists, and race-leaders, who "are at a loss to account for him" because they do not understand his parentage (3). The myth of New Negro "changelings," in other words, precludes the very existence of the generationally determined women whose psychology Fauset seems compelled to explore.

One way to understand the continuing presence of the Hegelian master/female slave dialectic in modern American life is to invoke the Freudian concept of fetish and make the claim that Black women become fetish objects for white men, and ultimately for American society. This may be the point Hortense Spillers is making in the opening sentences of "Mama's Baby, Papa's Maybe: An American Grammar Book": "Let's face it. I am a marked woman, but not everybody knows my name. 'Peaches' and 'Brown Sugar,' 'Sapphire' and 'Earth Mother,' 'Aunty,' 'Granny,' God's 'Holy Fool,' a 'Miss Ebony First,' or 'Black Woman at the Podium': I describe a locus of confounded identities, a meeting ground of investments and privations in the national treasury of rhetorical wealth. My country needs me, and if I were not here, I would have to be invented" (203). Whether we focus our attention on images in popular culture or the field of literary criticism, scholars such as Ann duCille, Michelle Wallace, and bell hooks, among others, have firmly established the idea of Black women in the role of "Other" in American society (see duCille, "Occult"; hooks; Michelle Wallace). By invoking the Freudian notion of fetish, however, I mean to suggest a very specific model

136

of "othering" in play in modern America, and to suggest further that Jessie Fauset both recognizes and responds to this "othering," this fetishization, of Black women.[6] Freud's concept of fetish allows us to see the othering of Black women as a phenomenon that combines white male castration anxiety with the eroticization of Black women's bodies. More significantly, it also allows us to see the "disavowal" related to the othering, or objectification, of Black women.[7] In Freudian terms, a fetish comes into being when a boy disavows his observation that women are phallus-less, thus making the fetish a substitute penis and the women who are fetishized "tolerable as sexual objects" so that the boy is saved "from becoming a homosexual" (Freud, "Fetishism" 954). However, this boy, our young white American, is not saved from being queer, and here I use the word "queer" in two senses: this white male desire that fetishizes Black women is almost homosexual, since race eroticizes the female body by fetishizing, or phallicizing it. More important, however, the eroticized Black female body, objectified as fetish, is constructed through disavowal, and as such, this fetishized sexuality is queer in Judith Butler's terms, a betrayal "of what ought to remain concealed"; that is, fetishized sex is queer in the ways that it acknowledges this disavowal, this refusal to acknowledge, that has created it in the first place.[8] In this latter way that fetishization is queer, it also carries and reveals secrets, and stories of miscegenation that acknowledge fetishized desire raise many questions. Among the most significant of these questions is how the fetishized Black woman, in the context of standpoint epistemology, understands *herself*. This, as I hope to demonstrate, is Jessie Fauset's question.

Waking from Confusion: Fauset's Early Writing

Early in her tenure as literary editor of *The Crisis* from 1919 to 1926, Fauset published her short story "The Sleeper Wakes," a story emblematic of Fauset's awakening to her own definition of the racial conundrum.[9] Here, we might say, Fauset portrays the modern "master/slave" moment of conflict, now invested with explicit sexual desire. Ultimately, her protagonist's question is how to understand herself as the object of this desire. In the story the light-skinned protagonist, Amy, is initially characterized as "a girl of seventeen" who "has no psychology, she does not go beneath the surface, she accepts" (2). Living on the surface allows Amy to run away from the colored family that has raised her since she was five, not, as the narrator explains, "that she was the least bit unhappy but because she must get out in the world" (3). In the world, Amy, whose parentage and racial identity are unknown to her, marries a very rich white man, Arthur Wynne, who has "a tradition," a family pride and a race pride that Amy finds inexplicable (10). When this pride brings him into conflict with his servants, because of the way in which he persists in racially insulting humiliation, Amy's empathy with these servants causes her to interfere with her husband's business practices and also brings her to conclude that she must be colored herself. In order to keep Wynne from deadly retaliation against one servant, Stephen, Amy tells Wynne that Stephen is her brother, then confesses that he really is not but that she, herself, is colored. Wynne believes her, promptly divorces her, but inevitably returns to her with the offer of an illegitimate relationship. And here, Fauset brilliantly characterizes the modern, sexualized conflict between people whose positions we might characterize as ex-master and ex-slave: Wynne insults Amy, insinuating she has already behaved as a whore. In return, Amy strikes him across his "hateful sneering mouth." Wynne strikes back and the narrator presents Amy's response, clearly from the depths of a consciousness that demonstrates that she now has a "psychology":

> As *she* fell, reeling under the fearful impact of his brutal but involuntary blow, her mind caught at, registered two things. A little thin stream of blood was trickling across his chin. She had cut him with the ring, she realized with a certain savage satisfaction. And there was something else which she must remember, which she *would* remember if only she could fight her way out of this dreadful clinging blackness, which was bearing down upon her—closing her in.
> . . .
> "Nigger," he had called her as she fell, "nigger, nigger," and again, "nigger."
> "He despised me absolutely," she said to herself wonderingly, "because I was colored. And yet he wanted me." (20)

A few pages later in the narration we find that Amy continues to focus on trying to understand this moment of conflict:

> She used to go over that last scene with Wynne again and again trying to probe the inscrutable mystery which she felt was at the bottom of the affair. She groped her way toward a solution, but always something stopped her. Her impulse to strike, she realized, and his brutal rejoinder had been actuated by something more than mere sex antagonism, there was *race* antagonism there—two elements clashing. That much she could fathom. But that he despising her, hating her for not being white should yet desire her! It seemed

to her that his attitude toward her—hate and yet desire, was the attitude in microcosm of the whole white world toward her own, toward that world to which those few possible strains of black blood so tenuously and yet so tenaciously linked her. (22)

This theme that Fauset identifies here, then, characterized as the concurrent hate and desire of white men for colored women, is, as her narrator concludes, also the larger American attitude toward African Americans generally, and the question of why this is so, and how one is to respond, will intrigue Fauset throughout her writing career. In this story, "The Sleeper Wakes," Amy's solution is to declare her own identity as "citizen of the world" and return to her colored home. As we shall see, however, in Fauset's later novels "home" is not such a safe place, but is itself implicated through Fauset's continued interrogation of the effect of racial antagonism within the African American family.

By reconsidering Jessie Fauset's vision of modern America as the place of racial entanglement where white Americans both hate and desire their colored brothers and sisters, and Fauset's literary quest as her exploration of African Americans' psychological responses to such conflicting emotions, we begin to see that her point of view, while at times bleak, is also stunning. By all accounts a central actor of the Harlem Renaissance, Fauset should not be considered peripheral to the main concerns of that literary movement, and indeed might be considered central if we reinterpret that movement along the lines that George Hutchinson suggests in *The Harlem Renaissance in Black and White*.[10] The "new story of the contexts, crosscurrents, and effectiveness of the Harlem Renaissance" that Hutchinson tells comes from rethinking American cultural history from a position of "interracial marginality" that allows us to see "'white' and 'black' American cultures as intimately intertwined, mutually constitutive," an understanding we would expect Fauset herself to have, given her position with *The Crisis* (2, 3). Indeed, other more recent explorations of the Harlem Renaissance as a construction rather than a phenomenon suggest that the complicated biases inherent in the 1970s literary scholarship that created and defined the Harlem Renaissance as a literary movement also disparaged Fauset in unfair ways.[11]

During Fauset's own lifetime her work met with both great praise and condescending dismissiveness, and it is the latter criticism of her work that is taken up by literary scholars in the 1970s.[12] Fauset herself, who is by all accounts an astute reader and editor of African American texts, specifically believed that she was not being treated fairly by some of her contemporaries, most notably

Alain Locke.[13] As Cheryl Wall suggests, Fauset's response to being misread can be found in her work ("Histories and Heresies" 68–73); and while *Plum Bun: A Novel Without a Moral* (1928) begins Fauset's response to her critics, *The Chinaberry Tree* and *Comedy: American Style* develop this response. By the late 1920s, Fauset was quite aware of attempts to write her off the public stage of African American letters. No longer literary editor of *The Crisis,* and unable to find work in the publishing field as she preferred, she instead was forced back to the high school classroom, and, according to her biographer, taught French at DeWitt Clinton High School in New York City from 1927 until 1944, during which time she wrote three of her four novels (Sylvander 66). While some critics suggest that Fauset's teaching duties and time pressures might account for flaws in her later novels (Sylvander 208–9), I would suggest that her own understanding of her position as both insider and outsider with respect to "New Negro" artistic and literary production contributes to her development of that "queer" narrative sensibility that insistently explores what Butler has named as questions of "what can and cannot be spoken, what can and cannot be publicly exposed" (*Bodies That Matter* 169).

As Wall most notably remarks, the publication of Fauset's first novel, *There Is Confusion,* was purportedly the reason for the March 21, 1924, dinner at the Civic Club, hosted by Charles S. Johnson, editor of the National Urban League's *Opportunity* magazine, yet neither Fauset nor her novel were the center of attention that evening ("Histories and Heresies" 59–62). The publication of *There Is Confusion* should have garnered Fauset attention. One year after publishing Jean Toomer's *Cane,* Horace Liveright at Boni and Liveright published Fauset's *There Is Confusion* to much anticipation and acclaim, and it was the first book-length work of fiction springing from the new literary activity centered in Harlem. As contributor to *The Crisis* since 1912 and literary editor since 1919, and with academic credentials that included degrees from Cornell and the University of Pennsylvania and additional study at the Sorbonne, Fauset had, as Wall states, "a claim to leadership and to honor" (61). Nevertheless, through the concerted efforts of Charles Johnson and Alain Locke, Fauset did not play a central role in this event, which ironically has come to be characterized as the Harlem Renaissance's moment of origin.[14] Instead, with Alain Locke as master of ceremonies, the "New Negro" was unveiled: young Harlem writers were introduced to prominent white editors, Paul Kellogg of the *Survey Graphic* invited Locke to edit a special issue of that magazine, and Locke's *New Negro* anthology was born. Meanwhile, after a full program of speakers—all men—Fauset said only a few words of thanks to her supporters. Later, she contributed one essay, "The Gift of Laughter," to Locke's *New*

Negro.[15] In a letter to Locke from 1934, however, and prompted by his criticism of her novel *Comedy: American Style,* Fauset makes clear what she did not say at the time: "I have always disliked your attitude toward my work dating from the time years ago when you went out of your way to tell my brother that the dinner given at the Civic Club for *There Is Confusion* wasn't for me" (qtd. in Davis, "Introduction" xxxii). It is in full knowledge of Locke's attitude toward her that Fauset contributes an essay to *The New Negro* anthology, and in this essay she begins to demonstrate the knowledge that this point of view as both insider and outsider allows. In "The Gift of Laughter" Fauset articulates her understanding of the performativity of race and in doing so demonstrates her line of thinking that rejects essentialist notions of racial identity in order to explore its edges and boundaries. While gender is not a subject taken up in "The Gift of Laughter," perhaps evidence that this essay is Fauset's own conscious "performance" of race, in later work it is the confluence of race and gender issues that brings Fauset to her complex understanding of the societal and psychological dimensions of race and racialized life.

"The Gift of Laughter" is a significant rewriting of Fauset's earlier essay from *The Crisis* titled "The Symbolism of Bert Williams."[16] In that earlier essay, a tribute to Bert Williams upon his death, Fauset begins an inquiry into three areas that she later develops in her novels: first, the idea of types, and the way in which a racial type becomes symbolic; second, the relation between African American comedy and "that deep, ineluctable strain of melancholy, which no Negro in a mixed civilization ever lacks," that is, the relation between comedy and tragedy (255); and third, a philosophy of life suggested by Bert Williams's example, that circumstances are to be met "with a tear, a sigh, a shrug, a brave smile and the realization that this is life," and that in the face of adversity the only choice is to "buckle down to life and try it again" (259). As she examines the character that Williams presents on the stage, that of the "poor, shunted, cheated, out-of-luck Negro" (255), she also notes her idea of the "symbolic" and the way that it operates through the "*rôle*"[17] that Williams plays. In ways that suggest Lacan's symbolic, particularly as it is contrasted to the "imaginary" as referenced by Abdul R. JanMohamed in the context of colonialist literature, Fauset's symbolic Bert Williams is "the racial type itself."[18] Specifically, even in this earlier essay, we see Fauset interested in Williams's creation of an "Other" that embodies "radical intersubjectivity" so that the "Other" created on stage is a mirror, rather than a mirror image, for his Black, and white, audience—and as such demonstrates to his audience the ways in which this racial type that he plays is a "structuring projection" of American society that allows it to see itself.[19]

In "The Gift of Laughter," which rewrites "The Symbolism of Bert Williams," and which more generally considers African American contributions to theater, Fauset expands her ideas about the symbolic Bert Williams in order to characterize the ways in which Williams performs race. She makes it quite clear that Williams, who is from Nassau, spent years perfecting his imitation of "the Negro," studying various walks and speech patterns in order to portray the type which "the white world thinks is universal but also the special types of given districts and localities with their peculiar foibles of walk and speech and jargon" (164). Further, her interest in Williams's performances extends to understanding the way in which he made people laugh, as compared with the performances by Black comedians on the stage a few years later, during the era of the Broadway "colored" musicals. In the latter instance, she identifies an operating aesthetic that she names "purely subjective," as compared to Williams, where "the laughter which he created must be objective" (165). Partially, what Fauset characterizes here is the difference between laughing *at* and laughing *with*, the difference between an audience's objectification of or identification with a stage performer. In the later performances, for example, she describes the humor as radiating from the funny man himself: "The spector is infected with his high spirits and his excessive good will; a stream of well-being is projected across the footlights into the consciousness of the beholder" (165). Yet, her interest in Williams continues, and here she names not only his talent and professional success, but also his personal pain. She quotes W. C. Fields as saying that Williams was "the funniest man I ever saw and the saddest man I ever knew," and she characterizes Williams's sadness as the "sadness of hopeless frustration" where "the gift of laughter in his case had its source in a wounded heart and in bleeding sensibilities" (164–65). This characterization of Williams, written by Fauset for Alain Locke's anthology, perhaps allows a certain insight into the more personal feelings of Fauset herself. It also demonstrates to us that Williams's "objective" performances of race are of continued interest to Fauset and serve as examples to her of how to proceed with art even when quite conscious of being objectified through it.

In "The Gift of Laughter," Fauset characterizes the ideal she continues to work toward in her novels, an ideal embodied by Bert Williams on the stage: ever aware of the limits placed upon him, says Fauset, he portrayed his character in an objective rather than subjective role, which requires that his audience objectify his character so that they continue to feel distance from, as well as identification with the character he plays—and ultimately themselves. Williams, the apostle "of the 'legitimate' on the stage for Negroes," who with George Walker was "no matter how dimly" seeking "a method whereby the colored man might enter the 'legitimate,'" also recognized, about himself, "that his color would probably keep him from ever making the 'legitimate'" (163); and so, portraying his character as ever objectified by his audience is Williams's way, Fauset implies, of making his illegitimacy the point of the performance. In this focus on issues of Williams's illegitimacy, it is as if Fauset is working out her own relation to the issue. Her essay in Locke's anthology is legitimate; her subject position as the knowledgeable writer of this essay about drama, the diviner who can articulate what she sees as the Black man's gift to the American stage, is accepted rather than objectified by her African American peers. Her first novel, *There Is Confusion*, is not legitimate, however, at least insofar as she is treated by her male peers at the *Opportunity* dinner in ways that did not honor her accomplishment. As a writer of novels, then, she too is in the role of apostle for the "legitimate," in this case New Negro literature, but herself never quite legitimate, and as such, objectified and acutely aware of her objectification. Another way, then, to characterize Fauset's novels subsequent to *There Is Confusion* is in their working out, as Willams does in his performances, these same issues of objective versus subjective portrayals of characters within the texts, in relation to the interrogation of what constitutes legitimate and illegitimate American lives. In doing so, Fauset's way of articulating "what ought to remain concealed," as we will see, follows Williams's example of how to make illegitimacy the point of the matter, which does, in a queer way, also turn it legitimate.

"This Queer Intangible Bugaboo" Called Color:
There Is Confusion, Plum Bun, and *The Chinaberry Tree*

Toward the end of *There Is Confusion*, Peter names "color" as "this queer intangible bugaboo" that wreaks havoc in the lives of African Americans (284). This pronouncement also serves quite well as Fauset's own statement of the way in which she sees color, and its antecedent, whiteness, as she explores them in her subsequent fiction. In *Plum Bun*, as Cheryl Wall remarks, Fauset responds to her own neglect as a female artist, which the infamous Civic Club dinner made so clear. "What she [Fauset] was too polite to say in her remarks" at that dinner, says Wall, "she writes indirectly in her second novel, *Plum Bun*" (68). Focusing once again on a female artist in New York, Fauset revises *There Is Confusion*'s "happy" ending to more carefully represent her female character's home-life desires and gender constraints. But more significantly, while *There Is Confusion* ends with Peter Bye's simplistic ideas about his lack of responsibility and irresoluteness as coming from "that strain of white Bye blood" (297), *Plum Bun* challenges such ideas. For this reason, as Wall also remarks, the novel "mitigates against the concept of a unitary racial subject" (172), and argues against racial essentialism of any kind. *Plum Bun* ultimately suggests "that there are certain things in living that are more fundamental even than colour" (171), and through this sentiment Fauset begins to deconstruct the blood fetish that operates within the psyche of her own female characters as an overdetermined desire for "whiteness" in response to their fetishized positions as Black women in American society. Later in her career, through *The Chinaberry Tree* and *Comedy: American Style*, Fauset interrogates the idea of the protective, nurturing African American family, almost dismissing it completely, and probes the inner workings of family systems as they collude and collide with vectors of social power—race, class, and gender. By doing so in these latter two novels, she also presents specifically Black female responses to the color "bugaboo." *The Chinaberry Tree* revisits the ex-master/ex-slave dialectic, revising the miscegenation story of *There Is Confusion* by entangling it with the threat of incestuous love, while *Comedy: American Style*, Fauset's darkest novel by far, takes up the issue of passing once again, recasts the New Negro "changeling" as a color-struck African American mother, and rewrites the American family romance. Both *The Chinaberry Tree* and *Comedy: American Style*, by probing the psychology of secret knowing, expose the confluence of sexuality and race and thereby complicate the color "line" problem dimensionally, ultimately pointing toward a "poly"lectical, rather than dialectical, model for social power and self-consciousness.

There Is Confusion demonstrates Fauset's early interest in "New Negro" psychology, which for her also takes up the question of how a people can recreate themselves as self-reliant arbiters of their own destiny rather than powerless victims of racial oppression. Read in this way, the main character of the novel is Peter Bye, whom we first meet as a child but who grows up to become one of the fighting men who returns from "the double battle in France, one with Germany and one with white America," and so is feted by all of Harlem.[20] Unlike David Levering Lewis's history of the Harlem Renaissance, however, this moment does not open Fauset's story; instead, like Pauline Hopkins's *Contending Forces*, *There Is Confusion* specifically addresses what it means that a protagonist's ancestor was a slave and so focuses on the family and personal history that preceded Peter's decision to become a soldier. Peter Bye traces his lineage through his father, Meriwether, to *his* father, Isaiah, to *his* father, Joshua, who had been emancipated as a very small boy. According to Fauset's narrator, the legacy from slavery changes generationally: "[Peter] grew up with the feeling that he and his had been unusually badly treated. His grandfather's connection with white people resulted in pride, his father's in shiftlessness; in Peter it took the form of a constant and increasing bitterness" (34). Peter, it seems, although further removed from slavery than his grandfather, is nevertheless caught up in its reverberations. Later, Peter's difficulties are described by his friend Brian Spencer as part of "the complex of color" that "comes to every colored man and every colored woman, too, who has any ambition" (179). According to Brian, however, "Peter's got it worse than most of us because he's got such a terrible 'mad' on white people to start with" (179). This complex of color that Brian refers to is also the source of the "confusion" referenced in the title of Fauset's novel. Again according to Brian, "if a fellow sticks it out he finally gets past it [the complex], but not before it has worked considerable confusion in his life" (179).

The question posed in *There Is Confusion*, then, is how to be free of the confusion that racism brings to African American life, how to truly obtain and retain a "New Negro" psychology. For Peter, freedom manifests itself as psychological freedom from the white Byes. Peter obtains this freedom only at the very conclusion of the novel, after he learns from the white Meriwether Bye, a distant relative, that the white and Black Byes are related by blood as well as past economic entanglements, and thus he has the opportunity to repudiate that blood relation. In terms of secrets kept and told, however, the white Meriwether is not this secret's teller. In fact, even as he lets Peter in on Aaron Bye's relation to the enslaved Judy Bye, he also indicates his unwillingness to make this relation public. Meriwether simply confirms the truth of the secret relation between the white and Black Byes; it had been told, in writing, by Judy and her husband Ceazer many years before. The crucial aspect of Peter's psychological freedom is that its key is handed down to him through his family's generations. Through the white Meriwether, then, Peter simply learns how to interpret the written testimony that has been available to him all his life.

Symbolically, Peter's freedom depends on his recovery of the slave mother in his family, Judy Bye, in her relation to her master, so that once again this modern, African American man develops his own subjectivity through unearthing the master/female slave moment and its attendant colored consciousness. Not until Peter realizes Judy Bye's declaration that his family begins with her, rather than with her son, Joshua, is he able to begin changing the attitude he has inherited from the males in his family. Fauset puts further emphasis on this figure when, during old Meriwether Bye's visit, the white man tells Peter about this woman, "old Judy Bye, whom I've seen often sitting in Isaiah's house, her eyes straining, straining into the future—perhaps she saw this, who knows?" (295). But "this," the future that Judy saw, is one thing for old Meriwether Bye, yet quite another for Peter. Old Meriwether realizes that "whatever slavery may have done for other men it has thrown the lives of all the Byes into confusion" (296). For him, Judy, sitting mute in her grandson's house, represents just this state of confusion. For Peter, however, Judy is not mute. She becomes the determined writer of her name, the mother who insists, on paper, that her son Joshua is descended from both her and Aaron Bye. For Peter, then, surrounded by confusion, Judy represents the way through it.

With the end of *There Is Confusion*, Fauset suggests, as does James Weldon Johnson in *The Autobiography of an Ex-Coloured Man*, that love matters most.[21] As Joanna Marshall tells Peter, "Oh, if you've suffered half as much as I have, you've suffered horribly. I learned that nothing in the world is worth as much as love. For people like us, people who can and must suffer—*Love* is our refuge and strength" (283–84). By "people like us," Joanna means colored people, and here Fauset begins to interrogate the idea of what it means to be colored in ways that she will develop in her later novels. "Why, nothing in the world is so hard to face as this problem of being colored in America," Joanna says in a conversation with Peter (283). Being colored has driven two of their friends "away from everybody they've ever known, so that they can live in—in a sort of bitter peace"; has forced Peter to consider abandoning his "wonderful gift as a surgeon to drift into any kind of work"; and drives Joanna herself, whom "the critics call . . . a really great artist . . . to consider ordinary vaudeville" (283). In the descriptions of Joanna's career, in particular, we see that Fauset works with the language, and the concepts, that she initially began to explore in her essay "The Symbolism of Bert Williams" and which she continued to revise in "The Gift of Laughter," namely, this question of what it means to be objectified by an American public. Further, Fauset quite deliberately marks Joanna's dancing as objectified self-presentation, and she does so by characterizing it as "queer." In her earliest understanding of what she means to do with her life, after telling Peter that "colored people . . . can do everything that anybody else can do,"[22] Joanna says that her dancing will not be "ordinary dancing, you know, but queer beautiful things that are different from what we see around here" (45). As Joanna begins to explore what she means to do with dance, she declares that she is "going to do a dance representing all the nations, some day," and with this in mind, sits in Central

Park, and Morningside Park, and watches people. In language that brings to mind Bert Williams, she is characterized as "studying types" (100). When the very queer Miss Vera Sharples (with "her graying bobbed hair straggling a bit over her mannish tweed coat, her feet encased in solid tan boots" so that "only her eyes, looking straightforwardly and appraisingly from under the unbecoming hat, kept her from being dubbed a 'freak'"), who represents the board of directors of the District Line Theater, asks her to audition for their production titled "The Dance of the Nations," Joanna does so, and in such a way that queer and colored conjoin. Joanna brings the children's dance she has learned, originally performed "out in the middle of the street" by "a band of colored children . . . with no thought of spectators" (47), into the Greenwich Village auditioning space and before the group that includes Francis, at the piano, pale with long black hair that "ran in unbroken strands from his forehead to the top of his coat collar," so that he is "unlike any American the girl had ever seen" (228). As the show transforms, Joanna's role expands so that she not only dances the part of the Black American "element," but also the Indian and (white) "America" itself. Thus, with a mask on her face so that she is "made as typically American as anyone could wish," Joanna is introduced as "the new 'America'" in a show that becomes so successful with her in the leading role that it immediately moves to Broadway (232).[23]

Joanna's ability to represent America does not last, however, and while she feels somewhat comfortable in Greenwich Village settings, she also tastes "the depths of ennui" and has visions of "life as a ghastly skeleton" (233). Socializing with such privileged New Yorkers makes her aware of the limitations race has put on her life, makes her realize "for the first time how completely colored Americans were mere on-lookers at the possibilities of life" (235). As a consequence of this new understanding, she wants to *do* something, "be needed . . . be useful," work toward some "worthy visible end" (236). Dancing has brought her fame—she's recognized on the street as the "dancer,"—but this fame, she realizes when she sees a fan in "Russian boots and a hat with three feathers sticking up straight, Indian fashion (274), is "an empty thing," not much different, as Jane Kuenz remarks, from the fame of a minstrel act, and something easily reproduced by anyone who visits the local department store (Kuenz 103). In the language of Fauset's drama criticism, in other words, Joanna understands the ways in which her career as a dancer traps her in an objectified "*rôle*" without providing her access to agency. Further, even this intrinsically limited "*rôle*," the best that her performance career offers, cannot last: after a brief tour in three northern cities, it ends. "Southern newspapers had started to editorialize against her," her manager says. "'A negress,' a Georgia newspaper had said, 'in the rôle of America. Shameful!'" (275). She is offered "a high-class vaudeville house" and a continuing career if they take the show "cross the pond" to Europe. In this context, then, with only an unsatisfactory career as a performer for her future, Joanna Marshall leaves the stage, marries Peter Bye, and becomes a devoted wife and mother.[24] As such, her baby boy then becomes the new American, representative of both white and Black, in a moment we might read as another moment of uplift, another presentation of a "Young Colored American" like Pauline Hopkins's.[25] Consequently, as with her earlier short story "The Sleeper Wakes," Fauset once again presents her protagonist's return to the colored family as a solution to her objectification, her fetishization, within larger American circles.

In *There Is Confusion*, the social justice worker, Joanna's brother Philip, says on his death bed that the great mistake of his early life was that he did not "look out for life first, then color and limitations" (287). *Plum Bun* continues this sentiment through Mattie Murray, Angela's mother, whose dictum is "Life is more important than colour" (266).[26] We might say that a perverted sense of this idea moves the young Angela Murray, but the real sense of her mother's words finally influences the more mature Angela. Eventually she reaches a position with regard to race that seems comfortable to her. "So far as sides are concerned," she declares, she is on the "coloured side," that is, her consciousness is colored, but she also knows that at times she will pass for white in spite of herself (373). By the end of the novel, Angela is no longer color struck; instead, she is simply intending to live her life as best she can. Her desire for "whiteness," the blood fetish, recognized for what it is, has for her given way to a larger sense of desire for life and living. A crucial moment in her transformation makes this point clearly. At her lowest point, when she contemplates suicide, Angela begins to think of "black people, of the race of her parents and of all the odds against living which a cruel, relentless fate had called on them to endure" (309). Yet she begins to see her people "as a people powerfully, almost overwhelmingly endowed with the essence of life. They had to persist, had to survive because they did not know how to die" (309). This sense of life is soon personified by a woman Angela meets in the beauty shop, a woman who is about to return to Ku Klux Klan territory in Texas. This Black woman is described as "frail . . . daintily dressed and shod." Further, she is soft-spoken and Southern. "But Angela saw her sharply as the epitome of the iron and blood in a race which did not know how to let go of life" (328). Here, blood transforms its fetishistic qualities to become synonymous with life itself. While, then, her mother's dictum has been that "life is more important than colour," Angela comes to know that color means life.

While *Plum Bun* seems to provide some answers to America's racial conundrum, it is important to consider Deborah McDowell's point that to read the novel simply as a novel of racial passing "is to miss its complex treatment of the intricacies of gender oppression, as well as the irony and subtlety of its artistic technique" (xv). Unlike James Weldon Johnson's *The Autobiography of an Ex-Coloured Man*, where the protagonist lives a life of racial secrets, yet through the narrative structure of the text tells those secrets, Fauset's *Plum Bun* presents Angela Murray as a character who ultimately tells racial secrets as her way of life, yet textually, and structurally, the narrative itself conceals rather than yields. Our narrator tells us, after Angela has more or less settled her racial identity, that while at one time Angela "thought that stolen waters were sweetest . . . now it was the unwinding road and the open book that most intrigued" (324). When we examine *this* open book, however, we find that the main title and section titles of the novel make reference to the novel's nursery rhyme epigraph:

> "To Market, to Market
> To buy a Plum Bun;
> Home again, Home again,
> Market is done."

This structuring of the text, together with the subtitle, "A Novel Without a Moral," suggests the necessity of turning from metonymy to metaphor in *Plum Bun*.[27] When we do so, we see, as Jacquelyn McLendon remarks, that "the metaphorical coding of the narrative, through use of the fairy-tale motif and the nursery rhyme that structures the novel, is the means by which Fauset attempts to dismantle hegemonic constructs of color, race, class, and gender" (29). However, as McLendon also concludes, "the problems Fauset foregrounds throughout the book are unsolved at the end. . . . Indeed, the novel itself resists closure, disrupting accepted discursive practice to allow the simultaneous expression of 'black' textuality and an emerging black woman's voice" (49). In some ways a revision of the "happy" ending of *There Is Confusion*, where the ongoing development of the female protagonist is sacrificed for the development of the male, *Plum Bun* does not end in marriage, and the lovers Angela and Anthony are not even in the United States at the close of the novel. All we really know, as readers, from the structural apparatus of the novel rather than from the story line, is that the concluding section of the novel represents

"Market Is Done," presumably meaning that Angela's interest in marriage as commodity is over. This does not mean, however, that Fauset is willing to put forth simplistic ideas of love and family as answers for Black female life. Indeed, her continued interrogation of the blood fetish, as we will see in her novel *The Chinaberry Tree*, implicates both Black heterosexual relationships and Black families as problematic constructions for Black women.

Jessie Fauset's "Double Trouble," published in *The Crisis* in 1923, is her earlier rendition of the story presented as *The Chinaberry Tree*, and like the novel introduces us to two female cousins who both have difficulties establishing social roles for themselves in the small New Jersey town where they live. While the short story is sketchy, and its characters emblematic rather than developed, Fauset establishes the theme she continues into the novel: that the townspeople interpret both young women as having "bad blood" because of the sexual liaisons of their mothers, and that these townspeople consequently believe that such liaisons by the mothers mean that these daughters cannot "be good" and so should be shunned (38–39). In the short story, the very beautiful and bitter Laurentine presents the townspeople's blood fetish as something that determines her and her cousin's fate. The story ends as Laurentine's pitiful cousin, here named Angélique, tries to evade her fate by promising, hysterically, to "be good" yet ironically falling into the arms of Aunt Sal, who has been a white man's mistress and is presumably the source of some of Angélique's trouble, yet nevertheless still imploring Aunt Sal, as the story ends, to help and protect her. In "Double Trouble," Angélique's favorite boyfriend is Malory, whom she also ultimately discovers is her half-brother. This theme of incest is developed in *The Chinaberry Tree* in ways that it is not in "Double Trouble," however, so that in the novel the incest taboo becomes the lens through which Fauset revises modern understanding of the miscegenation taboo and the legacy of master/female slave relationships. As a consequence, Fauset's young female characters in *The Chinaberry Tree*, Laurentine and Melissa, unlike her characters in "Double Trouble," begin to have access to a self-consciousness that takes into account their societal role as fetishized objects, yet manage also to find "breathing-spells, in-between spaces where colored men and women work and love and go their ways with no thought of the 'problem'" (*Chinaberry Tree* xxxi). By exploring and breaking sexual taboos, *The Chinaberry Tree* succeeds in redefining normative female desire to include cross-racial liaisons, thereby presenting a revised version of the legacy daughters receive from colored mothers.

In her foreword to *The Chinaberry Tree*, Fauset declares her intention to present her characters within their "homelife" environment, which she characterizes as that place of "breathing-spells, in-between spaces" where inter-racial prejudice is not the main source of drama. In this way her characters live according to the dictum from *Plum Bun* that "life is more important than colour," or at least attempt to do so. The novel opens with the sentence, "Aunt Sal, Laurentine, and even Melissa loved the house," and continues to describe the way their house looks in color and style, including its grounds and landscaping, in order to introduce the focal point of the home and the primary image of this family's homelife, which is its chinaberry tree. This tree is a gift from Colonel Halloway, who years ago "fetched it from Alabama," where both he and Aunt Sal are from, as part of establishing Aunt Sal in this residence (1). The tree itself, a popular ornamental sometimes referred to as an umbrella tree because of its umbrella-like foliage, becomes the favorite place for the three main characters of this novel, Aunt Sal, Laurentine, and Melissa, but for different reasons.[28] For Aunt Sal the tree represents the past, and becomes the place where she can best remember Halloway and their passionate love for one another (2, 339–40). For Laurentine, however, daughter of this union, the tree "casts its shadow" but represents the future, "other people, other places" she thinks at one point, while the narrator tells us that for her the "Chinaberry Tree and the future were intextricably blended" (2, 9). For Melissa, daughter of Aunt Sal's sister Judy, who comes to live with Sal and Laurentine because she has no other place to go, the chinaberry tree that catches her eye immediately upon her arrival represents "the happy, happy present": "Here she would stay, here in this house, in the shade of this Tree she must and would live" (27, 16). At the novel's conclusion, the characters are finally so much at peace that the chinaberry tree, as final image, represents "the immanence of God" and is "a Temple" (341).

In order to understand Fauset's chinaberry tree image, it is important to understand her use of the incest taboo as a way to recharacterize the miscege-nation taboo. The "white house and the beautiful grounds and the Chinaberry Tree" continue to bring Aunt Sal and Laurentine to the attention of the town. According to the narrator, "the affair was the town's one and great scandal. It condemned it and was proud of it. It could not take too open a stand against the Halloways for the family for generations had afforded the township its existence. But it never forgot it" (2). At a later point in the novel, the narrator is even more precise in the ways that the town responds to Laurentine and her mother:

> Gradually, like the old definition of a simile, the case of Sal Strange and her daughter, Laurentine, became confused, the sign was accepted for the

thing signified and a coldness and despite toward this unfortunate mother and child became a fetish without any real feeling or indignation on the part of the executioners for the offenses committed. Neglect of the two women became crystallized. On the other hand a reversion though still extant and occasionally revived was beginning to be something quite apart and remote from the Mrs. Strange and her daughter whom colored Red Brook observed occasionally at church or community entertainment. (22)

Fauset carefully dissects this fetishized treatment of Laurentine and her mother through conversation between Melissa and the noble Asshur, the young man who represents Melissa's future at the conclusion of the novel. When Melissa attempts to cast aspersions on the relationship between her aunt and Halloway, Asshur responds, very carefully, by suggesting, first, that the Colonel's "whiteness has nothing to do with" why the relationship should be understood as wrong, and might be "a sort of redeeming feature" (71). What Asshur attempts to understand while "wrestling with a big problem" is that because Melissa's aunt was born in the South, in Mississippi, "a state where to this day all possible stress is laid on a white skin" and "lots of colored people made a fetish of it, and of course all white people did"; because, in other words, of the legacy of slavery, here really the legacy of white superiority, society characterizes this interracial relationship as the horror it labels miscegenation, but for Asshur the very concept of miscegenation itself begins to seem ignorant and immoral.[29] For him, the relationship between Melissa's Aunt Sal and Halloway represents an extraordinary love story that deserves respect.

Through these passages we also see that Fauset works with the concept of fetish in this novel as a way to represent, and criticize, the very idea of racial essentialism. Sarah Strange, most often referred to as Aunt Sal, and her daughter Laurentine are, in Fauset's terms, fetishized by the Red Brook, New Jersey, townspeople because of the legacy from the past, and particularly from the South, of fetishized whiteness, that is, whiteness essentialized into a materiality. This whiteness fetish, also a "blood fetish," carries and sustains the ideology of racial superiority. Significantly, because whiteness is defined by what it is not (not "one drop" of Black blood), it also already carries within it an enforced sexual prohibition. White women, of course, become the "safeguards" of whiteness through their "purity"; white men, who have by their own admission "put a lot of 'white blood into black veins,'" live by the admonition to keep such relationships secret, or at least illegitimate.[30] In this context, women of color like Sarah Strange, so obviously involved in an interracial relationship, and living with her child who is the proof of interracial heterosexuality, also become fetishized, in the Freudian sense, because of the interracial sexuality that they symbolize. As with other acts of fetishization, we might see this instance as also bringing with it a disavowal; and here, the townspeople attempt to disavow the very existence of Laurentine, or at least to disavow any relation she herself has to "whiteness." Consequently, and particularly because there is no recognition of partial whiteness (whiteness is either "pure" or it is not whiteness), Laurentine is labeled not as having "white" blood but as having "bad blood," and her "bad blood," a way to sexualize her, brings with it her fetishized treatment by the townspeople.[31]

After Sarah's sister Judy comes to town, stays for a short time, and then quickly departs, Laurentine feels the acceptance she has just begun to experience from her peers end, and "the feeling which she somehow guessed the town had possessed for that unusual union of her father and mother, recrudesced, shot up and spattered over her anew like the lava from a miniature Vesuvius" (7). A child who had been a new friend is no longer allowed to play with her because, as the child says, "Mumma say I dasn't. She say you got bad blood in your veins" (8). In order to point to the blood fetish's lack of materiality, the child, Lucy, who would really like to still play with Laurentine, grabs a knife from her tea party setting and asks Laurentine, "Don't you want me to cut yo' arm and let it out?" (8). By naming Sarah and her daughter Laurentine with the patronym "Strange," Fauset draws even more attention to the blood fetish that the town fixes upon them, because their bad blood is also "Strange blood," which on the one hand simply names them familially, but on the other hand is also a euphemism for "queer" and another way to signify the mother and daughter as something that "ought to remain concealed" according to the townspeople (25). Because of the way she is treated by the townspeople, this queerness is an identity that Laurentine internalizes during her childhood; and when Judy's daughter Melissa comes to live in Red Brook, Laurentine's queerness is something that Melissa, too, discerns, but at a careful distance from herself, because, as she explains to the Reverend Simmons's wife, her mother was not Judy Strange, but Judy Paul, who left Red Brook and married John Paul, Melissa's father (25). Rather than question or reject the fetishized treatment of Sarah and Laurentine Strange, Melissa accepts it, and while she joins their household she also maintains her identity as something other than what they are. In her diary, for example, which Laurentine inadvertently discovers and then reads, she compares "her own unstained, unimpeachable integrity" with her aunt's and Laurentine's "ancient shame" (128).

Melissa does not understand the ways of the blood fetish, however. She believes that Laurentine is marked by her illegitimacy, by the fact that her mother and Colonel Halloway were never married, and she compares herself, or what she believes about her own birthright, to Laurentine's situation. What Melissa does not understand is how she, too, is being fetishized by the local boys other than Asshur. Harry Robbins, who wants her "with a devastating desire that balked and wasted him" (47), has attempted to tell Asshur the town's common thinking: "'Her aunt was a slut if ever there was one and everybody in Red Brook says that her mother—,'" but is cut off by Asshur's fist. Nevertheless, in spite of Asshur's intervention, as Melissa realizes, the town begins to shun her, too. Her own complicity, however, not so much in the fetishization of Aunt Sal and Laurentine, but in wrongfully judging them, means that she misses the crucial aspect of her newfound ostracism: that it is based not just on the relationship Sal has had with Halloway, but also on her own mother's behavior while she lived for a short while in Red Brook. Melissa's unwillingness to look more carefully at her mother's behavior, which springs from her need to self-righteously compare herself with Laurentine and give herself a "legitimate" identity, almost brings her, in the novel's terms, to complete ruin.

Because Melissa does not know her mother's past, or her own patrimony, she begins to date her half-brother, Malory Forten, and with this plot turn Fauset explores the incestuous relationship between a brother and sister fathered by the same man, Sylvester Forten. The relationship between Malory and Melissa, kept secret by the two because Laurentine will not permit Melissa to have male company, and because some of the townspeople seem to act so oddly toward them as a couple, becomes queerly telling in its similarity to that other, earlier prohibited relationship between Melissa's Aunt Sal and Colonel Halloway. Particularly after Melissa and Malory begin to play with the real passion they feel toward one another ("It was great fun, both Melissa and Malory thought, to play such indifference before others and yet to be so tinglingly aware, he of her, she of him" [239]) and make plans to elope (270–73), the reader also gets the distinct sense, in a derivative fashion, of the details of living that must also have been part of Sal and Halloway's "secret" relationship. And yet the passion of this incestuous relationship springs, in some ways, from a source that is presented as distinctly different from the passion between Sal and Halloway. After having their own secret Christmas dinner at the Greek tavern at Pompton Lakes, Melissa voices "some indefinable doubt" about her relationship with Malory but concludes, "It must be all right Malory for us to love each other and to get married—we feel so good about it" (216–17). Malory responds by telling Melissa that she is "just the girl" for him and when she asks how he can know that, he replies: "Because you are me—I'm you. I recognized you the moment I met you. You're the other part of me—like—like a shell and what it contains. I had in me all these dark, vacant spaces, and you had the gifts with which to fill them—light, richness, life itself,—why Melissa, if I were to lose you now, I guess I'd die" (217). Here, Fauset is presenting the idea of an incestuous relationship as one of sameness, in contrast to "miscegenation," always thought of as a relationship of extreme difference.

To some extent, Malory is simply expressing the "Greek" definition of erotic love as found in Aristophanes' speech about love in Plato's *Symposium* (189c-193e), where *eros* is a desire for the lost "other half," springing from a time before humans were cut in half because of the ways in which they threatened the gods. Nevertheless, there is also the clear implication that sameness, or "oneness," can become extreme.[32] Unknown to Malory but obvious to readers is the way that the darkness in his life is answered, quite literally, by Melissa: Malory's family life changes, becomes irrevocably dark, depressed, traumatized, because Malory's father has an affair with Melissa's mother, Judy, and then returns home and dies. This knowledge is kept from the young Malory, and, consequently, this family's secret turns him into this shell with vacant spaces, as he characterizes himself, while Melissa's existence, as his sister rather than his lover, as the family secret made flesh, speaks to the void stemming from these events in his young life. In the moment of confrontation on Romany Road, when he turns to Melissa with the information that she is his sister, his face has become the Greek mask of Comedy that has been plaguing Melissa in her dreams, "the face . . . terrible! . . . his mouth set in that unspeakably awful rictus," (330) and in the end he leaves Melissa "lying stricken in the black, black abyss into which she had fallen" (331).[33]

Fauset assumes her readers' own belief in the incest taboo and never seeks to explain why and how the relationship between Malory and Melissa is wrong. More than once, however, there is the implication that this incestuous relationship is an affront to God. Malory himself exclaims, "Oh God, how could You do it? You knew I loved her . . . You knew I wanted her . . . and she's my sister!" (331). When Mr. Stede discovers that the two are secretly meeting, "at night,—at her home—under that Chinaberry Tree" (296), he shows "faded eyes at last scared and miserable": "'God!' he whispered. . . . 'God, You know, they hadn't oughta do that'" (296). Gertrude Brown's sister, Kitty, has a similar reaction when she hears the story:

> "Oh God!" Kitty said again and again as Gertrude . . . told her what she had learned. "Oh God!" she murmured, hiding her face, as though in pain, in the pillow. "But Gertrude, Gertrude how could He, how could He permit it?"

"Who?" asked Gertrude in some natural bewilderment.

"God. . . ." She lifted her pallid face, ravaged with tears. "Gertrude, that poor girl! . . . You know for the first time I'm really afraid . . . I'm afraid of life, Gertrude . . . I think I'll sleep with you to-night . . . I'm scared." (301)

Stephen Denleigh, too, who plays a role in trying to stop Melissa and Malory from eloping, understands that "he had really been badly frightened. He mused: 'There actually is such a thing as Greek Tragedy even in these days. . . . We were almost swamped with it'" (340). All of these responses suggest the Oedipal influences at work here. Breaking the incest taboo transforms everyday life into something so supernaturally horrific and awful that members of the community feel themselves almost to have been forsaken by God, almost to have been left utterly bereft and alone, which points to the psychological power of blood and blood relations, and to the power, as well, of the prohibition not to beget too close to one's own source of life. This also suggests an inverse prohibition, significant in a novel so focused on recasting an interracial love affair in language other than prohibited miscegenation: avoid *overrating* blood relations—for example, claims of same-race identity in marriage partnering.[34]

The point made very clear, in contrast to the potential relationship between Malory and Melissa, is that the interracial relationship between Sal Strange and Colonel Halloway is not offensive to God. As we have previously noted, Asshur understands this relationship as an extraordinary example of love. Denleigh, too, the man in love with Laurentine, says, "I deliberately found out all I could about your mother and Colonel Halloway and from all I hear the two of them must have loved each other devotedly" (122). While this does not quite convince Laurentine that she should give up her own notion that she has "bad blood," Denleigh later continues his conversation with Laurentine about her parents, "trying hard to exorcise her ghost" (160). "This was a true love match," he tells Laurentine. Dismissing the idea of her "bad blood," he continues: "As I see it, the two of them were defying, not the laws of God, nor the laws of man speaking universally. Simply the laws of a certain section of America" (160). And here, the narrator indicates, Laurentine is beginning to be persuaded to reject the blood fetish that she has come to internalize: "The old familiar burden was loosening; someday it would disappear" (161). Through Asshur and Denleigh, the men who love them, then, Melissa and Laurentine come to a new understanding of themselves. Aunt Sal sees both of them as finally "safe," and in response she feels free, herself, "to think of her dead lover . . . with ease and gratefulness and the complete acceptance which always made their lack of conformity of absolutely no moment" (339–40). She thinks, in other words, how their lives were characterized by "happiness, terrible, devastating happiness. 'Happiness like fiah [fire],' she had told herself more than once," and here the force of the sexual desire each felt for the other begins to come into focus (168).

While Aunt Sal thinks of her daughter and niece as safe, the cousins, according to the narrator, are "sensing with all their being, the feel of the solid ground beneath their feet, the grateful monotony of the skies above their heads" (341). They are "rather like spent swimmers" who suddenly meet with rescue after giving up all hope of it, as the narrator describes, and so, in image, we picture women who, unlike Kate Chopin's character Edna Pontellier, know desire, know "fiah," but do not drown (341).[35] Instead, everyone in this story is queerly happy, and the fairy-tale ending conceals the near-tragedy that has almost wrecked them all. In the last moments of the novel, as the cousins are "sensing with all their being," they glimpse a kind of wholeness, a oneness with life that precludes objectification. There are no fetishes here, and no transcendent signifiers. Instead, these modern Black women feel "everywhere about them the immanence of God," and this internalized and immanent, rather than transcendent, God portends an acceptance of self expressed in later Black feminist literature: "i found god in myself / & i loved her / i loved her fiercely" (Shange 63). The way of knowing represented by this immanence turns the chinaberry tree into "a Temple," so that it symbolizes those ordinary "breathing-spells, in-between spaces where colored men and women work and love, "and at the same time represents the extraordinariness of such ordinary colored life.

Fauset's Last Laugh: *Comedy: American Style*

In her introduction to the 1995 reprint of *Comedy: American Style*, Thadious Davis reminds us that "Fauset had quite strong convictions about what she was doing in her narratives and about how to read her fiction" (xxxii). In response to Alain Locke's criticism of *Comedy: American Style*, Fauset is particularly careful to cite his misreading of the text. In a letter to Locke she states: "I wasn't telling the story of 'one dark child in a family' etc. If I had been even I, poor mid-Victorian, sentimental, perservering [*sic*] Miss Fauset would have told the story from a different angle. I was telling the story of a woman who was obsessed with the desire for whiteness" (xxxii). Locke's misreading of this text, as Fauset implies, again reflects his gender bias and the quite masculinist assumptions associated with New Negro psychology that so specifically write colored mothers out of the sphere of influence. Ironically, however, Fauset's novel *Comedy: American Style*, more than any other except *There Is Confusion*, works specifically with the Lockean conceptualization of New Negro psychology, and particularly the idea of the New Negro as "changeling." However, the focus for Fauset's experiment here is the mother Olivia rather than the son Oliver, a regendering of the changeling that Locke seems to have entirely missed. By presenting this changeling, Fauset seems also to be positing the likely scenario if Locke's bias is carried to extreme and colored mothers really do renounce their identities as such. It seems clear that Fauset has very purposefully created a female "changeling" whose psychology really cannot be explained by anyone, including her parents. Fauset allows this character to grow up, marry, and become a mother, and then presents a new family drama with this mother at its center, allowing this mother to bring with her all of her psychological difficulties stemming from the ways in which she wants whiteness as *her* fetish. By setting up such a story, Fauset's novel quite clearly serves at least two purposes: it emphasizes the ways in which the changeling psychology, as a psychology for women, creates a pathology that causes incredible, yet recognizably familiar, dysfunction in individuals and their families; and it points to the extreme importance, for Fauset, of mothers in the formation of individual identity. Clearly not a comedy in any typical sense of the genre, Fauset here seems determined to show how few choices African American women have as they face the "othering" of them that American society perpetuates.

In "The New Negro," as we have previously noted, Locke declares that "the three norns who have traditionally presided over the Negro problem," that is, the Sociologist, the Philanthropist, and the Race Leader, "have a change-ling in their laps" that "simply cannot be swathed in their formulae" (3). By characterizing the New Negro as a changeling, by cutting him off from his parentage, in other words, Locke implicitly suggests an individualistic psychol-ogy at work and, at the same time, brings forward the question of what, in its infancy, this creature has changed from and into. While Locke claims, in his essay, a kind of new race pride as part of the new psychology he delineates, he also claims that this New Negro is very American and, by implication, a changeling infant in the all-American (and consequently, white) family. Here, then, we might make the connection to Freud's idea of the family romance, where a child fantasizes for him or herself a different set of parents, and par-ticularly a different father, believing him or herself to be either adopted or a stepchild.[36] In Fauset's *Comedy: American Style*, it is the female character, Olivia, who has just this fantasy. When she is called a "nigger" by another child, she returns home to her father, who is ill with pneumonia, and whom she sees, in his bronze-brown complexion, as the cause of her own coloring. According to the narrator: "Olivia almost hated them both [her parents] with a flaring intensity no less violent for the immaturity of the heart which engendered it. How could they—how *could* they have made her colored?" (4). This idea of the child's, which implies her feeling of being in the wrong family, has already been noticed by her parents, who have decided that she is "a changeling," named her as such, and "thereafter to themselves they frequently [refer] to her as 'C'" (8). In *Comedy: American Style*, then, Fauset presents us with a problem story that considers what happens when the "New Negro" changeling is female and color struck, an African American so influenced by the American way that she renounces her heritage in an attempt to convert to, rather than simply pass as, white. As we consider Olivia's attempts to become her fetish, so to speak, and we witness her thorough embrace of white identity, we also begin to comprehend just how null and void this whiteness is which she so desires to embrace.

In form, *Comedy: American Style* is experimental and, as Jacquelyn McLendon remarks, its sections are named as the divisions of a drama; first there is "The Plot," then "The Characters," then "Teresa's Act," "Oliver's Act," and "Phebe's Act." Finally, there is the section titled "Curtain." In the three chapters that comprise "The Plot," Olivia's color obsession becomes fixed and she realizes that she can pass for white and wants to do so as often as possible. Her mother has impressed upon her the importance of class, however, and she also understands that "it was highly unlikely that she would meet and marry a white man" whose social class was as high as the African American college students who board with her mother in Cambridge (28). When her mother remarries a man who is as light-skinned as she is, and they have very light twin babies with "thick dark hair and blue eyes," Olivia realizes that she, too, can marry a light-skinned African American man and have "white children" who might then redefine her as white herself (29). By the end of "The Plot," Olivia has married the fair Christopher Cary, a medical student at Harvard, "forerunner of the modern young colored man" in his individualism (25), and who was taught by his own "staunch 'old Philadelphian'" mother to value passionless, sexually ignorant women with light skin (26–27). Thus, this marriage and Olivia's desire for "white children" set the stage for the novel by characterizing what we might retrospectively call the Cary family "curse," if we are thinking in terms of *The Chinaberry Tree* and Greek drama; or, if we are paying attention to Fauset's use of double entendre, we realize that by the end of "The Plot," we are also aware of the specifics of Olivia's "plotting" to be white. The remainder of the novel then unfolds as spectacle rooted in both the "The Plot" and the "plotting."

Before we witness the succeeding dramas, however, we are treated to the second section of the novel, "The Characters." Here we meet Olivia and Christopher Cary and their children, as well as select and significant friends of their children. Here we also begin to clearly see that *Comedy: American Style* is not a novel about Olivia Cary, but rather a novel about Olivia Cary's children and the effects she has on them and on their development. The three "Acts" that follow focus on each of Olivia's children, except that the last "Act" is named for the woman Olivia's oldest son, Christopher, marries, rather than for Christopher himself, and so also presents an alternative to Olivia's choices and obsessions. As we consider the material that Fauset presents in "The Characters," however, we also realize that she is once again employing double entendre and introducing us to the main characters of the drama that follows, but she is also here presenting to us a sense of the character of the characters, the disposition or type of person each of her main figures is destined to become. Thus, Olivia's oldest child, Teresa, with her white skin and "thick, 'good' dark hair," demonstrates herself to be almost completely overwhelmed by her mother's color prejudices, but her two friends, Marise, with "dark brown skin," and Phebe, "a very fair blonde with dark blue eyes," yet also "colored too," are not (37, 33). Phebe, we should note, figures into the later drama with her own "Act" because she becomes Christopher's wife but also because she is so light as to appear white and yet unwilling to renounce her colored identity.

Olivia's second child, her son Christopher, with very fair skin and "features finer and better chiselled" than his sister's, is much more influenced by his father's sensible attitudes about race than by his mother's, and determines, despite his mother's desire, that he will not "become white." "I'm perfectly satisfied the way I am," he tells his father, and with this statement also conveys something fundamental about who he is (53). The third child of the family, Oliver, whom Olivia names after herself before he is born, she determines will "be her very own" so that "in appearance, in rearing, in beliefs he should be completely, unrelievedly a member of the dominant race" (40). According to the narrator, Oliver is "handsomer and more attractive than the other children," but, as Olivia discovers a full month after his birth he is also "the exact bronze gold complexion of Lee Blanchard," Olivia's father. Thus, Olivia rejects Oliver in ways that he senses "even from babyhood" when he feels the "one lack which early automatically destroyed any root of undue self-esteem. He knew that he did not have his mother's love" (42). This lack, as we discover later, is not something from which he ever recovers. By the end of "The Characters," then, we have not only met our main protagonists, but have also been apprised of their "character," their psychological makeup and their type.

The three "Acts" that then follow "The Plot" and "The Characters" give us the major storyline development of this novel, and here Fauset carefully demonstrates the consequences when an African American woman who fully believes in white racial superiority acts upon those beliefs and determines to become white through her children's white connections. Olivia's daughter Teresa, who is not really interested in passing for white, does so to please her mother when she leaves home to attend an exclusive boarding school. She finally manages to convey to another African American student that she is passing, visits that student's family and meets a handsome, dark-skinned young man, falls in love, and plans to secretly marry. She forsakes this young man when her mother discovers the relationship, however. Pushed, finally, to either directly oppose her mother or not, Teresa finds herself asking her young man if he couldn't use his Spanish and "pass for a Mexican" (143). Teresa never really recovers from losing this relationship. In an attempt to regain her health, she and her mother travel to France where Teresa attends classes at a university in Toulouse, meets a small-minded professor interested in the American girl's money, and marries him. This marriage, of course, is just what her mother had hoped would happen so that she might say, "My son-in-law; he is a professor at the University of Toulouse" (177), and thereby live among and as a white person herself ("all of these people would be white . . . she would be white"[177]). At the end of "Teresa's Act" her life is almost as hopeless as Helga Crane's at the end of Nella Larsen's *Quicksand:* Teresa "thought back over her life. . . . She dwelt in some wonder on her mother's ambitions. Was this all it was to bring to her, life in this little southern town . . .? Absurd but true. Gradually her expectation of a change died away and she settled down into an existence that was colorless, bleak and futile" (183). Teresa's life is effectively over.

As bleak as the end of "Teresa's Act" is, "Oliver's Act" is much more so. Oliver himself is gorgeous and talented, a very handsome, sensitive young man with artistic aptitude and musical genius. His undoing, however, is his "great need to bestow and to receive love" and his "strong instinct for family life" (189). For these reasons, he cannot understand his mother's coldness toward him, and he cares about her affections deeply. Those "chilly spaces, those blank moments when his mother's indifference, her almost obvious dislike, cast their shadows about him" (199) create an anguish in him "that no tears could wash away" (201). He is not always unhappy in his life, but the absence of his mother's love creates an emotional disturbance that runs deep. He is not aware of the cause of his mother's treatment of him, however, until he happens to read a letter from her to his father, where she mentions "Oliver and his unfortunate color" (221). The narrator describes his reaction to this characterization of him: "Across his shadowed eyes the kaleidoscope of his life flashed. . . . He remembered vague words, broken whispers, suppressed phrases, which now he translated into pity. . . . He could see and understand it now—all so plainly" (221). When his sister, too, writes him to say that her husband is prejudiced about color, does not know that she, herself, is colored, and that Oliver with his "tell-tale color" therefore cannot visit, the shame he has kept at bay overtakes him and combines with a complete loss of faith "in all that was good in the world" (225). He takes out "the pistol with which he had done his target practice" (226). His brother Christopher hears the shot, and finds him "lying there, the light of the declining day athwart his smiling face" (226).

"Phebe's Act" completes the narratives of the lives of Olivia's children by telling us about Christopher's life as it connects with that of his childhood friend, Phebe Grant, whom he marries. "Phebe's Act" also most obviously conveys the double entendre contained within each of these sections that Fauset titles "Acts." Phebe, the child of a white father who left her colored mother, is a woman who knows real poverty in her young life, becomes a successful businesswoman as a young adult, and thinks herself engaged to another childhood friend, Nicholas Campbell, because he has given his attention to her throughout their young lives. She is ultimately rejected by him, however, because he loves another, but also because her light skin causes confusion and creates situations where people think that he is a Black man dating a white woman. Phebe also dates a very wealthy white man, Llewellyn Nash, without telling him of her color. When he proposes marriage, she takes responsibility for the way she has been playing with him, warns him that she is about to make him forget he ever loved her, then tells him that she is "a colored woman," "probably the whitest colored girl . . . you every saw" (286). Only after these events in Phebe's life does Christopher Cary call on her and ask her to marry him. He loves her, but he also needs help in "his life's work," which is to try to restore his father, who is "a broken man since Oliver's death" (298). When Christopher realizes that his father has lost absolutely everything, the "house on Eleventh Street . . . his insurance . . . his holdings, his investments" (300), he thinks he must release Phebe from their engagement because of his extreme poverty and family obligations, but Phebe, with a house and plenty of money herself, offers all she has. After Phebe and Christopher marry, and Phebe and her mother and Christopher and his parents all move in to Phebe's house together, the household scene becomes too much for her, particularly because Olivia continuously insults Phebe's mother and makes life wretched for everyone. Phebe leaves for New York, intending to have an affair with her former love, Nicholas, who now tells her that he has always loved her, in spite of his marrying someone else. She stands before the house where Nicholas is waiting on the sixth floor. She thinks about her husband, Christopher, who has said that he will always love her "with loyalty," and then she turns away and walks "as fast as her feet could carry her down the dingy uninviting thoroughfare," leaving Nicholas waiting (311). Phebe's act, the double entendre of this section, is this turning and leaving Nicholas waiting, of remaining true to Christopher and returning to him with love, "still a decent, faithful wife" (315).

The major actions of the three "Acts" of this drama, then, are Teresa's renunciation of her brown-skinned love, Oliver's suicide, and Phebe's return to Christopher. Teresa's and Oliver's acts are clearly influenced by their mother's belief in white racial superiority. They are a direct consequence of the family dynamic created when color prejudice becomes embedded in the family structure. Phebe's act, however, is more complex. On one hand Phebe is the alternative to Olivia, both in influence and in racial philosophy, as she is clearly transforming the Cary family and yet does so as a colored woman, the identity within which she lives her life. Before her "Act," the novel seems verging toward tragedy rather than comedy; that is, quite clearly the endings of "Teresa's Act" and "Oliver's Act" are in no way happy. Because "Phebe's Act" not only follows these two previous acts, however, but also continues the Cary family story past Oliver's suicide, it also asks us to examine more closely the question of happy endings and what makes them so. When we do, we recognize the conundrum now familiar to us through our reading of *Plum Bun*. Phebe's "act," deciding not to engage in an extramarital affair, drops us back into the difficulties that the confluence of race and gender brings to modern Black women. If "Phebe's Act" brings us the happy ending, then this novel is affirmation of conventional values. By choosing to remain faithful to her husband, Phebe may well have made the choice that will ensure that the newly reformed and fragile family will thrive. The cost to Phebe of this family's future, however, brings this reading into question. During a moment when Phebe is trying to understand herself before Christopher again enters her world, she recites the Mother

Goose nursery rhyme, "'Riddle me, riddle me, ree!/Perhaps you can tell me what this may be!'" (295). As the narrator then says: "She was a colored woman loving a colored man. But her skin was too white for him. So he had given her up. . . . She was a white woman, deeply interested in a white man. But for him her blood was too black. So he offered her insult" (295). In this light, when we examine her subsequent marriage to Christopher, and her decision, when tested, to remain faithful, we may not be persuaded that Phebe's choice brings resolution to difficulties or answers to riddles. In this part of *Comedy: American Style*, as with *Plum Bun*, it seems Fauset is once again presenting a novel of modern Black female sexuality passing as a novel about racial passing. If this is the case, then "Phebe's Act" does not present Phebe as an alternative female model to Olivia, but instead complicates the story of the Cary family by focusing on Phebe's choices rather than Christopher's gains. In other words, to the extent that this final "Act" is Christopher's, the story indeed ends happily; but, of course, Fauset purposely writes this section as "Phebe's Act," and names it such, in order to deepen her presentation of modern Black women in their knowledge of themselves. As a consequence, also, the question of the happy ending remains open.

If queering is, as Judith Butler suggests, an articulation of "what ought to remain concealed," then we see that the choice that Phebe makes in her "Act" queers *Comedy: American Style*, and for two distinct reasons. The two men whom Phebe ultimately rejects for Christopher Cary are Llewellyn Nash, the rich white man she dates for a time, and Nicholas Campbell, the young Black man who had initially rejected her. These are the two men who cause her, earlier, to invoke the nursery rhyme words, "Riddle me, riddle me, ree!" to mark the puzzle that the confluence of race, gender, and sexuality have presented in her life. By reaffirming Christopher as her sexual choice, she may not be affirming the sanctity of marriage and conservative family morals so much as she is rejecting both men who have marked her with the race fetish, whether that fetish be color or whiteness. Both of these rejections are queer, meaning that they conceal as much as they reveal about Phebe, and are marked as such by Fauset's narrative. When Phebe tells Llewellyn that she is colored, and that she is not interested in passing because she just prefers "being colored," he responds by saying, "You live in a queer world, Phebe" (289), which marks that world as not only distinct from but also signifying upon his white privilege and upper-class life. Yet his interest is clear: "I'd like to live in it for a few months and see what it was like," he says (289). There is also sexual implication here. Phebe, however, clearly rejects Llewellyn as a sexual partner, thereby establishing her own priorities and her own agency. In yet another example of a woman of color in relationship with a white man, we see here that Phebe is neither objectified nor objectifies.[37] Her parting words to Llewellyn, "Goodbye Llewellyn, forget me. I shall certainly forget you" (289), indicate the formation of a new kind of relationship between people in the positions of ex-master and ex-slave, one that hints of a rearrangement of the vectors of societal power.

The other queer moment, named as such in "Phebe's Act," is occasioned by Phebe's rejection of Nicholas. While Fauset has revealed to us how Llewellyn responds to Phebe's rejection, we never learn of Nicholas's feelings upon being rejected. We do know Christopher's feelings, however, because he tells Phebe that he "had the queerest feeling last night . . . or rather this morning . . . about three," during the time, in other words, when Phebe is in New York and after she has determined not to pursue a sexual relationship with Nicholas but before she has come home (317). Here, Christopher feels "queer," an indication that something is being concealed from him, but also that *he* is concealing something. After all, he is involved in conversation with his father while he is also worried about whether or not Phebe has left him, and there is no indication that he in any way mentions this worry. Queer family dynamics continue through the end of "Phebe's Act." While Christopher and Phebe affirm their love for one another, they too persist in not communicating fully. The last line of "Phebe's Act," "He could not understand why she cried when he kissed her," indicates that Phebe is not talking about her absence and Christopher is not asking. That this turn of events has made Christopher, not Phebe, feel queer should not be surprising. He is, after all, even as husband afforded neither the ultimate agency nor his own "Act" in this drama. In relation to Phebe, he is what we might call queerly, rather than clearly, patriarchal.

Comedy: American Style presents one final section, appropriately titled "Curtain," which focuses on Olivia in Paris, where she has retreated so as not to continue living in the reconstructed Cary household. Within this final section we are confronted, once again, with the question of happy endings as well as the question of genre that Fauset raises by calling this novel a comedy, American style. If we return to Fauset's example of Bert Williams, we might claim the ending of this novel as one that invites us to laugh at Olivia and the situation her ways of whiteness create, although doing so becomes a journey into the looking-glass, so that our objectification of her mirrors back to us not only ourselves but also the whole structure of racialized American society. Yet even by this reading, laughing at Olivia is not entirely satisfactory because it overlooks the pathos that Fauset sees as inherent in "objective" comedy. In

"The Gift of Laughter" she states that "not without reason has tradition made comedy and tragedy sisters and twins" and that "the capacity for one argues the capacity for the other" (167). Based on statements such as this one, we might attribute to Fauset's story an indeterminate genre at once both comedy and tragedy. But here we must also interject with the double entendre that "Curtain," like every other section of this novel, employs. "Curtain" provides us with a kind of finale yet also suggests the image of life's veil, and as veiled presentation this final glimpse of Olivia is even more puzzling, not less so. What, we ask, is the racial implication of this veil, and is it Olivia's sight and therefore her insight that is veiled, or is it our own sight or insight in relation to her? The way that we do not know is queer indeed.

"Riddle me, riddle me, ree!/ Perhaps you can tell me what this may be!" As this fairy tale language reverberates within this ending, we pause to consider Jessie Fauset as she is characterized by Langston Hughes—as the midwife who brought "the so-called New Negro literature into being" (*Big Sea* 218). Having played such a *rôle*, we suspect she knows a great deal about change-lings. Through her novels, I am suggesting, we see her orchestrate two major transformations. First, Fauset ultimately develops secrets kept and told into a psychology of modern American consciousness. But if, by the end of *Comedy: American Style*, Fauset's readers are embroiled in Olivia's racial tangle, then secrets are no longer simply the content of African American fiction but have themselves become embodied, as formal element. This is the second transformation we should attribute to Fauset. *Comedy: American Style*, in other words, is itself a formal changeling and a puzzle. Perhaps Fauset writes tragedy; but in her America, where Bert Williams can only play for laughs, she knows enough to call it comedy.

Afterword:
Telling in the Twentieth Century

◄◦⟩ ⟨◦►

Go curse your God, boy, and die.

—Ralph Ellison, *Invisible Man*

Well, you know what dey say 'uh white man and uh nigger woman is de freest thing on earth.' Dey do as dey please.

—Zora Neale Hurston, *Their Eyes Were Watching God*

I conclude this study of secrets in African American literature by briefly considering the appeal of two novels, Ralph Ellison's *Invisible Man* and Zora Neale Hurston's *Their Eyes Were Watching God*, both celebrated as exemplary American, as well as African American, texts. *Invisible Man* and *Their Eyes Were Watching God* are also telling narratives, structured in significant ways such that what readers hear in these texts, too, is—secrets. Telling (secrets), then, might be one way for Black writers to gather an audience we call "American," that is, a multiracial and perhaps even predominantly white audience. In some ways a negotiation of how to speak truth to power, telling is, nevertheless, neither a voice of public proclamation nor a vernacular and thereby in-group (*kept* secret) phenomenon. Instead, because telling narratives develop *secret* telling, the telling voice can be characterized as an intimate vocalization directed to one group but kept from another, such that a new in-group composed of telling voice and readers is formed. Further, as an African American vocalization reverberating within American consciousness, telling, when it goes deep, seems to find that all-American touchstone, the master/female slave moment, and to speak in some ways from or to this referent.

Both *Invisible Man* and *Their Eyes Were Watching God* are crossover novels, that is, African American texts that have found their way into the American literary canon. About Ralph Ellison, Morris Dickstein writes in a late 1990s essay for *Raritan*, "Of all African-American writers and intellectuals, Ellison stakes the greatest claims—not for a separate black culture or literary tradition, but for an inestimably great role within *American* culture" ("Ralph Ellison, Race, and American Culture" 33). In this same essay, when Dickstein poses James Baldwin's question, "Do I really *want* to be integrated into a burning house?" to an imaginary Ralph Ellison, he has Ellison answering, "Yes, because it's *my* house" (33). Dickstein is, of course, in good company as he declares *Invisible Man* to be one of the great American novels. As Robert Butler catalogs, in the mid-1950s to early 1960s, R. W. B. Lewis, Robert Bone, and Leslie Fiedler were among the first major critics to suggest the significance of *Invisible Man* in American literary studies, and since then, while there has been some critical discussion of whether or not Ellison should be considered representative as an *African* American writer, there has been very little disagreement about his representative American-ness (xix–xl).

Similarly, although with skepticism about why it has come to be so, Hazel Carby discusses the rediscovery and positive critical reception of Hurston's *Their Eyes Were Watching God* from the mid-1970s through the early 1990s, pointing to the many facts that indicate that after years of neglect, the novel has entered the "American literary mainstream" ("Politics of Fiction" 28). According to Carby, the text "is common to a wide variety of courses, whether African American studies, American studies, English, or Women's studies," and Hurston studies are "a veritable industry and an industry that is very profitable" (28–29). Carby worries that the cultural life of *Their Eyes* outside of African American studies contexts is simply a fad, and, worse, that the commodification of Hurston demonstrates yet another example of Black female exoticization. She asks critics to ask themselves whether *Their Eyes* has "become the most frequently taught black novel because it acts as a mode of assurance that, really, the black folk are happy and healthy" (41). Even when scholars answer Carby's question in the negative, however, the question itself remains key: why, if true, has *Their Eyes* become "the most frequently taught black novel"? And here I extend Carby's question to include Ellison's text as well: why are *Their Eyes* and *Invisible Man* so often read as representatively Black in an American context? My suggestion, here, refers us to the telling nature of these texts.

Consider the first epigraph, above, "Go curse your God, boy, and die," a comment directed to the narrator of *Invisible Man* by an old woman, "singer of spirituals," an ex-slave, a "colored mother," as I will claim (10). This woman appears during the narrator's reefer-induced hallucination, and these are among the first words she speaks to the narrator. In some ways, these words suggest the male mulatto's tragedy, which Invisible Man ultimately rejects since this point marks the beginning rather than the end of his journey into his subconscious. Ellison's prologue presents Invisible Man's hallucination springing out of the depths of Louis Armstrong's "What Did I Do to Be So Black and Blue" as a meditation on origin, not a statement of fate. In a descent that invokes Dante, Invisible Man first meets this "old woman singing a spiritual"; beneath her "lay a still lower level on which I saw a beautiful girl the color of ivory pleading in a voice like my mother's as she stood before a group of slaveowners who bid for her naked body"; and below that he finds "a lower level and a more rapid tempo" where "someone" is delivering a sermon on "the 'Blackness of Black- ness'" (9).

This "blackness of blackness" might be paraphrased, in Hegelian terms, as "the consciousness of consciousness," or more precisely, the racial con- sciousness of racial consciousness, which would indicate the moment of *self- consciousness*; in other words, within these depths Invisible Man is uncover- ing buried racial knowledge accessible only through the master/female slave moment. While the content of the sermon delivered to the congregation within ever-deeper levels of the subconscious focuses on the ludicrous aspects of racialized life ("Black will make you . . . Black . . . or black will un-make you"), the call and response structure seems designed to seduce Invisible Man into this community of the absurd; he breaks away from the congregation only when a voice screams, "Git out of here, you fool! Is you ready to commit treason?" (10). It is at this point that Invisible Man's attention turns back to "the old woman singing a spiritual," who is now moaning, "Go curse your God, boy, and die" (10),[1] and this woman becomes the center of Invisible Man's subconscious experience.

When Invisible Man asks the old woman why she is moaning, she explains, "I dearly loved my master, son"; and when Invisible Man responds by tell- ing her that she should have hated him, she explains further: "He gave me several sons . . . and because I loved my sons I learned to love their father though I hated him too." This woman, then, lover and hater of her master, is the "colored" mother of Invisible Man's subconscious, and in relation to the figurative sons more generally, of an African American male subconscious. Taking her existence into account places Invisible Man in a position he rec- ognizes well because her love and hate form an ambivalence he recognizes as his own. While he would like to simplify this ambivalence, to simply hate, for example, he cannot—and this mother's description of her sons cautions him against such simplification. Invisible Man's own agency is on hold in the prologue; he does not know how to act, and so he remains in "hibernation" (defined by him as "a covert preparation for a more overt action" [13]). Her sons act, or would act, but in inappropriate ways—"Them boys woulda tore [their father] to pieces with they homemade knives"; "They gits to laughing and wants to kill up the white folks"; and one son in particular is so upset by the way Invisible Man "makes Ma cry" that he strikes and then nearly strangles him. Yet, all the more confusing is the old woman's action. While her verbal response with regard to love and hate is clear (Invisible Man declares that maybe freedom lies in hating, and she replies, "Naw, son, it's in loving"), her consequent action might be troubling: she "loved" her master "and give him the poison and he withered away like a frost-bit apple" (11), an image that calls to mind impotence as much as death. This master/female slave relation, then, has generated sons, but it ultimately resolves when mastery, or at least its maleness, withers while the old woman, at least for now, endures.[2]

Invisible Man ascends from this "underworld of sound" and hears Louis Armstrong once again singing "What did I do/To be so black/And blue?" He reflects that "this familiar music had demanded action, the kind of which [he] was incapable"; like the old woman whose head spins every time she tries, as she says, "to say what I got up in my head," who says that every time she tries to walk, her head "gits to swirling" and she falls down, Invisible Man is caught in a dizzying racial paradox. The only way out according to the old woman is through loving; Invisible Man cannot understand this idea that the old woman herself just barely grasps. He concludes by stating that he has not smoked reefer since that time because "to see around corners is enough. . . . But to hear around them is too much" (13). Hearing around corners, hearing secrets, in other words, challenges Invisible Man to the core. Yet, Invisible Man finds his way by telling his story, and while in the epilogue he pays tribute to his grandfather's influence, he also suggests, through this descriptive language, that he is brought to the telling by this colored woman.

Invisible Man escapes an all-male and violent world by dropping below the street; and despite his protest that hearing around corners brings a paralyzing degree of understanding, in the epilogue he clearly has secret knowledge initially represented by the old woman of his prologue. What's more, he *tells* the secrets he gathers, and the telling itself changes him: "Here I've set out to throw my anger into the world's face, but now that I've tried to put it all down the old fascination with playing a role returns, and I'm drawn upward again" (579). Using the language that the old woman has given him as she tries to characterize her love for freedom ("First I think it's one thing, then I think it's another. It gits my head to spinning. I guess now it ain't nothing but knowing how to say what I got up in my head. But it's a hard job, son.

Ever' time I starts to walk my head gits to swirling and I falls down."), Invisible Man declares,

> The very act of trying to put it all down has confused me and negated some of the anger and some of the bitterness. So it is that now I denounce and defend, or feel prepared to defend. I condemn and affirm, say no and say yes, say yes and say no. I denounce because though implicated and partially responsible, I have been hurt to the point of abysmal pain, hurt to the point of invisibility. And I defend because in spite of all I find that I love. In order to get some of it down I *have* to love. (579–80)

Invisible Man does not credit these thoughts to the voice of the old woman within the depths of his soul. Instead, he wonders about his grandfather's influence and whether or not this is the message his grandfather meant to convey. Perhaps it is; perhaps his grandfather's and the old woman's messages are the same. The bitterness of native sons (the old woman's sons by the white slavemaster who has withered, about whom she declares, "They's bitter, that's what they is . . .") is tempered by mother love, however, in the same way that the brutal legacy of slavery's sexualized violence is transformed into love through the "colored" mother's uplifting, lifting up, her child. Ellison reveals in *Invisible Man* that this legacy redefined through the mothers is central to his twentieth-century exploration of Black male subjectivity: this is where his narrator has learned love.[3] And in his narrator's telling he offers the possibility that he speaks for us, his readers ("Who knows but that, on the lower frequencies, I speak for you?"), as well as himself. With this narrative denouement, his readers are effectively pulled "in" to the secret.

The second epigraph, above, "Well, you know what dey say 'uh white man and uh nigger woman is de freest thing on earth.' Dey do as dey please" (*Their Eyes* 189), is spoken by an unnamed male, presumably Black, who is talking about Janie after her trial for the murder of Tea Cake. In an uncanny way, this folk expression gives credence to the master/female slave moment and points to its powerful legacy in African American folk culture. It also revises as it echoes *Invisible Man*'s old woman as she says that freedom is in loving. In the context of Janie's trial, however, the statement represents a summary comment from the community about her jury's verdict. By defending herself verbally, Janie has gotten away with love, and this community is jealous of such freedom. This epigraph also, then, focuses our attention on the famous courtroom scene in *Their Eyes*, which has received so much critical attention because it represents contested issues of voice in the novel. As such, this scene is crucial to a discussion of *Their Eyes* as telling narrative.

There are at least two recorded versions of the conversation following the Modern Language Association session of 1979, when *Their Eyes* becomes the significant text under discussion. According to Mary Helen Washington, the conversation revolved around remarks made by Robert Stepto and Alice Walker (Washington xiii–xiv; Lauter 86). In the discussion period during the session titled "Traditions and Their Transformations in Afro-American Letters," Stepto "raised the issue that has become one of the most highly controversial and hotly contested aspects of the novel: whether or not Janie is able to achieve her voice in *Their Eyes*" (xi). Stepto's concern focused on the courtroom scene, "where Janie is called on not only to preserve her own life and liberty but also to make the jury, as well as all of us who hear her tale, understand the meaning of her life with Tea Cake" (xi). According to Washington, "Stepto found Janie curiously silent in this scene, with Hurston telling the story in the omniscient third person" and "was quite convinced (and convincing) that the frame story in which Janie speaks to Pheoby creates only the illusion that Janie has found her voice" (xi). In Washington's telling, this is the point where Alice Walker enters the conversation, "insisting passionately that women did not have to speak when men thought they should, that they would choose when and where they wish to speak because while many women *had* found their own voices, they also knew when it was better not to use it" (xii). This, as Washington describes, was "the earliest feminist reading of voice in *Their Eyes*, a reading that was later supported by many other Hurston scholars" (xii).

As Paul Lauter reads the courtroom scene in *Their Eyes*, and the MLA session discussion that brought Janie's trial to such critical scrutiny, Janie's story is "not a life, a story intended for white judgment, and therefore the courtroom may be an inappropriate forum" (*Canons and Contexts* 86). This point is important, yet appropriate or not the courtroom scene is specifically where Janie, a Black woman—or to be more precise, a "colored" woman—must tell her story to a group of white men who have the ultimate power of life or death over her; in other words, the courtroom scene represents a moment reminiscent of the master/female slave confrontation. Further, the shift from first-person to omniscient third-person narration places readers in the position of a third party decidedly not in the courtroom. We know about the confrontation between Janie and the men of the jury, but we do not overhear; our place, as readers, is not analogous to Frederick Douglass's as he watches his aunt Esther plead with Captain Anthony. It is as if, then, Alice Walker had declared during that MLA session discussion that Janie, or Hurston, tells secrets to which her readers are sometimes not party, that master/female slave moments might remain private still, and that these secrets do not signal a diminished power of voice but, rather, a strategic one.

Lorraine Bethel characterizes the overall reading experience of *Their Eyes* as like an "overheard conversation," and Carla Kaplan reiterates this point (see Bethel 180; Kaplan 131). Because Janie is speaking to her friend Pheoby, reading *Their Eyes* is analogous to being let in on a secret. As Pheoby characterizes, everyone, including the porch-sitters, wants to hear secrets; that is the reason, according to Pheoby's husband, Sam, that most people go to church: so that they will be present on Judgment Day, "de day dat every secret is s'posed to be made known. They wants to be there and hear it *all*" (6). Within this context of Judgment Day secrets, Janie tells Pheoby she has no intention of sharing her story with the porch-sitters, but gives Pheoby permission to do so and declares that Pheoby's telling will be the same thing "'cause mah tongue is in mah friend's mouf" (6). As Kaplan points out, this suggests Pheoby's "sensuality and erotic openness to Janie" (133) in ways that call readers' own positionality into question. Whether we see ourselves as kissing friends of Janie's or not, however, we are swept up into "that oldest human longing—self-revelation" and so, like readers who hear Ellison's Invisible Man as speaking for us, too, we place ourselves in secret concert with Janie.

Ralph Ellison declares in his introduction to *Invisible Man*, written for the thirtieth-anniversary edition of the novel, that the task he initially set before himself "was one of revealing the human universals hidden within the plight of one who was both black and American" (xxii). In order to make it possible for readers, white readers in particular, to identify with the narrator, says Ellison, his task was to provide his narrator "with something of a worldview, give him a consciousness in which serious philosophical questions could be raised" (xxii). Mostly, however, as Ellison declares, as writer he is "gambling with the reader's capacity for fictional truth" (xxii). This is the gamble inherent in *telling*, this leap of faith in the reader's capacity for full humanity, and such a gamble sometimes challenges the reader *into* fuller humanity. As narrative strategy, this *telling* depends upon developing an intimacy between writer and reader such that detachment, ironic distance, and other trademarks of new critical reading strategies and later twentieth-century theoretical postures do not fit. "Quiet as it's kept,"[4] one telling voice begins, and in response, if we lean close, we feel perhaps exclusively, singularly, secretly beloved; loved as reader. For better or worse, I conclude, this is the power of telling secrets, and this telling, whether on the lower frequencies or "with each others' tongues in our mouths,"[5] fathoms all kinds of love affairs as it fulfills its soft promise.

NOTES

◆◗ʃ ʅ◖◆

INTRODUCTION

1. Frances Smith Foster repeats Morrison's opening to *The Bluest Eye* in her own first chapter of *Written by Herself.* Foster's point is, "Quiet as it's kept, black women have been recording and influencing American history since their earliest arrival upon these shores" (1).

CHAPTER I: THE MASTER/FEMALE SLAVE MOMENT AS SLAVERY'S LEGACY

1. According to Hegel, the relation between man and woman is natural, not dialectical. As such, no woman can be "master" because, as nature, she has no contradiction between herself and nature to negate; no woman can be "slave" because, as the bearer of life she cannot risk life. For a review and critique of Hegel's position, see O'Brien, *Politics of Reproduction* 70–73. Many readers of *The Second Sex* see Beauvoir as attempting to locate man as master and woman as slave. For an interesting rereading of Beauvoir on this point, see Lundgren-Gothlin.

2. According to Hegel's schema, while men become citizens and thus achieve self-consciousness, women remain within the family (*Phenomenology of Spirit*, para. 457, 274–75). Hegel's understanding of woman's role is dependent upon his interpretation of Sophocles' *Antigone*. See Mills, "Hegel's *Antigone*," for a complete interpretation and critique of Hegel's reasoning.

3. Note that here I am quoting from Sojourner Truth's address at the Ohio Women's Rights Convention, May 1851, as recorded by Marius Robinson, not Frances Gage, since Painter has so carefully documented the inaccuracies of Gage's text.

4. Chapter 4 of *Phenomenology of Spirit* (trans. Miller) focuses on "Self-Consciousness." Paragraphs 166–77 introduce "The Truth of Self-Certainty"; within that heading is subheading A, "Independence and Dependence of Self-Consciousness: Lordship and Bondage" (para. 178–96), which is the primary focus here. Subheading B, "Stoicism, Scepticism, and the Unhappy Consciousness" (para. 197–230) is also significant to this discussion. Barnett reviews the French reception of Hegel (13–26). See also Kelly.

5. For Taylor, the three terms of "the historical dialectics" are "the basic purpose or standard, the inadequate reality, and an inadequate conception of the purpose which is bound up with that reality." More crucially:

> But the ontological dialectics also involve three terms. We start off with an inadequate notion of the standard involved. But we also have from the beginning some very basic, correct notions of what the standard or purpose is, some criterial properties which it must meet. It is these criterial properties which in fact enable us to show that a given conception of the standard is inadequate. For we show that this conception cannot be realized in such a way as to meet the criterial properties, and hence that this definition is unacceptable as a definition of the standard or purpose concerned. But we show the inadequacy of the faulty formula by trying to "realize" it, that is, construct a reality according to it. This is what brings out the conflict with the standard. So that reality is our third term. (133)

6. The account Patterson uses is from Douglass *Life and Times*, where Douglass not only gives the details of his resistance to the slavedriver Edward Covey, who is attempting to beat him, but also reflects upon the meaning of this resistance. "I was a changed being after that fight," says Douglass. "I was nothing before—I was a man now" (143).

7. This phrase is, of course, the subtitle of Eugene D. Genovese's study of slavery, *Roll, Jordan, Roll*.

8. The classic example of an African American author signifying on the denied African American or Black presence in America is the paint factory incident in Ralph Ellison's *Invisible Man*. The protagonist is taught that in order to mix the paint labeled "Optic White," described as "White! . . . the purest white that can be found," intended for the government and white enough for any "national monument," it is necessary to add ten drops of a liquid that is "dead black" (200–202).

9. In Thomas Nelson Page's "Marse Chan: A Tale of Old Virginia" (from *In Ole Virginia*), the story's narrator meets an ex-slave in the summer of 1872 who proceeds to tell the story of his loyalty to his "Marse Chan," who died during the war. In Joel Chandler Harris's "A Story of the War," Uncle Remus tells of how he saved his "Mars Jeems" by shooting the Yankee who was about to shoot his master; the "Yankee" has subsequently fallen in love with "Mars Jeems's" sister, "Miss Sally," and so become part of the Southern family.

10. In the illustration, drawn by W. T. Smedley, the young slave stands between the white pillars on the front porch of the big house, holding the white baby in his arms and looking into its face. "Old master," with his hands on his hips, stands beside the two, looking down at them. The other slaves are gathered below these three, and all look up at the baby in the young slave's arms.

11. Other scholars who have written about the spirituals as coded speech include Genovese (*Roll, Jordan, Roll*), Levine (*Black Culture*), and Raboteau (*Slave Religion*).

12. Those enslaved cannot, of course, trust all people of slave status. The shared

conversion experience is the key to trustworthiness, not race or shared oppression. Further, it could be argued that some people who are not enslaved also share in this collective consciousness. We would expect these people to be abolitionists, and while we might not include William Lloyd Garrison as part of this group, it would be difficult to exclude John Brown.

13. This conversation is also reported in Chesnut, *A Diary from Dixie* 122. Mary Boykin Chesnut's diaries have been published in a number of different forms, for which both she and later editors are responsible. Chesnut kept a diary during the Civil War years. Later, in the early 1880s, she wrote a book based on her diaries. This book manuscript, in carelessly edited form, was published in 1905 and again in 1949 as *A Diary from Dixie*. In 1981, C. Vann Woodward published *Mary Chesnut's Civil War*, a scholarly edition of Chesnut's 1880s book manuscript that also includes additional excerpts from the 1860s diaries and corrects many of the editorial mistakes made in the 1905 and 1949 editions of *A Diary from Dixie*. In 1984, C. Vann Woodward and Elisabeth Muhlenfeld edited and published *The Private Mary Chesnut: The Unpublished Civil War Diaries*, an edition of the wartime diaries themselves.

14. Jean Fagan Yellin identifies this woman as Martha Hoskins Rombough Blount (1777–1858), whose first husband was William Rombough, whose sister became John Horniblow's wife. John Horniblow was the hotel-keeper who bought Jacobs's grandmother after she had been captured as a child while on her way to St. Augustine. Because of these family connections, she had known Molly Horniblow, Jacobs's grandmother, all her life (Jacobs 275n3).

15. I am working with ideas presented in a number of essays collected in Mills *Feminist Interpretations*, a volume in the series "Re-reading the Canon." For an informative review of this series, and the volume on Hegel in particular, see Alcoff.

16. This is Heidi M. Ravven's paraphrase of Irigaray (Ravven 249n34).

17. Part of the history of this debate involves the positions of Simone de Beauvoir and Luce Irigaray. As Patricia Mills notes in the introduction to *Feminist Interpretations*, Beauvoir's subject is Hegelian, and as such sovereign and transcendent. Women can become subjects, but only by embracing freedom. Irigaray, on the other hand, defines a postmodern subject whose "main attribute is language, not activity." To achieve subjectivity for Irigaray, then, it is necessary to "speak woman." An interesting aspect of Mills's characterization of Beauvoir and Irigaray's thinking is the way that she sees these "radically different theories of woman's subjectivity" as "articulating two sides of the same problem." According to Mills, Beauvoir is analyzing the process of "othering," while Irigaray explores the process of "saming" (2–10).

18. Readers familiar with *Gender Trouble* and other writing by Butler may find it helpful to be reminded that *Subjects of Desire* is Butler's revised dissertation, which suggests just how formative thinking about/through Hegel's philosophy has been to her work.

19. In this context, it is significant that Jacobs decides to defeat Dr. Flint by having children through consensual relations with another man, Mr. Sands.

20. Douglass tells us of this incident in *Narrative;* in this text Douglass's aunt's name is Hester (51–52). In *My Bondage,* Douglass's more complete version of this incident, he names his aunt Esther, and does so in *Life and Times* as well. For the sake of consistency, I will refer to Douglass's aunt as Esther throughout my analysis.

21. For interpretations of Douglass's narratives in relation to the construction of Black masculinity, see Maurice Wallace; Cunningham; and Van Leer.

22. There is also a clear correlation here to Dr. Flint's behavior as reported by Harriet Jacobs; Flint constantly makes his desires known, through speech and in writing.

23. Douglass's *Narrative* reports this moment in slightly different fashion, but the reflection as presented in *Life and Times* is quoted by Orlando Patterson in *Slavery and Social Death* (13). Some critics read this as Douglass's reaction to his earlier witnessing of his Esther's brutalization. See Maurice Wallace 252–55.

24. In some ways, of course, the answer is Douglass himself. Anthony is most probably Douglass's father, and Esther is Douglass's mother's sister. On this point see Cunningham 122.

25. Cassuto's article presents a significant reinterpretation of Douglass's story as indeed transformational to American consciousness, in Hegelian terms.

26. It is worth quoting O'Brien at length, in order to be clear about what reproductive labor is and is not:

> Reproductive labour, like all human labour, creates value. What sort of value can this be said to be? Historically, instances can be found of the attribution to children of use value and exchange value, but this value inheres in the potential of the child. . . . Further, the child has a human value simply by virtue of being human, of growing and maturing in all the wonder of nature's most stunning performance. For this, the child is not appropriated: it is loved. This is the value of the child's distinct personality, and is not the product of reproductive labour. . . .
>
> The value which is produced by reproductive labour might be called synthetic value. It represents the unity of sentient beings with the natural process and the integrity of the continuity of the race. These are what men lose in the alienation of the seed, and, in a very real sense, nature is unjust to men. She includes and excludes at the same moment. It is an injustice, however, which male praxis might reasonably be said to have overcorrected. (*Politics of Reproduction* 69–70).

27. See Walker; Gates *Figures in Black;* and McDowell "In the First Place" for a full treatment of the varying ways Douglass refers to and understands his relation to his father and mother.

28. Harryette Mullen also sees a distinction between the ways in which Douglass and Jacobs deal with information about sexual relations between white men and enslaved women:

> Jacobs deals more explicitly with the slave woman's sexual subjugation than

Douglass, who is always reluctant, in the 1845 *Narrative*, to rely upon information transmitted orally by slaves, which he generally treats as unsubstanti-
ated gossip or "whispered" opinion, inferior to authenticating (written) documents, perhaps anticipating the skepticism of contemporary historians who
are reluctant to state that black women were raped in slavery, and who not
surprisingly find scarce documentation of sexual abuse in the journals of slaveholders. (251)

29. For a contemporary analysis of these issues see Patricia Williams.

30. Bleser notes that this letter is with the James Henry Hammond Papers at the
South Carolina Library.

31. This also brings new meaning to the question that opens Gilbert and Gubar's
Madwoman in the Attic: "Is a pen . . . a penis?"

32. This passage is pointed out by Fleischner.

CHAPTER 2: FATHER/SON RELATIONS IN AFRICAN
AMERICAN ABOLITIONIST FICTION

1. For one significant reading of this text, see Sollors 163–67.

2. For a discussion of the ways that identity is relational that adds an interesting
dimension to my claims about the construction of African American manhood, see
Eakin.

3. Baker's idea of the "sound of Caliban" is constructed as critique of post-Enlight-
enment dualism, particularly as it manifests itself in postcolonial criticism. See Baker,
"Caliban's Triple Play" (*Critical Inquiry* 13.1) 182–96, qtd. in Baker, "Caliban's Triple
Play" (Chicago, 1986), 389.

4. For a review of the historical scholarship surrounding the controversy of Thomas
Jefferson and Sally Hemings, see Reed 1–5. While it most likely is true that Jefferson
fathered children by Sally Hemings, and owned them as slaves, it is improbable that
any were sold as slaves since two were runaways from Monticello and two were freed
in 1826 in accordance with Jefferson's will.

5. My analysis is of *Clotel; or, The President's Daughter: A Narrative of Slave Life in
the United States; With a Sketch of the Author's Life*, published in London, 1853. Brown
also published three other versions of this novel: *Miralda; or, The Beautiful Quadroon;
A Romance of American Slavery, Founded on Fact*, serialized in the *Weekly Anglo-African*;
Clotelle: A Tale of the Southern States; and *Clotelle; or, The Colored Heroine; A Tale of the
Southern States*. In all versions but the first the title character lives happily at novel's
end. Also, *Clotel* (1853) is the only version of the novel originally published outside
the United States, and the only version published with William Wells Brown's fugitive slave narrative as a preface.

6. See Peterson for an analysis of the cultural power of the myth of Ham and Japheth
in the antebellum South.

7. Olney outlines the "conventions of slave narratives" and includes a list of four

conventions having to do with the prefatory material to accompany a slave narrative: "an engraved portrait," "a title page that includes the claim . . . 'Written by Himself,'" "a handful of testimonials," and "a poetic epigraph." Olney then identifies twelve conventions of the narrative itself, most of which can be found in Brown's narrative, and then ends his outline with a sketch of the conventional material placed in appendices to slave narratives.

8. Brown paraphrases from Matthew 25:33–40 and implies that Wells Brown, through his acts toward William Wells Brown, is one of the righteous who will be recognized as such on the day of judgment because of his willingness to take in and take care of "the least of my brethren" as Christ taught.

9. Actually, even Brown's first name was changed, at the whim of Dr. Young, his master, who had a nephew by the name of William and would not allow his slave to be called by that same name. Brown's mother subsequently renamed him "Sandford" (*Narrative of William W. Brown* 97–98).

10. See "Novelization," where Andrews uses Barbara Herrnstein Smith's concept of the "fictive" as a way to discuss the radical experimentation with narrative voice that characterizes early African American novels.

11. According to Farrison, as a famous fugitive Brown would have been "immediately arrested and remanded into slavery" upon returning to the United States (177).

12. This letter, written from St. Louis on January 10, 1848, was addressed to Edmund Quincy, Esq. (*Narrative of the Life and Escape* 44).

13. As Gilmore explains, he takes the term "professional fugitive" from Larry Gara, "The Professional Fugitive in the Abolition Movement." See Gilmore 180.

14. Brown's other versions of *Clotel*, *Miralda* and *Clotelle*, are published in the United States and are not subtitled "The President's Daughter."

15. For an account of the well-known rumors about Jefferson's slave daughters, see Brodie 339–56; and Jordan, 182–93. For an assessment of Brodie's historical accuracy, see Gordon-Reed. Brodie notes that "on July 10, 1802, the *Port Folio*, a Federalist literary sheet in Philadelphia, published an anonymous ballad hinting that the President preferred black women" (347).

16. For an interesting review and analysis of the Jefferson-Hemings controversy, including the recent DNA analysis that renewed this controversy in fall 1998 by concluding that there are strong possibilities that descendants of Jefferson and Hemings are who they say they are, see Ann duCille, "Where."

17. According to Brodie, Meriwether Jones denounced the exposé as "filth, blasphemy, lies, and pollution" in the *Richmond Examiner*, September 18 and 22, 1802. The editor of the Lynchburg *Virginia Gazette*, on the other hand, believed the story and scolded Jefferson for not marrying a white woman instead (reprinted in the *Richmond Recorder*, November 3, 1802). See Brodie 349, 353.

18. As previously noted, this most likely did not happen.

19. The first three stanzas of "Jefferson's Daughter," as printed in the *Anti-Slavery Harp* are as follows:

Can the blood that, at Lexington, poured o'er the plain,
    When the sons warred with tyrants their rights to uphold,
Can the tide of Niagra wipe out the stain?
    No! Jefferson's child has been bartered for gold!

Do you boast of your freedom? Peace, babblers—be still;
    Prate not of the goddess who scarce deigns to hear;
Have ye power to unbind? Are ye wanting in will?
    Must groans of your bondman still torture the ear?

The daughter of Jefferson sold for a slave!
    The child of a freeman for dollars and francs!
The roar of applause, when your orators rave,
    Is lost in the sound of her chain, as it clanks.

20. In Brown's 1847 *Narrative of William W. Brown* he tells the story of a beautiful woman whom the slave trader, Walker, held as a slave. This woman creates "anxiety" among the passengers, who want to learn her history. At St. Louis, however, she is "removed to a boat bound for New Orleans, and the history of the beautiful slave-girl remained a mystery" (34–35). In reflecting on his life as a slave, perhaps Brown believed that this woman was Jefferson's daughter, and perhaps this gave him a personal reason to write a story about her. This event in Brown's life would have occurred in 1829 or so, roughly the time just after Monticello was sold and Jefferson's slaves auctioned.

21. "Woman's fiction" is Nina Baym's term for a genre of American novels by and about women in the mid-nineteenth century.

22. The name of the historical leader of the revolt aboard the *Creole* is Madison Washington; thus, this name is not Douglass's creation. In the *Heroic Slave*, however, when Washington tells Listwell his name, he also says that this is the name his mother gave to him (*Heroic Slave* 33).

23. See "Frederick Douglass," where Sundquist argues that "Douglass's act of self-fathering is embedded in the rhetoric and ideals of the Revolutionary fathers," and also that "the ambiguity of his origins has itself become a part of his rhetorical strategy" (124, 126).

24. This is Maggie Sale's point in *Slumbering Volcano* (239n3).

25. This story, a popular one to fictionalize, was the basis for Brown's "Madison Washington" (*Black Man*); Child's "Madison Washington"; and Hopkins's "A Dash for Liberty."

26. While Washington later explains to Listwell that the cause of his need to soliloquize is a brutal beating by his master or overseer, the novella begins after that moment has passed, thus excluding the conflict itself.

27. Deborah McDowell presents an important reading of this passage in her essay "In the First Place: Making Frederick Douglass and the Afro-American Narrative Tradition."

28. One way that Douglass resists turning this story into the personal story of Madi-

son Washington concerns his treatment of Susan, Washington's wife. In the versions of the story by William Wells Brown, Lydia Maria Child, and Pauline E. Hopkins, Susan is also a captive on board the *Creole*, and the two are happily reunited at the end of the story, as a consequence of the freedom Washington has gained for everyone on the slave ship. In Douglass's *The Heroic Slave*, however, Susan is killed in Virginia when Washington attempts to help her escape, after which he is subsequently captured, sold, and placed onboard the *Creole*. While Susan's fate, in Douglass's version of the story, seems harsh, it does preclude the happy ending that Brown, Child, and Hopkins write, thus allowing Douglass to explore a story with a much different focus and a conclusion that has nothing to do with one ex-slave's individual happiness.

29. It is possible that Delany did tell the details of the secret insurrection in the last, missing chapters of the novel, which were printed in the May 1862 issues of the *Weekly Anglo-African* but have not yet been rediscovered. My argument, however, would suggest not.

30. Robert Reid-Pharr makes an important argument about the way Delany presents the boy, Rube, described as a "queer animal," and abused in a display of sadomasochism by his master for the benefit of other white male visitors. I would complicate this argument by also adding a second scene from *Blake* to Reid-Pharr's analysis of the role that sadomasochism plays in the novel, this one found in part 2, where again a boy child is beaten, this time by mistress rather than master, and also, at the command of mistress, by his own mother. See *Blake* 169–70.

31. Maggie is described, in looks, as of "zambo complexion." "Zambo" is a variation of "sambo," which, by the terminology of racial classification, technically means the child of a mulatto and a negro, or someone three-quarters Black. See Williamson xii.

32. It is significant that the final indignity that seems to move Blake to declare war against "the whites" is the mistreatment of Ambrosina Cordora, the daughter of Madame Montego, who, after being horsewhipped, makes her way home "with the clothes half torn from her person" (311). As Ambrosina is recovering, she says, "I wish I was a man, I'd lay the city in ashes this night, so I would" (313). Ambrosina continues her thoughts by declaring: "One thing I do know, if our men do not decide on something in our favor, they will soon be called to look upon us in a state of concubinage," but then she interrupts her own reasoning: "I'll destroy myself first!" (313). It is this state of affairs that brings Blake to say, "Woe be unto those devils of whites, I say!"—the line that concludes the last currently known chapter of this novel.

33. For an account of these interests and their relation to *Blake*, see Sundquist, *Wake* 182–221, It is important to realize that in the 1850s there was a strong movement within the United States to reopen the African slave trade. Also in the 1850s, pro-slavery political groups advocated United States annexation of much of Central and South America, as well as many of the Caribbean islands, including Cuba, with the idea of adding pro-slavery "territory" to the United States.

34. Part 1 bears this epigraph, attributed to Harriet Beecher Stowe:

By myself, the Lord of Ages,
I have sworn to right the wrong,
I have pledged my word unbroken,
For the weak against the strong.

The epigraph for part 2, also from Stowe, is:

Hear the word!—who fight for freedom!
Shout it in the battle van!
Hope! For bleeding human nature!
Christ the God, is Christ the Man!

Both epigraphs are from Stowe's poem "Caste and Christ." (5–6).

35. Floyd J. Miller, in his introduction to *Blake*, claims that "it is likely that [Delany] began formulating his story—in mind, if not on paper—sometime late in 1852 or in 1853" (xix). Miller's reasons for tracing the beginning of the novel to these years are based on biographical information about Delany. Robert Levine disagrees with Miller's chronology (178). My only claim is that Delany was beginning to formulate the novel in 1853. When, precisely, he wrote it is another matter.

36. This problem, the forty-seventh proposition of book 1 of Euclid's *Elements*, which proves that the square of the hypotenuse of a right triangle equals the sum of the squares of its legs, is an emblem in the Master's degree of Freemasonry (see Mackey). Duncan's *Masonic Ritual and Monitor* also explains the forty-seventh problem of Euclid:

This was an invention of our ancient friend and brother, the great Pythagoras, who, in his travels through Asia, Africa, and Europe, was initiated into several orders of priesthood, and raised to the sublime degree of a Master Mason. This wise philosopher enriched his mind abundantly in a general knowledge of things, and more especially in geometry or masonry. On this subject he drew out many problems and theorems, and, among the most distinguished he erected this, which in the joy of his heart he called "Eureka," in the Grecian language signifying, "I have found it"; and upon the discovery of which he is said to have sacrificed a hecatomb. It teaches Masons to be general lovers of the arts and sciences. (129)

My gratitude to William M. Burgan for assistance with this information.

37. According to Loretta Williams, "Individual Masons and lodges were involved in the abolition movement" (114). The Black Masonic organization in Washington, D.C., was known to be one such lodge and was a part of the "underground railroad" system.

38. In *Official Report*, Delany not only presents the quotation correctly, but he also tells his readers that he has spoken with the "eminent black clergyman and scholar" Rev. H. H. Garnet about the meaning of the verse, particularly the word "soon" (122). In *Principia*, Delany also quotes the passage correctly (95).

39. Mammy Judy first tells Blake that the word of God says "Stan still an' see de salvation" (21), meaning he should wait for deliverance from the Lord. Blake rein-

terprets this biblical passage to suit his needs, and, subsequently, this phrase becomes understood in a new way and repeated again and again by the people Blake talks with as he travels through the South and Southwest with his message of organized insurrection. (See *Blake* 41, 73, 79, 108, 122.) The biblical passage itself is from Exodus 14:13: ("And Moses said unto the people, Fear ye not, stand still, and see the salvation of the Lord, which he will shew to you to day") and refers to God parting the Red Sea so that the children of Israel could escape the Egyptians, and then God's drowning of the Egyptians as they tried to pursue the Israelites.

The Biblical verse that Abyssa repeats, introduced in part 2 of *Blake*, "Arm of the Lord, awake!" (224, 257, 260) is from Isaiah 51:9 ("Awake, awake, put on strength, O arm of the Lord; awake, as in the ancient days, in the generations of old.") The verses that follow this one make reference to the earlier parting of the Red Sea and conclude, joyfully, that "the redeemed of the Lord shall return, and come with singing unto Zion" (Isaiah 51:11).

40. In an earlier passage from *Principia*, Delany suggests that Africans are the original Christians and adds that evidence "certainly points to a higher and holier mission designed for that [African] race than has yet been developed in the progress of civilization" (73).

CHAPTER 3: SLAVE MOTHERS AND COLORED CONSCIOUSNESS

Portions of this chapter appeared in a different form in Ann L. Ardis and Leslie W. Lewis, eds. *Women's Experience of Modernity, 1875–1945*, 31–46. © 2003 the Johns Hopkins University Press. Reprinted with permission of the Johns Hopkins University Press.

1. Hegel's history of consciousness clearly relegates women, as wives, to the family, a "natural" institution and therefore prehistoric. Consequently, as Mary O'Brien comments, "the separation of public and private life becomes a condition of *history*, rather than, as it actually is, a working structure of patriarchal hegemony" (O'Brien, "Hegel" 187). Female slaves are not wives, however; not relegated to the family and consequently not written out of history even according to Hegel's model. In another context, yet equally significant, Black women writers challenge the binary of "separate spheres," around which "much criticism of nineteenth-century American literature written during the last quarter century has structured itself" (Davidson, "Preface" 443). For a recent assessment of the metaphoric significance of "separate spheres" ideology, see the "No More Separate Spheres!" special issue of *American Literature* edited by Cathy Davidson.

2. Sometimes incorrectly considered a typographical error that should instead read "norms," Locke indeed refers to "norns," the three Norse goddesses of fate.

3. Harper was one of only six African American women to address the international delegation during the three-day forum. See Carby 3–6 for a contemporary account of this event.

4. Deborah Gray White, in *Too Heavy a Load*, presents editorials from the *Woman's Era* (September 1894 and June 1894) along with other evidence to support her point that Black women felt a "sad loss of confidence in the ability of most Black men to deal effectively with the race problem" (36–37).

5. See Carby *Reconstructing Womanhood*, 117; Carby quotes Elizabeth Lindsay Davis, *Lifting as They Climb: The National Association of Colored Women* 19.

6. Margaret Murray Washington, Booker T. Washington's third wife, was chair of the executive committee of the National Association of Colored Women's Clubs in 1900, and president of the National Association of Colored Women from 1912–16.

7. For an earlier analysis of Pauline Hopkins's fiction along these lines, see Leslie W. Lewis, "Towards."

8. As Maya Angelou's "Still I Rise" concludes:

Out of the huts of history's shame
I rise
Up from a past that's rooted in pain
I rise
. . .
Leaving behind nights of terror and fear
I rise
Into a daybreak that's wondrously clear
I rise
Bringing the gifts that my ancestors gave,
I am the dream and the hope of the slave.
I rise
I rise.

9. Hurston's *Their Eyes Were Watching God* posits Nanny as a victim of slavery, while two generations later Janie becomes self-determined; Morrison's *Beloved* rewrites rape in terms of motherhood and presents Sethe's survival despite the stealing of her milk; Butler's *Kindred* culminates as the time-traveling Black female character murders her white slave-owning ancestor just as he begins to rape her, thereby setting herself free from the past.

10. As F. James Davis makes clear, these numbers are undoubtedly too low since the "mulatto" designation depended on visible white ancestry.

11. While installments of the magazine are missing, and consequently the details of her death are unclear, there is a reference in the conclusion to the Ku Klux Klan. See *Minnie's Sacrifice* 90.

12. As quoted from Frances Harper's 1859 essay, "Our Greatest Want," in *A Brighter Coming Day: A Frances Ellen Watkins Harper Reader* (104) by Foster in her introduction to *Minnie's Sacrifice* xxvii.

13. In *Moses: A Story of the Nile*, Moses speaks of his mother, saying, ". . . from her lips I/Learned the grand traditions of our race that float/With all their weird and

solemn beauty, around/Our wrecked and blighted fortunes" (*Brighter Coming Day* 143).

14. Miriam is, of course, the name of Moses's sister in Exodus, another indication that Harper is revising the old legend.

15. The passage from *Moses: A Story of the Nile* is as follows:

> If slavery only laid its weight of chains
> Upon the weary aching limbs, e'en then
> It were a curse; but when it frets through nerve
> And flesh and eats into the weary soul,
> Oh then it is a thing for every human
> Heart to loathe, and this was Israel's fate,
> For when the chains were shaken from their limbs,
> They failed to strike the impress from their
> Souls. (*Brighter Coming Day* 162–63)

16. For more information about the missing installments of the novel see Foster, "Editor's Note."

17. I am reading Gloria Anzaldúa's *Borderlands/La Frontera: The New Mestiza*, which is in many ways a work specific to Chicana lesbian experience, as also a metaphysics of mixed heritage peoples more generally. In the chapter "*La conciencia de la mestiza/* Towards a New Consciousness," Anzaldúa speaks about the kind of transformation that Iola Leroy experiences. The passage, in its entirety is as follows:

> She can be jarred out of ambivalence by an intense, and often painful, emotional event which inverts or resolves the ambivalence. I'm not sure exactly how. The work takes place underground—subconsciously. It is work that the soul performs. That focal point or fulcrum, that juncture where the *mestiza* stands, is where phenomena tend to collide. It is where the possibility of uniting all that is separate occurs. This assembly is not one where severed or separated pieces merely come together. Nor is it a balancing of opposing powers. In attempting to work out a synthesis, the self has added a third element which is greater than the sum of its severed parts. That third element is a new consciousness—a *mestiza* consciousness—and though it is a source of intense pain, its energy comes from continual creative motion that keeps breaking down the unitary aspect of each new paradigm. (79–80)

18. Harper's new consciousness, in other words, is specifically not W. E. B. Du Bois's bifurcated double consciousness.

19. *Colored American Magazine* 1.3 (August 1900) includes Angelina Grimke's "Black Is, As Black Does (A Dream)" (160–63) and part 1 of "Beth's Triumph" (152–59) by Anne Bethel Scales, presumably Anne Spencer. Spencer was Annie Bethel Bannister prior to her marriage to Edward Spencer, but since her mother was Sarah Scales, she could also have referred to herself, in public as well as in writing, as Anne Bethel Scales prior to her marriage.

20. For a list of Hopkins's publications, see Walther. Additionally, I think there is good reason to believe that the author of "Furnace Blasts I: The Growth of the Social Evil Among All Classes and Races in America" (*Colored American Magazine* 6.4: 259–63) and "Furnace Blasts II: Black or White—Which Should Be the Young Afro-American's Choice in Marriage (*Colored American Magazine* 6.5: 348–52), J. Shirley Shadrach, is a pseudonym for Pauline Hopkins herself (and certainly an article titled "Furnace Blasts" written by "Shadrach" is pseudonymous). Comments made and quotations used in the "Furnace Blasts" editorials are also found in writing attributed to Hopkins. For example, there are language similarities between "Furnace Blasts II" and the novel *Of One Blood*, serialized in *Colored American Magazine* as "Furnace Blasts II" was published. Further, we know Hopkins wrote under other pseudonyms, for example as Sarah A. Allen. Finally, the article "Charles Winter Wood; or, From Bootblack to Professor," advertised in a preview of the next issue's table of contents lists Sarah A. Allen as its author, but switches authorship to J. Shirley Shadrach in the issue when published—another indication that Allen and Shadrach are one and the same. See *Colored American Magazine* 5.4 advertisement, and 5.5: 345.

21. For an excellent overview of Hopkins's difficulties with Booker T. Washington, and his role in the publishing of the *Colored American Magazine*, see Johnson and Johnson.

22. Carby's analysis (135–36) of "Talma Gordon," part of her larger discussion of Hopkins's views on imperialism, has shaped my summary presentation of this story.

23. In "Talma Gordon" one of the characters, a college president, had responded earlier to the inevitability of amalgamation as argued by Doctor Thornton, saying, "Among the lower classes that may occur, but not to any great extent" (272). Interestingly, another member of the Canterbury Club who appears in "Talma Gordon" is the Hon. Herbert Clapp, who argues for the "the increase of wealth and the exalted position which expansion would give the United States" (271). This same Hon. Herbert Clapp appears in *Contending Forces* where he speaks on the subject of lynching, and argues that "the quickest execution" is best for a "fiend who robs a virtuous woman of her honor to gratify his hellish diabolism" (248).

24. "Furnace Blasts II: Black or White—Which Should Be the Young Afro-American's Choice in Marriage," by J. Shirley Shadrach, was also published in the same issue with the serialized *Of One Blood* and Cornelia Condict's letter of complaint about Hopkins's serialized fiction. This piece also points to the inevitability of interracial relations, and concludes by saying: "The grand finale of this racial drama is about to begin, the key-note of which lies in the affirmation: 'Of one blood have I made all nations of men.' Today we can say how wonderfully the law of evolution is fulfilling old Bible prophecies!" (6.5 [March 1903]: 352). If J. Shirley Shadrach is one of Hopkins's pseudonyms, her position on amalgamation is even clearer.

25. Kassanoff ("'Fate'") makes this argument. Her claim, with which I disagree, is that "although *Of One Blood* explicitly argues for a brotherhood of man, subtexts . . . dispute this claim" (171).

26. The sexual connotation of this description suggests an analogy between white male rape of African American women and the expansionist forces of colonization as they enter Africa.

27. Elizabeth Ammons has noted the implications of Hopkins's use of female names with classical ties, exploring, for example, Dianthe as virgin goddess of the hunt (218). It is also significant that Dianthe Lusk is the exact name of the famous abolitionist John Brown's first wife. Certainly this is no accident on Hopkins's part.

28. Aubrey Livingston is revealed by his grandmother to be a colored changeling, but nevertheless has the position of a white man in the world.

29. On epistemic privilege see Harding, esp. chap. 6.

CHAPTER 4: NARRATIVE FATHERING AND THE EPISTEMOLOGY OF SECRET KNOWING

1. Carby is here quoting Philip Brian Harper, x.

2. According to Carby, *Souls* aims, through its "representations of individuals," "to bring into being a community" as Benedict Anderson defines this process, particularly as it includes "performing . . . unifying rites." See *Race Men* 13, 195n16; Anderson, 56. Carby goes on to suggest:

> Because *The Souls of Black Folk* was so successful in the creation and imagining of a black community, it was an important text to academics and political activists outside of the academy who fought to establish African American Studies as a coherent and structured field of knowledge—a process which also needed to bring its own imagined community into being through the intellectual and political work of identifying intellectual ancestors; situating and classifying their texts; establishing literary canons and genres of writing; and establishing traditions of thought and intellectual practice. (14)

3. In "Black English," Baldwin states:

> We are the only people in this country, in this part of the North American wilderness, who have never denied their ancestors. A very important matter, for the price of the American ticket—from Russian, from Italy, from Spain, from England—was to pretend you didn't know where you came from. . . . The price of the ticket was to cease being Irish, cease being Greek, cease being Russian, cease being whatever you had been before, and to become "white." And *that* is why this country says it's a white country and really believes it is. . . . Now one hears from a long time ago that "white is merely a state of mind." I add to that, white is a moral choice. It's up to you to be as white as you want to be and pay the price of that ticket. You cannot tell a Black man by the color of skin either. But this is a democracy. (56–57)

Later in the same essay, Baldwin continues:

> I attest to this, the world is not white; it never was white, cannot be white. White is a metaphor for power, and that is simply a way of describing Chase

Manhattan Bank. That is all it means, and the people who tried to rob us of identity have lost their own. (59)

4. This is a point made by Andrews, who quotes Chesnutt's Second Journal, May 29, 1880:

The object of my writings would be not so much the elevation of the colored people as the elevation of the whites—for I consider the unjust spirit of caste which is so insidious as to pervade a whole nation, and so powerful as to subject a whole race and all connected with it to scorn and social ostracism—I consider this a barrier to the moral progress of the American people; and I would be one of the first to head a determined, organized crusade against it.

For the context in which he is using this quotation, see Andrews, *Literary Career* 13. Joyce Pettis also includes this quotation in her essay "The Literary Imagination and the Historic Event: Chesnutt's Use of History in *The Marrow of Tradition* (38).

5. This is James Baldwin's term, from his essay "Stranger in the Village," when he characterizes Black and white men confronting one another:

The black man insists, by whatever means he finds at his disposal, that the white man cease to regard him as an exotic rarity and recognize him as a human being. This is a very charged and difficult moment, for there is a great deal of will power involved in the white man's naiveté. Most people are not naturally reflective any more than they are naturally malicious, and the white man prefers to keep the black man at a certain human remove because it is easier for him thus to preserve his simplicity and avoid being called to account for crimes committed by his forefathers, or his neighbors. (166)

6. It seems clear that "race men," by popular convention and according to Du Bois's definition, do not include those who are biologically white. In this case, Chesnutt is rather obviously signifying on the racial imperative.

7. This phrase is from Rich, "Split at the Root."

8. A similar portrait of a secret keeper is found in Paul Laurence Dunbar's *Sport of the Gods*, where Maurice Oakley keeps secret the theft to which his own brother confesses, thus continuing the stay in prison for the innocent former servant Berry Hamilton. By not confessing white guilt, and by keeping his brother's letter to himself, Maurice's life so revolves around his secret that it becomes perverted and is, eventually, completely destroyed.

9. This editorial presents an opinion similar to one written by Alexander Manly and published in the *Wilmington Record* on August 18, 1898. For a discussion of this editorial in relation to *Marrow of Tradition*, see Sundquist, *Wake* 408–35.

10. William Andrews makes a similar point in his literary biography of Chesnutt. In a reading of comments that Chesnutt makes about *The Marrow of Tradition*, Andrews says: "Historical change and social adjustment are . . . crucial themes in Chesnutt's analysis of the contemporary southern scene. Whites *and* blacks, South *and* North, he believed, must accept the inescapable fact that theirs was an era of social and political

transition" (182). Chesnutt's own comments are from a short article in the *Cleveland World*, where he says, with regard to *The Marrow of Tradition*, "It is the writer's belief that the forces of progress will in the end prevail" (magazine section 5).

11. See Giles and Lally. In this article the authors summarize two of the earliest critical positions about the novel, that of Bone (*Negro Novel*) and Gayle (*Way of the New World*). Gleason "Voices" offers a version of this reading, as does Delmar ("Moral Dilemma").

12. For a reading of *The Marrow of Tradition* that focuses on the counterplot involving the two half-sisters, see Kawash's chapter "A Question of Justice" (85–123).

13. According to West in "Malcolm X and Black Rage" (*Race Matters* 135–51), Malcolm X's notion of a psychic conversion is a needed process whereby Black people can free themselves from "the quest for white approval and disappointment owing mainly to white racist assessment" (139).

14. See chapter 11, *Black Feminist Thought*.

15. For a fascinating reading of the child's near death experience with croup as "judicial strangulation," see Kawash 121–23.

16. In the last sentences of *Paul Marchand*, Chesnutt makes reference to the attempt in Louisiana in 1921 to make "marriage a felony between a white person and a person of colored blood to the thirty-second degree inclusive" (185). Joel Williamson documents such animus against miscegenation that lynching is proscribed by some southern whites for "any white man who so sinned" (94). In May 1907, according to Williamson, citizens of Francisville, Louisiana, "raised a vigilance committee to oppose the keeping of black women by white men. Simultaneously, in Vicksburg, Mississippi, citizens actually organized an 'Anti-Miscegenation League'" (94).

17. References here are to the Vintage edition of *The Autobiography of an Ex-Coloured Man*, which according to a "Note on the Text" is an exact reprinting of the 1927 Knopf edition of *The Autobiography of an Ex-Coloured Man*. In this edition, spelling has been changed from the 1912 *Autobiography of an Ex-Colored Man* in order to attract British sales (Wilson, *Complete Poems* xxxii).

18. See the opening of Fleming's "Irony," in which he places his own reading focused on the "artistic elements of the work" in juxtaposition to Sterling Brown's and Hugh M. Gloster's readings of the novel as "objective presentation of Negro manners in various parts of the country" (Fleming 83; S. Brown 73–96; Gloster, 78–83). See also Van Vechten's introduction to the 1927 edition where he says the novel is "a composite autobiography of the Negro race in the United States in modern times" (xxxiv).

19. Other critics who, according to Skerrett, read the novel as ironic include Bone, Fleming, Garrett, and Margolies.

20. In Chesnutt's *Marrow of Tradition*, for example, Dr. Miller, when segregated into the "colored" railway car, muses:

> It was an old car, with faded upholstery, from which the stuffing projected here and there through torn places. Apparently the floor had not been swept for several days. The dust lay thick upon the window sills, and the water-cooler,

from which he essayed to get a drink, was filled with stale water which had made no recent acquaintance with ice. There was no other passenger in the car, and Miller occupied himself in making a rough calculation of what it would cost the Southern railroads to haul a whole car for every colored passenger. It was expensive, to say the least; it would be cheaper, and quite as considerate of their feelings, to make the negroes walk. (56)

Chesnutt also characterizes the "Blue Vein Society" in the title story from the collection *The Wife of His Youth*, a society popularly known to be open only to African Americans "white enough to show blue veins" (1). And in *Their Eyes Were Watching God*, Hurston presents the character Mrs. Turner, who is so color-struck that she has "built an altar to the unattainable—Caucasian characteristics for all" (145).

21. Kawash makes this point quite clearly when she explains that "to read the *Autobiography* without resorting to the critical fallacies involved in pronouncing moral or sociological judgment on a fictional character, we must take the narrator not for what the cultural logic of passing decrees him to be, a truly Black man passing for white, but for what the narrative presents him as—unnameable" (154).

22. In *Ex-Coloured Man* Johnson's narrator says:

As I listened to the singing of these songs, the wonder of their production grew upon me more and more. How did the men who originated them manage to do it? The sentiments are easily accounted for; they are mostly taken from the Bible; but the melodies, where did they come from? Some of them so weirdly sweet, and others so wonderfully strong. Take, for instance, "Go down, Moses." I doubt that there is a stronger theme in the whole musical literature of the world." (181)

In the preface to *The Book of American Negro Poetry* Johnson says:

I never think of this music but that I am struck by the wonder, the miracle of its production. How did the men who originated these songs manage to do it? The sentiments are easily accounted for; they are, for the most part, taken from the Bible. But the melodies, where did they come from? Some of them so weirdly sweet, and others so wonderfully strong. Take, for instance, "Go Down, Moses"; I doubt that there is a stronger theme in the whole musical literature of the world. (17)

23. For a careful and complex analysis of lynching as disciplinary act, see Wiegman 81–113.

24. Wald states that this scene is "based on his own experiences as a witness to lynchings as an NAACP representative," which is not correct (*Crossing the Line* 38). As Sondra Kathryn Wilson points out in her chronology accompanying *Complete Poems*, while *Ex-Colored Man* is published in 1912, Johnson becomes a member of the NAACP in 1915 and joins the staff as field secretary in 1916 (xxx–xxxi). There is an interesting resonance, however, in the kind of social protest against lynching that

Johnson envisions, which includes organizing the 1917 New York City silent protest march (Gates, "Introduction" viii).

25. This is Marjorie Garber's term, defined by her as "a failure of definitional distinction, a borderline that becomes permeable, that permits of border crossings from one (apparently distinct) category to another; black/white, Jew/Christian, noble/bourgeois, master/servant, master/slave" (16).

26. A related reading is Kawash's, who proposes "reading 'ex-coloured' not as a temporal event, being first colored and then not, but as a superimposition of X and *colored*, effectively negating both terms of the racial binary: colored negating whiteness, X negating colored, thereby rendering impossible both whiteness and blackness without restoring by default the relation of opposition that is presumed to prevail between them" (138).

27. It may be significant to note that photographs of James Weldon Johnson himself show him with a moustache.

28. According to Fleming, he seems to feel no pity for the victim, yet for himself he feels humiliation and shame (94).

29. This quotation is from the version of this poem as published in The Crisis *Reader*, ed. Sondra Kathryn Wilson, which reprints the poem as it appeared in *The Crisis*, February 1916. In the *Complete Poems*, also ed. Sondra Kathryn Wilson, the poem appears with the title "Brothers-American Drama," and stanzas are introduced with a parenthetical reference to either "the mob" or "the victim" as speaker (56–57). The text for *Complete Poems* is taken from Johnson's volume, *Fifty Years and Other Poems*, published in 1917.

30. An additional, contemporary text that we might consider with *Invisible Man* and *Ex-Coloured Man* would be David Bradley's *The Chaneysville Incident*, which relies on a narrator/historian who comes out of a kind of hibernation of his own, resolves numerous personal issues, and consequently reconciles with his white wife, agrees to father a child, and, presumably, makes the decision to "tell" the story of this time of his life.

CHAPTER 5: QUEERING AMERICA'S FAMILY

1. For a summary of earlier criticism of Fauset, see McDowell, "Neglected" 86–87; and Wall, *Women* 212n7. For a summary of more recent criticism, see Kuenz, 106n8. For an argument against the invocation of claims of authenticity, see L. Lewis, "Naming."

2. There is a striking difference between Wall's treatment of Fauset in *Women of the Harlem Renaissance* (1995) and in "Histories and Heresies: Engendering the Harlem Renaissance" (2001). It is the later work that I am referencing here.

3. This is, of course, a reference to the classic text in Black women's studies, *All the Women Are White, All the Blacks Are Men, But Some of Us Are Brave: Black Women's Studies*, ed. Hull, Scott, and Smith.

4. Robert Bone considers Fauset to be part of the "Rear Guard," characterized as

"those who lag behind" because they "still wished to orient Negro art toward white opinion." In contrast with Harlem School writing, according to Bone, "the work of the Rear Guard conformed to the canons of the early Negro novel" (97).

5. According to Sylvander, Fauset characterized her studies at Cornell University from 1901–5 as "'chiefly classical,' though including, 'of course,' a good deal of work in English as well as American History, German, French, Psychology" (29).

6. For other readings of fetish, particularly in a cultural context, see Pietz, "The Problem of the Fetish," I, II, III; Apter and Pietz; Krips; JanMohamed. Pietz's work is particularly suggestive here, because he traces fetish, "as an idea and a problem," to its origination "in the cross-cultural spaces of the coast of West Africa during the sixteenth and seventeenth century" ("Problem" I: 5). Significantly, Pietz also contextualizes Freud's concept of the fetish in Hegelian terms: "For Hegel, the African culture of the fetish represented a moment just prior to History, since the fetish was precisely that object of the Spirit that failed to participate in the Idea, which never experienced a negation and *Aufhebung* to a truth beyond its natural materiality. Marxism's commodity fetish, psychoanalysis's sexual fetish, and modernism's fetish as art object all in an essential way involve the object's untranscended materiality" ("Problem" I: 7).

7. Interestingly, Judith Butler discusses the "disavowal" necessary to Hegel's master/slave relationship. According to Butler, "the lord [master] postures as a disembodied desire for self-reflection, one who not only requires the subordination of the bondsman [slave] in the status of an instrumental body, but who requires in effect that the bondsman *be* the lord's body, but be it in such a way that the lord forgets or disavows his own activity in producing the bondsman, a production which we will call a projection." This would seem to suggest that in Butler's reading of Hegel, in the moment of self-consciousness where "othering" first takes place, disavowal of such an action does, as well. See *Psychic Life* 35.

8. To the extent, then, that the sex act inherent in miscegenation is a fetishized sex act, the miscegenation taboo, like the taboo on homosexuality, does indeed regulate normative heterosexuality, even without reference to "racially pure reproduction" (Butler, *Bodies That Matter* 167). Butler suggests that it is miscegenation's insistence on racial purity that makes it regulatory of heterosexuality, but since miscegenation carries a fetish within it, so to speak, it is already regulatory as fetishized sex.

9. The dates during which Fauset served as literary editor to *The Crisis* are sometimes confused. According to Sylvander (56–57), Du Bois announced in a September 1918 *The Crisis* editorial that a literary editor would be added to the staff. There was a delay, however, and the formal announcement of Fauset's position as literary editor did not come until the November 1919 issue.

10. Hutchinson does not consider Fauset central to his history, however. Allison Berg has noted that "Hutchinson repeats the critical commonplace that class was Jessie Fauset's 'chief shortcoming'" and contends more generally that gender does not factor into his analysis. See Berg; see also Hutchinson 225.

11. This is one of the main points of Cheryl Wall's article "Histories and Heresies."

12. As an example of the bifurcation of Fauset criticism during her lifetime, consider the January 1934 issue of *Opportunity* magazine, where William Stanley Braithwaite wrote that Fauset "stands in the front rank of American women novelists in general" and places her in the company of Sarah Orne Jewett, Mary E. Wilkins Freeman, Edith Wharton, Willa Cather, and Ellen Glasgow while Alain Locke dismisses Fauset and her "perservering [*sic*] and slowly maturing art" and "almost single-handed championship of upper and middle class Negro life as an important subject for fiction" (qtd. in Thadious Davis, "Introduction" xvi–xvii).

13. This point about Locke is also made by Davis in her introduction to *Comedy: American Style* (xxxii). In her work with *The Crisis* and *Brownie's Book*, Fauset published Langston Hughes's first poems. She also recognized the talent of Countee Cullen, Nella Larsen, Claude McKay, George Schuyler, and Jean Toomer, among others; for this support Hughes, for example, considers her a "midwife" to the Harlem Renaissance (see Hughes, *Big Sea* 218).

14. This history is presented in Wall, "Histories and Heresies"; Hutchinson 389–95; and D. L. Lewis 89–118.

15. We should note that Locke's editorial control over the anthology was formidable. In a letter to Charles S. Johnson he writes: "Did you see the snide remarks of Miss Fauset on the Reiss drawing? She has had the additional bad taste to go out of her way to insert a similar tirade in her article for the book. I am going to delete it if it deletes me from her list" (qtd. in Hutchinson 523n31).

16. Wall makes the point that an earlier version of "The Gift of Laughter" appeared as "The Symbolism of Bert Williams" in *The Crisis*, May 1922: 12–15 ("Histories and Heresies" 74n5). See also Wilson 255–59.

17. Note that Fauset uses the French *rôle*, and indicates this by her use of italics and the accented *o*.

18. "The racial type itself" is Fauset's characterization of Bert Williams's performance, used to indicate a positive attribute in Williams's work. Fauset contrasts the way Williams manages to be "the racial type itself" with the rendition by Charles Gilpin of the Emperor Jones, which "many colored theatregoers" find irritating because of the way that "the artistic interpretation of a type and the deliberate travestying of a race" are not distinguishable ("Symbolism" 255). Fauset's use of the term "symbolic" to characterize the way that Williams manages to portray "to us the racial type itself" fits well with JanMohamed's categorization of colonialist discourse into the imaginary and the symbolic, which is, of course, terminology derived from Lacan. While "imaginary" fiction "tends to fetishize a nondialectical, fixed opposition between the self and the native," which we might ascribe to Gilpin's version of the Emperor Jones as Fauset characterizes it, "symbolic" texts "thematize the problem of colonialist mentality and its encounter with the racial Other," often rigorously examining "the 'imaginary' mechanism of colonialist mentality." This is an interesting (and, I would

say, accurate) description of the effect of Williams's portrayal of his "poor, shunted, cheated, out-of-luck Negro" (see JanMohamed 84–87).

19. The phrases "radical intersubjectivity" and "structuring projection" are Jane Gallop's (59–63). The idea of a "structuring projection" also brings to mind James Baldwin's classic observation: "What one's imagination makes of other people is dictated, of course, by the laws of one's own personality and it is one of the ironies of black-white relations that, by means of what the white man imagines the black man to be, the black man is enabled to know who the white man is" ("Stranger in the Village" 167).

20. For Fauset, because this is but one moment in the life of Peter Bye, we continue to see her at odds with masculinist understandings of the 1920s and 1930s, even those contemporary to our own time such as David Levering Lewis's, where the image of the soldiers known as "Hell Fighters" opens the history told as *When Harlem Was in Vogue*.

21. Joanna does not entirely renounce a career in the arts. Like Johnson's ex-coloured man before he renounces his color, Joanna becomes a composer. According to the narrator, because "her mentality was essentially creative, she found herself more and more impelled toward the expression of the intense appreciation of living which welled within her." For this reason, "with her slight knowledge of composition she composed two little songs and glimpsing future possibilities, she began to study that most fascinating of all the sciences—harmony" (291).

22. In saying that "colored people . . . can do everything that anybody else can do," Joanna is relying upon her extensive knowledge springing from her Sunday reading about exemplary females, "notable women of color" (72). This is the kind of material that Pauline Hopkins published in the *Colored American Magazine*, particularly in the series titled "Famous Women of the Negro Race."

23. Jane Kuenz remarks that "Joanna's performance as America makes whiteness visible, but visible as a mask, the arbitrary sign of the power to which white people are thus only arbitrarily attached" (102).

24. But also, as previously noted, is perhaps beginning a new career as a composer.

25. By this I mean to suggest both the image in the *Colored American Magazine* of the "Young Colored American" and my reading of Sappho's son Alphonse in *Contending Forces*. When Old Meriwether Bye visits Peter and Joanna at the conclusion of the novel, Joanna sees this white man and her own husband as "the last of the old order and the first of the new," even while she also notes that Peter himself has not completely escaped the effects of "the ancient regime" (293). When the representative of the "old order" offers his inheritance to Peter and Joanna's son in an attempt to keep the Bye legacy alive, and Peter speaks up and not only rejects the inheritance but also repudiates the blood tie between the white and Black Byes, this repudiation places Peter and Joanna's young son in a position to become the first of a new order, yet this youngest Bye will also be the representative not only of the Black Byes but of all the Byes, and thus "the new American."

26. In *Plum Bun*, Fauset switches her spelling to "colour" and "coloured." In *There Is Confusion* and then subsequently in *The Chinaberry Tree* and *Comedy: American Style*, the spelling is "color" and "colored."

27. There is an interesting parallel here to Barbara Johnson's classic article "Metaphor, Metonymy and Voice in *Their Eyes Were Watching God.*" According to Johnson, "Hurston dramatizes the predicament not only of the anthropologist but also of the novelist: both are caught between the (metaphorical) urge to universalize or totalize and the knowledge that is precisely 'the near and the obvious' that will never be grasped once and for all but will only be (metonymically) named and renamed, as different things successively strike different heads" (209). This seems to me to be particularly apt with regard to racialized descriptions.

28. It is tempting to here include a reading of the chinaberry tree that takes into account its many other attributes: its poisonous fruit, its bitter foliage, its status as a naturalized rather than native tree.

29. The concept of miscegenation is problematic because it suggests that racial categories are discrete and that people of different races are distinct species. This is, of course, not true even though many racist beliefs stem from this idea.

30. This quotation is from Senator Theodore Bilbo of Mississippi (qtd. in F. J. Davis 174).

31. It is interesting to note here that Fauset includes Laurentine's white half-sisters in this story. As soon as both come of age they visit Laurentine to offer their assistance. According to the narrator's description of this meeting, "they were three well-bred women facing a problem for which not one of them was responsible" (12). From them, Laurentine accepts the training that enables her to be a dressmaker and earn her living.

32. In his "Appendix: The Oedipus Connection" (*Fetish: An Erotics of Culture* 185–86), Henry Krips reads Lévi-Strauss's interpretation of the Oedipus myth as one that serves to resolve the "initial cosmological contradiction between autochthony and sexual reproduction," that is, to solve the problem of whether humans originate from one (from "sameness") or from two (from "difference"). The incest taboo, according to this reading, represents a prohibition against too much "sameness."

33. Here, Melissa is called a "bastard" by Malory and falls into the "black, black abyss" (331). In "The Sleeper Wakes" Amy is called a "nigger" by Wynne and is enveloped in "dreadful clinging blackness" (20).

34. In *Oedipus the King*, Oedipus characterizes his own behavior as "a father seeing nothing, knowing nothing,/ begetting you from his own source of life" (1484–85). Also, as Krips "proves," "the logic of the Oedipus myth depends upon the system of associations that, according to Freud, structures dream thoughts and the unconscious. . . . Overrating blood relations as marriage partners results in offspring born of one blood. Thus, since dream logic associates effects with their causes, overrating blood relations is equivalent to being born of one. Since autochthony is to be born of

the earth, it too is equivalent to being born of one. Thus overrating blood relations is equivalent to autochthony, since both are equivalent to being born of one." The significance of this, as Krips goes on to say, is that according to Greek cosmology autochthones are monsters. Thus, "overintimacy with blood relations" creates monsters (187, 191–92).

35. Edna Pontellier "awakens" to her own sexual desire but takes that desire to sea, allowing it to enfold her body "in its soft, close embrace." She grows tired. "Exhaustion was pressing upon and over-powering her." She then drowns in her desire (Chopin 113–14).

36. According to Freud, "There are only too many occasions on which a child is slighted, or at least *feels* he has been slighted, on which he feels he is not receiving the whole of his parents' love, and most of all, on which he feels regrets at having to share it with brothers and sisters. His sense that his own affection is not being fully reciprocated then finds a vent in the idea, which is often consciously recollected from early childhood, of being a stepchild or an adopted child" ("Family Romances" 42). By thinking of him or herself as a stepchild or an adopted child, Freud continues, the child "is not getting rid of his father but exalting him. Indeed the whole effort at replacing the real father by a superior one is only an expression of the child's longing for the happy, vanished days when his father seemed to him the noblest and strongest of men and his mother the dearest and loveliest of women" (45). For a full account of this psychological phenomenon see "Family Romances" 41–45.

37. In this way, Phebe's encounter with Llewellyn is distinct from the encounter between Amy and Wynne in "The Sleeper Wakes" and Angela and Roger in *Plum Bun.*

AFTERWORD

1. As Valerie Lee points out in her introduction to *Granny Midwives and Black Women Writers: Double-Dutched Readings*, in a discussion of Alice Walker's story "The Revenge of Hannah Kemhuff," the question "Should I curse God and die?" contains a reference to the story of Job (Lee 15).

2. This is meant to suggest a Faulknerian echo in Ellison's writing. In his introduction to *Invisible Man*, Ellison declares himself in agreement with Faulkner about history's role in the present, saying, "What is commonly assumed to be past history is actually as much a part of the living present as William Faulkner insisted. Furtive, implacable and tricky, it inspirits both the observer and the scene observed, artifacts, manners and atmosphere and it speaks even when no one wills to listen" (xvi).

3. One very interesting aspect of *Juneteenth*, Ellison's work as edited and published posthumously by John F. Callahan, is the way in which the novel develops Ellison's ideas about mother love. In *Juneteenth*, Hickman becomes, as a young man, the midwife and then "mother" to the racially indeterminate child he names Bliss, who later becomes a race-baiting senator, and this mothering transforms Hickman's life. This

happens because the baby's mother, who has accused Hickman's brother of rape and so caused his death by lynching, comes to Hickman for help with the birth of her child (286–314).

4. The opening words of Toni Morrison's *The Bluest Eye.*

5. Marjorie Pryse's paraphrase of the relation between Janie's and Pheoby's tongues (see *Conjuring* 22).

WORKS CITED

Alcoff, Linda Martin. "Philosophy Matters: A Review of Recent Work in Feminist Philosophy." *Signs: Journal of Women in Culture and Society* 25.3 (Spring 2000): 841–82.

Ammons, Elizabeth. *Conflicting Stories: American Women Writers at the Turn into the Twentieth Century.* New York: Oxford University Press, 1992.

Anderson, Benedict. *Imagined Communities: Reflections on the Origins and Spread of Nationalism.* London: Verso, 1983.

Andrews, William. *The Literary Career of Charles W. Chesnutt.* Baton Rouge: Louisiana State University Press, 1980.

———. "The Novelization of Voice in Early African American Narrative." *PMLA* 105.1 (January 1990): 23–34.

Angelou, Maya. *I Know Why the Caged Bird Sings.* New York: Bantam, 1971.

———. "Still I Rise." *Still I Rise.* New York: Random House, 2001.

———. *To Tell a Free Story: The First Century of Afro-American Autobiography, 1760–1865.* Urbana: University of Illinois Press, 1986.

Anzaldúa, Gloria. *Borderlands/La Frontera: The New Mestiza.* San Francisco: Aunt Lute, 1987.

Apter, Emily, and William Pietz. *Fetishism as Cultural Discourse.* Ithaca, N.Y.: Cornell University Press, 1993.

Ardener, Shirley, ed. *Perceiving Women.* London: Malaby, 1975.

Ardis, Ann L., and Leslie W. Lewis, eds. *Women's Experience of Modernity, 1875–1945.* Baltimore: Johns Hopkins University Press, 2003.

Baker, Houston. *Blues, Ideology, and Afro-American Literature: A Vernacular Theory.* Chicago: University of Chicago Press, 1984.

———. "Caliban's Triple Play." *"Race," Writing, and Difference.* Ed. Henry Louis Gates Jr. Chicago: University of Chicago Press, 1986. 381–95.

Baldwin, James. "Black English: A Dishonest Argument." *Black English and the Education of Black Children and Youth.* Ed. Geneva Smitherman. Detroit: Wayne State University, 1981. 54–60.

————. "Stranger in the Village." *Notes of a Native Son*. Boston: Beacon, 1955. 159–75.

Ball, Edward. *Slaves in the Family*. New York: Farrar, 1998.

Barnett, Stuart. "Introduction: Hegel Before Derrida." *Hegel After Derrida*. Ed. Stuart Barnett. New York: Routledge, 1998. 1–38.

Baym, Nina. *Woman's Fiction: A Guide to Novels by and about Women in America, 1820–70*. Urbana: University of Illinois Press, 1993.

Beauvoir, Simone de. *The Second Sex*. New York: Vintage, 1989.

Bellman, Beryl L. "The Paradox of Secrecy." *Human Studies* 4 (1981): 1–24.

Berg, Allison. "The New 'New Negro': Recasting the Harlem Renaissance." *College Literature* 25.3 (Fall 1998): 172–80.

Bernardi, Debra. "Narratives of Domestic Imperialism: The African-American Home in the Colored American Magazine and the Novels of Pauline Hopkins, 1900–1903." *Separate Spheres No More: Gender Convergence in American Literature, 1830–1930*. Ed. Monika M. Elbert. Tuscaloosa: University of Alabama Press, 2000. 203–24.

Bethel, Lorraine. "'This Infinity of Conscious Pain': Zora Neale Hurston and the Black Female Literary Tradition." Hull et al. 176–88.

Bleser, Carol K. Rothrock, ed. *Secret and Sacred: The Diaries of James Henry Hammond, a Southern Slaveholder*. New York: Oxford University Press, 1988.

Bone, Robert. *The Negro Novel in America*. New Haven, Conn.: Yale University Press, 1958.

Boyd, Melba Joyce. *Discarded Legacy: Politics and Poetics in the Life of Frances E. W. Harper*. Detroit: Wayne State University Press, 1994.

Bradley, David. *The Chaneysville Incident*. New York: Harper, 1981.

Brodie, Fawn. *Thomas Jefferson: An Intimate History*. New York: Bantam, 1974.

Brown, Sterling. "A Century of Negro Portraiture in American Literature." *Massachusetts Review* 7 (Winter 1966): 73–96.

Brown, William Wells. *Anti-Slavery Harp: Collection of Songs for Anti-Slavery Meetings*. 2nd ed. Boston: Marsh, 1849.

————. *The Black Man, His Antecedents, His Genius, and His Achievements*. 1863. New York: Arno, 1969.

————. *Clotel; or, The President's Daughter: A Narrative of Slave Life in the United States*. 1853. New York: Carol, 1969.

————. *Clotelle: A Tale of the Southern States*. Boston: Redpath, 1864.

————. *Clotelle; or, The Colored Heroine: A Tale of the Southern States*. 1867. Miami: Mnemosyne, 1969.

————. "A Lecture Delivered before the Female Anti-Slavery Society of Salem, at Lyceum Hall, Nov. 14, 1847." Boston: Anti-Slavery Society, 1847.

————. *Miralda; or, The Beautiful Quadroon: A Romance of American Slavery, Founded on Fact*. Serialized. *Weekly Anglo-African*. Dec. 1, 1860–March 16, 1861.

————. *Narrative of the Life and Escape of William Wells Brown*. 1853. Published with *Clotel; or, The President's Daughter*. New York: Carol, 1969. 17–55.

―――. *Narrative of the Life of William W. Brown*. 1847. *Five Slave Narratives*. Ed. William Loren Katz. New York: Arno, 1969.

Butler, Judith. *Bodies That Matter: On the Discursive Limits of "Sex."* New York: Routledge, 1993.

―――. *The Psychic Life of Power: Theories in Subjection*. Stanford, Calif.: Stanford University Press, 1997.

―――. *Subjects of Desire: Hegelian Reflections in Twentieth-Century France*. New York: Columbia University Press, 1987.

Butler, Octavia. *Kindred*. Boston: Beacon, 1988.

Butler, Robert J. Introduction. *The Critical Response to Ralph Ellison*. Westport, Conn.: Greenwood, 2000. xix–xl.

Carby, Hazel, "The Politics of Fiction, Anthropology, and the Folk: Zora Neale Hurston." *History and Memory in African-American Culture*. Eds. Geneviève Fabre and Robert O'Meally. New York: Oxford University Press, 1994. 28–44.

―――. *Race Men*. Cambridge, Mass.: Harvard University Press, 1998.

―――. *Reconstructing Womanhood: The Emergence of the Afro-American Woman Novelist*. New York: Oxford University Press, 1987.

Cassuto, Leonard. "Frederick Douglass and the Work of Freedom: Hegel's Master-Slave Dialectic in the Fugitive Slave Narrative. *Prospects: An Annual Journal of American Cultural Studies* 21 (1996): 229–59.

Chesnut, Mary Boykin. *A Diary from Dixie*. Ed. Ben Ames Williams. Boston: Houghton, 1949.

Chesnutt, Charles W. *The Journals of Charles W. Chesnutt*. Ed. Richard Brodhead. Durham, N.C.: Duke University Press, 1993.

―――. *The Marrow of Tradition*. New York: Penguin, 1993.

―――. *Paul Marchand, F.M.C.* Princeton, N.J.: Princeton University Press, 1999.

―――. *The Quarry*. Princeton, N.J.: Princeton University Press, 1999.

―――. *The Wife of His Youth and Other Stories*. Ann Arbor: University of Michigan Press, 1968.

―――. *"To Be an Author": Letters of Charles W. Chesnutt, 1889–1905*. Eds. Joseph R. McElrath Jr. and Robert C. Leitz III. Princeton, N.J.: Princeton University Press, 1997.

―――. "What Is a White Man?" *New York Independent*, May 30, 1889: 5–6.

Child, Lydia Maria. "Madison Washington." *The Freedmen's Book*. Ed. Lydia Maria Child. Boston: Fields, 1869. 147–53.

Chopin, Kate. *The Awakening*. New York: Norton, 1976.

Christian, Barbara. *Black Women Novelists: The Development of a Tradition, 1892–1976*. Westport, Conn.: Greenwood, 1980.

Collins, Patricia Hill. *Black Feminist Thought: Knowledge, Consciousness, and the Politics of Empowerment*. 2nd ed. New York: Routledge, 2000.

―――. "Learning from the Outsider Within: The Sociological Significance of Black Feminist Thought." *Beyond Methodology: Feminist Scholarship As Lived Research*.

Ed. Mary Margaret Fonow and Judith A. Cook. Bloomington: Indiana University Press, 1991. 35–59.

Cooke, Michael G. *Afro-American Literature in the Twentieth Century: The Achievement of Intimacy*. New Haven, Conn.: Yale University Press, 1984.

Cooper, Anna Julia. *A Voice from the South: By a Black Woman of the South*. Xenia, Ohio: Aldine, 1892.

Cunningham, George. "'Called Into Existence': Gender, Desire, and Voice in Douglass' *Narrative of 1845*." *differences: A Journal of Feminist Cultural Studies* 1 (1989): 108–36.

Davidson, Cathy N. "Preface: No More Separate Spheres!" *American Literature* 70.3 (September 1998): 443–63.

Davis, Charles T., Jr., and Henry Louis Gates Jr. *The Slave's Narrative*. New York: Oxford University Press, 1985.

Davis, Elizabeth Lindsay. *Lifting As They Climb: The National Association of Colored Women*. Washington, D.C.: National Association of Colored Women, 1933.

Davis, F. James. *Who Is Black? One Nation's Definition*. University Park: Pennsylvania State University Press, 1991.

Davis, Thadious M. Foreword. *There Is Confusion*. Jessie Fauset. Boston: Northeastern University Press, 1989. v–xxvi.

———. Introduction. *Comedy: American Style*. Jessie Redmon Fauset. New York: Hall, 1995. xv–xxxv.

Delany, Martin R. *Blake; or, The Huts of America*. 1859–1861. Ed. Floyd J. Miller. Boston: Beacon, 1970.

———. *The Condition, Elevation, Emigration, and Destiny of the Colored People of the United States*. 1852. New York: Arno Press, 1968.

———. *Official Report of the Niger Valley Exploring Party*. Philadelphia: Rhistoric, 1969.

———. *The Origin and Objects of Ancient Freemasonry: Its Introduction into the United States, and Legitimacy among Colored Men*. Pittsburgh: Haven, 1853.

———. *Principia of Ethnology: The Origin of Races and Color, with an Archeological Compendium of Ethiopian and Egyptian Civilization from Years of Careful Examination and Enquiry*. 1879. Baltimore: Black Classic, 1991.

Delmar, P. Jay. "The Moral Dilemma in Charles W. Chesnutt's *The Marrow of Tradition*." *American Literary Realism* 14.2 (Autumn 1981): 269–72.

Dickstein, Morris. "Ralph Ellison, Race, and American Culture." *Raritan: A Quarterly Review* 18.4 (Spring 1999): 30–50.

Dixon, Melvin. "Singing Swords: The Literary Legacy of Slavery." Davis and Gates 298–317.

Douglass, Frederick. *The Heroic Slave*. 1853. *Three Classic African-American Novels*. Ed. William L. Andrews. New York: Mentor-Penguin, 1990. 23–69.

———. *Life and Times of Frederick Douglass*. 1892. New York: Macmillan, 1962.

———. *My Bondage and My Freedom.* New York: Dover, 1969.

———. *Narrative of the Life of Frederick Douglass, an American Slave, Written by Himself.* New York: Penguin, 1982.

Du Bois, W. E. B. "The Colored Magazine in America." *The Crisis* 5 (November 1912): 33–35.

———. *The Souls of Black Folk.* New York: Bantam, 1989.

DuCille, Ann. *The Coupling Convention: Sex, Text, and Tradition in Black Women's Fiction.* New York: Oxford University Press, 1993.

———. "The Occult of True Black Womanhood: Critical Demeanor and Black Feminist Studies." *Female Subjects in Black and White: Race, Psychoanalysis, Feminism.* Eds. Elizabeth Abel, Barbara Christian, and Helene Moglen. Berkeley: University of California Press, 1997. 21–56.

———. "Where in the World Is William Wells Brown? Thomas Jefferson, Sally Hemings, and the DNA of African-American Literary History." *American Literary History* 12.3 (Fall 2000): 443–62.

Dunbar, Paul Laurence. *The Sport of the Gods.* 1902. New York: Arno, 1969.

Duncan, Malcolm C. *Duncan's Masonic Ritual and Monitor; or, Guide to the Three Symbolic Degrees.* Chicago: Cook, 1972.

Eakin, Paul John. *How Our Lives Become Stories: Making Selves.* Ithaca, N.Y.: Cornell University Press, 1999.

Ellison, Ralph. *Invisible Man.* New York: Vintage, 1990.

———. *Juneteenth.* Ed. John Callahan. New York: Random House, 1999.

———. "The Little Man at Chehaw Station." *Going to the Territory.* New York: Random, 1986. 3–38.

Ernest, John. *Resistance and Reformation in Nineteenth-Century African-American Literature: Brown, Wilson, Jacobs, Delany, Douglass, and Harper.* Jackson: University Press of Mississippi, 1995.

Farrison, William Edward. *William Wells Brown: Author and Reformer.* Chicago: University of Chicago Press, 1970.

Fauset, Jessie Redmon. *The Chinaberry Tree: A Novel of American Life and Selected Writings.* Boston: Northeastern University Press, 1995.

———. *Comedy: American Style.* New York: Hall, 1995.

———. "Double Trouble." *The Sleeper Wakes: Harlem Renaissance Stories by Women.* Ed. Marcy Knopf. New Brunswick, N.J.: Rutgers University Press, 1993. 26–39.

———. "The Gift of Laughter." *The New Negro.* Ed. Alain Locke. New York: Atheneum, 1970. 161–67.

———. *Plum Bun: A Novel without a Moral.* Boston: Beacon, 1990.

———. "The Sleeper Wakes." *The Sleeper Wakes: Harlem Renaissance Stories by Women.* Ed. Marcy Knopf. New Brunswick, N.J.: Rutgers University Press, 1993. 1–25.

———. "The Symbolism of Bert Williams." Wilson, *Reader* 255–59.

Felski, Rita. *The Gender of Modernity*. Cambridge, Mass.: Harvard University Press, 1995.

Fleischner, Jennifer. *Mastering Slavery: Memory, Family, and Identity in Women's Slave Narratives*. New York: New York University Press, 1996.

Fleming, Robert. "Irony as a Key to Johnson's *The Autobiography of an Ex-Coloured Man*." *American Literature* 43.1 (March 1971): 83–96.

Fortune, T. Thomas. "False Theory of Education Cause of Race Demoralization." *Colored American Magazine* 7.6: 473–78.

Foster, Frances Smith. *A Brighter Coming Day: A Frances Ellen Watkins Harper Reader*. New York: Feminist, 1990.

———. Editor's Note. *Minnie's Sacrifice, Sowing and Reaping, Trial and Triumph: Three Rediscovered Novels*. Boston: Beacon, 1994. xli–xliii.

———. Introduction. *Minnie's Sacrifice, Sowing and Reaping, Trial and Triumph: Three Rediscovered Novels*. Boston: Beacon, 1994. xi–xxxvii.

———, ed. *Minnie's Sacrifice, Sowing and Reaping, Trial and Triumph: Three Rediscovered Novels by Frances E. W. Harper*. Boston: Beacon, 1994.

———. *Written by Herself: Literary Production by African American Women, 1746–1892*. Bloomington: Indiana University Press, 1993.

Freud, Sigmund. "Family Romances." *The Sexual Enlightenment of Children*. New York: Macmillan, 1963. 41–45.

———. "Fetishism." *The Norton Anthology of Theory and Criticism*. Ed. Vincent B. Leitch. New York: Norton, 2001. 952–56.

Gaines, Ernest. *The Autobiography of Miss Jane Pittman*. New York: Bantam, 1982.

Gaines, Kevin K. *Uplifting the Race: Black Leadership, Politics, and Culture in the Twentieth Century*. Chapel Hill: University of North Carolina Press, 1996.

Gallop, Jane. *Reading Lacan*. Ithaca, N.Y.: Cornell University Press, 1985.

Gara, Larry. "The Professional Fugitive in the Abolition Movement." *Wisconsin Magazine of History* 48 (Spring 1965): 196–204.

Garber, Marjorie. *Vested Interests: Cross-Dressing and Cultural Anxiety*. New York: Harper, 1993.

Garrett, Marvin P. "Early Recollections and Structural Irony in *The Autobiography of an Ex-Colored Man*." *Critique: Studies in Modern Fiction* 13.3 (1971): 5–14.

Gates, Henry Louis, Jr., ed. *Black Literature and Literary Theory*. New York: Methuen, 1984.

———. *Figures in Black: Words, Signs, and the "Racial" Self*. New York: Oxford University Press, 1987.

———. Introduction to the Vintage Edition. *The Autobiography of an Ex-Coloured Man*. New York: Vintage, 1989. v–xxiii.

———. *The Signifying Monkey: A Theory of Afro-American Literary Criticism*. New York: Oxford University Press, 1988.

Gayle, Addison. *The Way of the New World: The Black Novel in America*. Garden City, N.Y.: Anchor, 1976.

Genovese, Eugene D. *Roll, Jordan, Roll: The World the Slaves Made.* New York: Vintage, 1976.

Giddings, Paula. *When and Where I Enter: The Impact of Black Women on Race and Sex in America.* New York: William Morrow, 1984.

Gilbert, Sandra M., and Susan Gubar. *The Madwoman in the Attic: The Woman Writer and the Nineteenth-Century Literary Imagination.* New Haven, Conn.: Yale University Press, 1979.

Giles, James R., and Thomas P. Lally. "Allegory in Chesnutt's *Marrow of Tradition.*" *JGE: The Journal of General Education* 35.4 (1984): 259–69.

Gilmore, Paul. *The Genuine Article: Race, Mass Culture, and American Literary Manhood.* Durham, N.C.: Duke University Press, 2001.

Gilroy, Paul. *The Black Atlantic: Modernity and Double Consciousness.* Cambridge, Mass.: Harvard University Press, 1993.

Gleason, William. "Voices at the Nadir: Charles Chesnutt and David Bryant Fulton." *American Literary Realism* 24.3 (Spring 1992): 22–41.

Gloster, Hugh M. *Negro Voices in American Fiction.* New York: Russell, 1965.

Gordon-Reed, Annette. *Thomas Jefferson and Sally Hemings: An American Controversy.* Charlottesville: University Press of Virginia, 1997.

Grimké, Angelina. "Black Is, as Black Does (A Dream)." *Colored American Magazine* 1.3 (August 1900): 160–63.

Gruesser, John Cullen, ed. *The Unruly Voice: Rediscovering Pauline Hopkins.* Urbana: University of Illinois Press, 1996.

Harding, Sandra. *Whose Science? Whose Knowledge? Thinking from Women's Lives.* Ithaca, N.Y.: Cornell University Press, 1991.

Harper, Frances E. W. "An Address Delivered at the Centennial Anniversary of the Pennsylvania Society for Promoting the Abolition of Slavery." *Masterpieces of Negro Eloquence, 1818–1913.* Ed. Alice Moore Dunbar. Mineola, N.Y.: Dover, 2000. 64–68.

———. *Iola Leroy; or, Shadows Uplifted.* 1892. Introd. Hazel V. Carby. Boston: Beacon, 1987.

———. *Minnie's Sacrifice.* 1869. *Minnie's Sacrifice, Sowing and Reaping, Trial and Triumph: Three Rediscovered Novels by Frances E. W. Harper.* Ed. Frances Smith Foster. Black Women Writers Series. Boston: Beacon, 1994. 1–92.

———. "Woman's Political Future." *World's Congress of Representative Women.* Ed. Mary Wright Sewell. Chicago: McNally, 1894. 433–38.

Harper, Philip Brian. *Are We Not Men? Masculine Anxiety and the Problem of African American Identity.* New York: Oxford University Press, 1996.

Harris, Joel Chandler. *Uncle Remus: His Songs and His Sayings.* New York: Grosset and Dunlap, 1921.

Hegel, G. W. F. *Phenomenology of Spirit.* Trans. A. V. Miller. Oxford: Oxford University Press, 1977.

hooks, bell. *Black Looks: Race and Representation.* Boston: South End, 1992.

Hopkins, Pauline. "Club Life among Colored Women." *Famous Women of the Negro Race*. Pt. 9. *Colored American Magazine* 5.4 (August 1902): 273–77.

———. *Contending Forces: A Romance Illustrative of Negro Life North and South*. Introd. Richard Yarborough. Schomburg Library of Nineteenth-Century Black Women Writers. New York: Oxford University Press, 1988.

———. "A Dash for Liberty." *Colored American Magazine* 3 (August 1901): 243–47.

———. *Of One Blood; or, The Hidden Self*. 1902–3. *The Magazine Novels of Pauline Hopkins*. Introd. Hazel V. Carby. Schomburg Library of Nineteenth-Century Black Women Writers. New York: Oxford University Press, 1988. 439–621.

———. "Talma Gordon." *Colored American Magazine* 1.5 (October 1900): 271–90.

Hughes, Langston. *The Big Sea*. New York: Hill, 1940.

———. "Cross." *The Collected Poems of Langston Hughes*. New York: Vintage, 1995. 59–59.

Hull, Gloria, Patricia Bell Scott, and Barbara Smith, eds. *All the Women Are White, All the Blacks Are Men, but Some of Us Are Brave: Black Women's Studies*. Old Westbury, N.Y.: Feminist, 1982.

Hurston, Zora Neale. *Their Eyes Were Watching God*. New York: Harper, 1990.

Hutchinson, George. *The Harlem Renaissance in Black and White*. Cambridge: Harvard University Press, 1995.

Irigaray, Luce, "The Eternal Irony of the Community." Trans. Gillian C. Gill. Mills, *Feminist Interpretations* 45–57.

———. *Speculum of the Other Woman*. Trans. Gillian C. Gill. Ithaca, N.Y.: Cornell University Press, 1985.

Jacobs, Harriet. *Incidents in the Life of a Slave Girl*. Ed. Jean Fagan Yellin. Cambridge, Mass.: Harvard University Press, 1987.

JanMohamed, Abdul. "The Economy of Manichean Allegory." *The Post-Colonial Studies Reader*. Eds. Bill Ashcroft, Gareth Griffiths, and Helen Tiffin. London: Routledge, 1995. 18–23.

Japtok, Martin. "Between 'Race' as Construct and 'Race' as Essence: *The Autobiography of an Ex-Colored Man*." *Southern Literary Journal* 28.2 (Spring 1996): 32–47.

Johnson, Abby Arthur, and Ronald M. Johnson. "Away from Accommodation: Radical Editors and Protest Journalism, 1900–1910." *Journal of Negro History* 62 (October 1977): 325–28.

Johnson, Barbara. "Metaphor, Metonymy and Voice in *Their Eyes Were Watching God*." Gates, *Black Literature* 205–19.

Johnson, Charles S. "The Rise of the Negro Magazine." *Journal of Negro History* 13 (January 1928): 7–21.

Johnson, Georgia Douglas. "The Riddle." *The New Negro*. Ed. Alain Locke. New York: Atheneum, 1970. 147.

Johnson, James Weldon. *Along This Way: The Autobiography of James Weldon Johnson*. New York: Da Capo, 2000.

———. *Autobiography of an Ex-Coloured Man*. New York: Vintage, 1989.

————. *Black Manhattan*. New York: Da Capo, 1991.

————, ed. *The Book of American Negro Poetry*. New York: Harcourt, 1969.

Johnson, James Weldon, and J. Rosamond Johnson. *The Books of American Negro Spirituals*. New York: Da Capo, 1969. 1–187.

Jordan, Winthrop D. *The White Man's Burden: Historical Origins of Racism in the United States*. New York: Oxford University Press, 1974.

Kalkavage, Peter. "Hegel's Logic of Desire." *St. John's Review* 43.2 (1996): 1–19.

Kaplan, Carla. "The Erotics of Talk: 'That Oldest Human Longing' in *Their Eyes Were Watching God*." *American Literature* 67.1 (March 1995): 115–42.

Kassanoff, Jennie A. "'Fate Has Linked Us Together': Blood, Gender, and the Politics of Representation in Pauline Hopkins's *Of One Blood*." Gruesser 158–81.

Kawash, Samira. *Dislocating the Color Line: Identity, Hybridity, and Singularity in African-American Literature*. Stanford, Calif.: Stanford University Press, 1997.

Kelly, Michael. "The Post-War Hegel Revival in France: A Bibliographic Essay." *Journal of European Studies* 12 (1983): 199–216.

Knopf, Marcy. Foreword. *The Chinaberry Tree: A Novel of American Life and Selected Writings*. Jessie Redmon Fauset. Boston: Northeastern University Press, 1995. ix–xxix.

Kojève, Alexandre. *Introduction to the Reading of Hegel*. Ed. Allan Bloom. Trans. James H. Nichols Jr. Ithaca, N.Y.: Cornell University Press, 1969.

Krips, Henry. *Fetish: An Erotics of Culture*. Ithaca, N.Y.: Cornell University Press, 1999.

Kuenz, Jane. "The Face of America: Performing Race and Nation in Jessie Fauset's *There Is Confusion*." *Yale Journal of Criticism* 12.1 (1999): 89–111.

Lauter, Paul. *Canons and Contexts*. New York: Oxford University Press, 1991.

Lee, Valerie. *Granny Midwives and Black Women Writers: Double-Dutched Readings*. New York: Routledge, 1996.

Levine, Lawrence W. *Black Culture and Black Consciousness: Afro-American Folk Thought from Slavery to Freedom*. New York: Oxford University Press, 1977.

Levine, Robert S. *Martin Delany, Frederick Douglass, and the Politics of Representative Identity*. Chapel Hill: University of North Carolina Press, 1997.

Lewis, David Levering. *When Harlem Was in Vogue*. New York: Knopf, 1981.

Lewis, Leslie W. "Naming the Problem Embedded in the Problem That Led to the Question 'Who Shall Teach African American Literature?'; or, Are We Ready to Discard the Concept of Authenticity Altogether?" *White Scholars/African American Texts*. Ed. Lisa A. Long. New Brunswick, N.J.: Rutgers University Press, 2005. 52–67.

————. "Towards a New 'Colored' Consciousness: Biracial Identity in Pauline Hopkins's Fiction." *Women's Experience of Modernity, 1875–1945*. Baltimore: Johns Hopkins University Press, 2003. 31–46.

Lewis, Vashti Crutcher. "Mulatto Hegemony in the Novels of Jessie Redmon Fauset." *College Language Association Journal* 35.4 (June 1992): 375–86.

Lindsay, Elizabeth Davis. *Lifting as They Climb: The National Association of Colored Women*. Washington, D.C.: National Association of Colored Women, 1993.

Litwack, Leon E. *Been in the Storm So Long: The Aftermath of Slavery*. New York: Knopf, 1979.

Locke, Alain. Foreword. Locke, *New Negro* xv–xvii.

———. "Negro Youth Speaks." Locke, *New Negro* 47–53.

———, ed. *The New Negro*. New York: Atheneum, 1970.

———. "The New Negro." Locke, *New Negro* 3–16.

Lundgren-Gothlin, Eva. "The Master-Slave Dialectic in *The Second Sex*." *Simone de Beauvoir: A Critical Reader*. Ed. Elizabeth Fallaize. New York: Routledge, 1998. 93–108.

Mackey, Albert G. *A Lexicon of Freemasonry: Containing a Definition of All Its Communicable Terms, Notices of Its History, Traditions, and Antiquities, and an Account of All the Rites and Mysteries of the Ancient World*. Philadelphia: Moss, Brother and Co., 1858.

"Madison Washington: Another Chapter in His History." *Liberator*, June 10, 1842: 89.

Margolies, Edward. *Native Sons: A Critical Study of Twentieth-Century Negro American Authors*. Philadelphia: Lippincott, 1968.

McCoy, Beth A. "'Is This Really What You Wanted Me to Be?' The Daughter's Disintegration in Jessie Redmon Fauset's *There Is Confusion*." *MFS: Modern Fiction Studies* 40.1 (Spring 1994): 101–17.

McDowell, Deborah E. "'The Changing Same': Generational Connections and Black Women Novelists." *New Literary History: A Journal of Theory and Interpretation* 18.2 (Winter 1987): 281–302.

———. "In the First Place: Making Frederick Douglass and the Afro-American Narrative Tradition." *African American Autobiography: A Collection of Critical Essays*. Ed. William L. Andrews. Englewood Cliffs, N.J.: Prentice Hall, 1993. 36–58.

———. "The Neglected Dimension of Jessie Redmon Fauset." Pryse and Spillers 86–104.

Mills, Patricia Jagentowicz, ed. *Feminist Interpretations of G. W. F. Hegel*. University Park: Pennsylvania State University Press, 1996.

———. "Hegel's *Antigone*." Mills, *Feminist Interpretations* 59–88.

Morrison, Toni. *Beloved*. New York: Knopf, 1987.

———. *The Bluest Eye*. New York: Penguin, 1994.

———. *Playing in the Dark: Whiteness and the Literary Imagination*. Cambridge, Mass.: Harvard University Press, 1992.

———. "Unspeakable Things Unspoken: The Afro-American Presence in American Literature." *Michigan Quarterly Review* 28.1 (Winter 1989): 1–34.

Mullen, Harryette. "Runaway Tongues: Resistant Orality in *Uncle Tom's Cabin, Our Nig, Incidents in the Life of a Slave Girl*, and *Beloved*." *The Culture of Sentiment: Race, Gender, and Sentimentality in Nineteenth-Century America*. New York: Oxford University Press, 1992. 244–64.

O'Brien, Mary. "Hegel: Man, Physiology, and Fate." Mills, *Feminist Interpretations* 177–207.

———. *The Politics of Reproduction*. Boston: Routledge, 1981.

Olney, James. "'I Was Born': Slave Narratives, Their Status as Autobiography and as Literature." Davis and Gates 148–75.

Page, Thomas Nelson. *In Ole Virginia*. Plantation Edition. New York: Scribner's, 1906.

Painter, Nell Irvin. Introduction. *The Secret Eye: The Journal of Ella Gertrude Clanton Thomas, 1848–1889*. Ed. Virginia Ingraham Burr. Chapel Hill: University of North Carolina Press, 1990. 1–67.

———. *Sojourner Truth: A Life, a Symbol*. New York: Norton, 1996.

Patterson, Orlando. *Slavery and Social Death: A Comparative Study*. Cambridge, Mass.: Harvard University Press, 1982.

Peterson, Thomas Virgil. *Ham and Japeth: The Mythic World of Whites in the Antebellum South*. Metuchen, N.J.: Scarecrow, 1978.

Pettis, Joyce. "The Literary Imagination and the Historic Event: Chesnutt's Use of History in *The Marrow of Tradition*." *South Atlantic Review* 55.4 (November 1990): 37–48.

Pietz, William. "The Problem of Fetish, I." *Res* 9 (Spring 1985): 5–17.

———. "The Problem of Fetish, II." *Res* 13 (Spring 1987): 23–45.

———. "The Problem of Fetish, IIIa." *Res* 16 (Autumn 1988): 105–23.

Pryse, Marjorie. "Critical Interdisciplinarity, Women's Studies, and Cross-Cultural Insight." *NWSA Journal* 10.1 (Spring 1998): 1–22.

———. Introduction: "Zora Neale Hurston, Alice Walker, and the 'Ancient Power' of Black Women." Pryse and Spillers 1–24.

Pryse, Marjorie, and Hortense Spillers, eds. *Conjuring: Black Women, Fiction, and Literary Tradition*. Bloomington: Indiana University Press, 1985.

Raboteau, Albert J. *Slave Religion: The "Invisible Institution" in the Antebellum South*. New York: Oxford University Press, 1978.

Rampersad, Arnold. "Slavery and the Literary Imagination: Du Bois's *The Souls of Black Folk*." *Slavery and the Literary Imagination*. Eds. Arnold Rampersad and Deborah E. McDowell. Baltimore: Johns Hopkins University Press, 1989. 104–24.

Ravven, Heidi M. "Has Hegel Anything to Say to Feminists?" Mills, *Feminist Interpretations* 225–52.

Reid-Pharr, Robert. "Violent Ambiguity: Martin Delany, Bourgeois Sadomasochism, and the Production of a Black National Masculinity." *Representing Black Men*. Eds. Marcellus Blount and George Cunningham. New York: Routledge, 1996. 73–94.

Rich, Adrienne. "Split at the Root." *Blood, Bread and Poetry: Selected Prose 1879–1985*. New York: Norton, 1986. 100–123.

———. "Women and Honor: Some Notes on Lying." *On Lies, Secrets, and Silence: Selected Prose 1966–1978*. New York: Norton, 1979. 185–94.

Rushdy, Ashraf A. *Remembering Generations: Race and Family in Contemporary African American Fiction*. Chapel Hill: University of North Carolina Press, 2001.

Sale, Maggie Montesinos. *The Slumbering Volcano: American Slave Ship Revolts and the Production of Rebellious Masculinity*. Durham, N.C.: Duke University Press, 1997.

Scales, Anne Bethel [Anne Spencer]. "Beth's Triumph." Part I. *Colored American Magazine* 1.3 (August 1900): 152–59.

Séjour, Victor. "Le Mulâtre." Trans. Philip Barnard. *Norton Anthology of African American Literature*. 1st ed. New York: Norton, 1997. 163–67.

Senate Documents. 27th Cong., 2nd sess., January 21, 1842, no. 51, 1–46.

Shadrach, J. Shirley [Pauline Hopkins?]. "Furnace Blasts I: The Growth of the Social Evil Among All Classes and Races in America." *Colored American Magazine* 6.4 (February 1903): 259–63.

———. "Furnace Blasts II: Black or White—Which Should Be the Young Afro-American's Choice in Marriage?" *Colored American Magazine* 6.5 (March 1903): 348–52.

Shange, Ntozake. *For Colored Girls Who Have Considered Suicide When the Rainbow Is Enuf*. New York: Macmillan, 1975.

Singer, Peter. *Hegel: A Very Short Introduction*. New York: Oxford University Press, 1983.

Smith, Lillian. *Killers of the Dream*. 1949. Garden City, N.Y.: Anchor, 1963.

Smith, Theophus H. *Conjuring Culture: Biblical Formations of Black America*. New York: Oxford University Press, 1994.

Smith, Valerie. *Self-Discovery and Authority in Afro-American Narrative*. Cambridge, Mass.: Harvard University Press, 1987.

Sollors, Werner. *Neither Black Nor White Yet Both: Thematic Explorations of Interracial Literature*. New York: Oxford University Press, 1997.

Sophocles. *Antigone*. Trans. Richard Emil Braun. New York: Oxford University Press, 1973.

———. *Oedipus the King*. Trans. David Grene. *Sophocles I*. Ed. David Grene and Richmond Lattimore. Chicago: University of Chicago Press, 1954.

Spillers, Hortense. "Mama's Baby, Papa's Maybe: An American Grammar Book." *Black, White, and in Color: Essays on American Literature and Culture*. Ed. Hortense Spillers. Chicago: University of Chicago Press, 2003. 203–29.

Stepto, Robert. *From behind the Veil: A Study of Afro-American Narrative*. 2nd ed. Urbana: University of Illinois Press, 1991.

———. "Storytelling in Early Afro-American Fiction: Frederick Douglass's 'The Heroic Slave.'" Gates, *Black Literature* 175–86.

Stowe, Harriet Beecher. "Caste and Christ." *Autographs for Freedom*. Ed. Julia Griffiths. Cleveland: Jewett, 1853. 4–6.

———. *Uncle Tom's Cabin; or, Life Among the Lowly*. 1852. Ed. and introd. Ann Douglas. New York: Penguin, 1981.

Sundquist, Eric. "Frederick Douglass: Literacy and Paternalism." *Critical Essays on Frederick Douglass*. Ed. William L. Andrews. Boston: G. K. Hall, 1991. 120–32.

————. *To Wake the Nations*. Cambridge, Mass.: Harvard University Press, 1993.

Sylvander, Carolyn Wedin. *Jessie Redmon Fauset, Black American Writer.* Troy, N.Y.: Whitston, 1981.

Tate, Claudia. *Domestic Allegories of Political Desire: The Black Heroine's Text at the Turn of the Century.* New York: Oxford University Press, 1992.

Taylor, Charles. *Hegel.* Cambridge: Cambridge University Press, 1975.

Thomas, Ella Gertrude Clanton. *The Secret Eye: The Journal of Ella Gertrude Clanton Thomas, 1848–1889.* Ed. Virginia Ingraham Burr. Chapel Hill: University of North Carolina Press, 1990.

Toomer, Jean. *Cane.* 1923. New York: Liveright, 1951.

Van Leer, David. "Reading Slavery: The Anxiety of Ethnicity in Douglass' Narrative." *Frederick Douglass: New Literary and Historical Essays.* Ed. Eric Sundquist. New York: Cambridge University Press, 1990: 118–40.

Van Vechten, Carl. Introduction. Johnson, *Autobiography* xxxiii–xxxviii.

Virgil. *Aeneid.* Trans. Allen Mandelbaum. New York: Bantam, 1972.

Wald, Gayle. *Crossing the Line: Racial Passing in Twentieth-Century U.S. Literature and Culture.* Durham, N.C.: Duke University Press, 2000.

Walker, Peter. *Moral Choices: Memory, Desire, and Imagination in Nineteenth-Century American Letters.* Baton Rouge: Louisiana University Press, 1979.

Wall, Cheryl. "Histories and Heresies: Engendering the Harlem Renaissance." *Meridians: Feminism, Race, Transnationalism* 2.1 (2001): 59–76.

————. *Women of the Harlem Renaissance.* Bloomington: Indiana University Press, 1995.

Wallace, Maurice. "Constructing the Black Masculine: Frederick Douglass, Booker T. Washington, and the Sublimits of African American Autobiography." Davidson and Hatcher, *No More* 237–62.

Wallace, Michelle. *Invisibility Blues: From Pop to Theory.* New York: Verso, 1990.

Walther, Malin LaVon. "Works by and about Pauline Hopkins." Grueser 221–24.

Washington, Booker T. *Up from Slavery.* New York: Doubleday, 1924.

Washington, Mary Helen. Foreword. Hurston ix–xvii.

West, Cornel. *Race Matters.* New York: Vintage, 1994.

White, Deborah Gray. *Too Heavy a Load: Black Women in Defense of Themselves, 1894–1994.* New York: Norton, 1999.

White, Walter. *The Fire in the Flint.* Athens: University of Georgia Press, 1996.

Wideman, John Edgar. *Fatheralong: A Meditation on Fathers and Sons, Race and Society.* New York: Random, 1995.

Wiegman, Robyn. *American Anatomies: Theorizing Race and Gender.* Durham, N.C.: Duke University Press, 1995.

Williams, Loretta J. *Black Freemasonry and Middle-Class Realities.* Columbia: University of Missouri Press, 1980.

Williams, Patricia J. *The Alchemy of Race and Rights: Diary of a Law Professor.* Cambridge, Mass.: Harvard University Press, 1991.

Williamson, Joel. *New People: Miscegenation and Mulattoes in the United States*. Baton Rouge: Louisiana State University Press, 1995.

Wilson, Sondra Kathryn. Introduction. *James Weldon Johnson: Complete Poems*. Ed. Sonra Kathryn Wilson. New York: Penguin, 2000. xv–xxi.

———, ed. The Crisis *Reader: Stories, Poetry, and Essays from the N.A.A.C.P.'s* Crisis *Magazine*. New York: Random House, 1999.

Woodward, C. Vann, ed. *Mary Chesnut's Civil War*. New Haven, Conn.: Yale University Press, 1981.

Woodward, C. Vann, and Elisabeth Muhlenfeld, eds. *The Private Mary Chesnut: The Unpublished Civil War Diaries*. New York: Oxford University Press, 1984.

Wright, Richard. "Between Laughter and Tears." *New Masses* 5 (October 1937): 22–23.

Yarborough, Richard. "Race, Violence, and Manhood: The Masculine Ideal in Frederick Douglass's 'The Heroic Slave.'" *Frederick Douglass: New Literary and Historical Essays*. Ed. Eric J. Sundquist. Cambridge: Cambridge University Press, 1990. 166–88.

INDEX

85–86; *Iola Leroy*, 14, 16, 70, 78–87;
and matrifocal knowledge, 68, 73, 75,
99; *Minnie's Sacrifice*, 73–78, 81, 87;
Moses: A Story of the Nile, 74–76; and
racial consciousness, *see* consciousness;
"Woman's Political Future," 68–69,
86–87
Harris, Joel Chandler, 13
Harrison, Hazel, 4
Hegel, G. W. F.: and desire 22–25; and
history of consciousness 184n1; and
labor 26–27; *Phenomenology of Spirit*, 9,
23; and *polis*, 21
Hegelian: consciousness and racial consciousness, 169; dialectic, 1, 8, 11–12,
16–17, 26–27, 92, 121, 136; self-con-
sciousness, 1–2, 7–12, 16–17, 92, 104,
130; third term, 36, 52
Henry, Patrick, 47
hooks, bell, 136
Hopkins, Pauline: as editor of *Colored
American Magazine*, 70, 72–73; *Contend-
ing Forces*, 71, 81, 88–95, 99–100, 144;
"Furnace Blasts," 187n20, 187n24;
Hagar's Daughter, 97; "Here and
There," 90; and matrifocal knowledge,
68, 99; *Of One Blood*, 97–100; "Talma
Gordon," 90, 97–98; *Winona*, 97
Hughes, Langston, 166
Hurston, Zora Neale: *Their Eyes Were
Watching God*, 167–68, 171–73, 185n9
Hutchinson, George, 139
hybridity, 32, 134
Hyppolite, Jean, 9

incest, 154–56
Irigaray, Luce, 21

Jacobs, Harriet: *Incidents in the Life of a
Slave Girl*, 17–19, 23–24
JanMohamed, Abdul R., 141
Jefferson, Thomas, 48; and Brown, Wil-
liam Wells, 44, 47; and Hemings, Sally,
45
Jewett, Sarah Orne, 194n12
Johnson, Barbara, 196n27

Johnson, Charles S., 96, 140
Johnson, Georgia Douglas, "The Riddle,"
67, 101
Johnson, James Weldon: *Along This Way*,
124–25, 128; *Autobiography of an Ex-
Coloured Man*, 2, 102, 106, 121–32,
146, 149; *Black Manhattan*, 125; *Book
of American Negro Poetry*, 124; *Books of
American Negro Spirituals*, 124; "Brothers," 130; *God's Trombones*, 124

Kalkavage, Peter, 23
Kaplan, Carla, 173
Kawash, Samira, 122
Keck, Charles, 103–4
Kellogg, Paul, 140
Kojève, Alexandre, 9–10, 22, 24
Kuenz, Jane, 147

Lacan, Jacques, 9, 11
Larsen, Nella, *Quicksand*, 161
Lauter, Paul, 172
Lewis, David Levering, 144
Lewis, R. W. B., 168
Liberator, 45
Litwack, Leon, 13–14, 31
Locke, Alain, 70, 120, 140, 157; *New
Negro*, 68, 140–41
Lusk, Dianthe, 99, 188n27
lying, 13, 25. See also denial, secrets

Manly, Alexander, 189n9
master/female slave moment, 7, 67–68,
92, 102–4, 133, 167, 175n1; in Delany's
Blake, 58; in Douglass's narratives, 53;
in Ellison's *Invisible Man*, 169–73; in
Fauset's novels, 135, 137–38, 150; in
Harper's novels, 78–82. *See also* Hegelian: dialectic
master/slave dialectic, 7–12, 16–17, 22–26,
33, 35, 130; and Delany's *Blake*, 57; and
Douglass's *Heroic Slave*, 48, 51–52; as
ex-master and ex-slave dialectic, 114;
and Hopkins's *Contending Forces*, 99. *See
also* Hegelian: dialectic
McDowell, Deborah, 149

LESLIE W. LEWIS is the dean of the School of Arts and Humanities and a member of the English faculty at the College of Saint Rose in Albany, New York. She is the author of "Naming the Problem Embedded in the Problem That Led to the Question 'Who Shall Teach African American Literature?'; or, Are We Ready to Discard the Concept of Authenticity Altogether?" in the anthology *White Scholars/African American American Texts* and coeditor with Ann L. Ardis of *Women's Experience of Modernity, 1875–1945*. Other articles have appeared in *African American Review* and *Critical Essays on John Edgar Wideman*. She teaches African American literature and American studies at Saint Rose, and she contributes to college-wide diversity and engaged urban campus initiatives.

⟡

The University of Illinois Press
is a founding member of the
Association of American University Presses.

Composed in 10/13 Janson Text
with Hoefler Text Fleurons ornaments
by Celia Shapland
at the University of Illinois Press
Designed by Dennis Roberts
Manufactured by Thomson-Shore, Inc.

University of Illinois Press
1325 South Oak Street
Champaign, IL 61820-6903
www.press.uillinois.edu